THE WORLDS OF
HUME
AND
KANT

THE WORLDS OF
HUME
AND
KANT

James B. Wilbur
The University of Akron
and
Harold J. Allen
Adelphi University

Ps Prometheus Books

700 East Amherst Street
Buffalo, N.Y. 14215

Originally published
in 1967 by
American Book Company
New York, New York

Published 1982 by Prometheus Books
700 East Amherst Street, Buffalo, New York 14215

Library of Congress Catalog Number: 82-80553
ISBN: 0-87975-163-0

Preface

This volume presents the philosophies of Hume and Kant through their actual writings and through commentary provided by the authors. The selections, which were taken from their major works, were chosen to reflect the wide perspectives of both philosophers. The commentary was designed to develop as well as to interpret the most salient aspects of each philosophy. As with the previous volume, *The Worlds of Plato and Aristotle,* by the same authors, the inclusion of the works of both philosophers in one volume presents a convenient opportunity for the comparison of their vision and perception of the world.

The overall conception of the work is shared, but primary responsibility for Hume belongs to Mr. Allen, and for Kant to Mr. Wilbur.

We wish to extend our thanks to Mrs. Priscilla Gaertner and Mrs. Anne Corney for their aid and assistance with the manuscripts and typing.

Table of Contents

KANT

Key to Selections
and Acknowledgments

Each selection is identified by a letter in parentheses immediately follow-ing the last line of the selection. This letter refers to the key below, which indicates the pages of the source from which the selection was taken.

Most of the footnotes of Hume and Kant have been retained and are des-ignated by astericks to distinguish them from the footnotes we have supplied.

HUME

All selections, with the exception of Selection XV, refer to either the Selby-Bigge edition of Hume's *A Treatise of Human Nature*, which was reprinted from the original edition in three volumes, or the second Selby-Bigge edition of Hume's *Enquiries Concerning the Human Understanding and Concerning the Principles of Morals*, reprinted from the posthumous edition of 1777. Both are works published by the Clarendon Press at Oxford. Selection XV may be found in the Norman Kemp Smith edition of Hume's *Dialogues Concerning Natural Religion*, a title in The Library of Liberal Arts, published by The Bobbs-Merrill Co., Inc.

Introduction

Treatise of Human Nature
(a) pp. 270–274

Part I

Enquiry Concerning the Human Understanding
(a) pp. 149–155

Treatise of Human Nature
(b) pp. 1–7   (d) pp. 10–13
(c) pp. 19–21   (e) pp. 66–68

Enquiry Concerning the Human Understanding
(f) pp. 25–27

Treatise of Human Nature

Enquiry Concerning the Human Understanding

Dialogues Concerning Natural Religion

Enquiry Concerning the Human Understanding

Part II

Enquiry Concerning the Human Understanding

Enquiry Concerning the Principles of Morals

KANT

We wish to acknowledge the publishers of the following texts for their kind permission to use material for our selections.

Conjectural Beginning of Human History from Immanuel Kant: *On History*, edited by Lewis White Beck, copyright © 1957 by the Liberal Arts Press, Inc., © 1963 by The Bobbs-Merrill Company, Inc., reprinted by permission of the Liberal Arts Press Division of The Bobbs-Merrill Company, Inc.

Selection I: The Nature of Man

Immanuel Kant: *Prolegomena to Any Future Metaphysics*, edited by Lewis White Beck, copyright © 1950 by The Liberal Arts Press, Inc., reprinted by permission of the Liberal Arts Press Division of The Bobbs-Merrill Company, Inc.

Selection II: Synthetic Judgments A Priori

Selection III: The Forms of Sensibility

Immanuel Kant: *Critique of Pure Reason*, translated and edited by Norman Kemp Smith, reprinted by permission of St. Martin's Press, Inc., New York,

Selection III: The Forms of Sensibility

(b) p. 67	(f) pp. 74–75
(c) pp. 67–68	(g) p. 76
(d) p. 68	(h) p. 77
(e) p. 71	(i) pp. 77–78

Prolegomena to Any Future Metaphysics

Selection IV: The Categories

(a) pp. 45–46	(f) p. 52
(b) pp. 47–48	(g) pp. 53–54
(c) pp. 48–49	(h) p. 60
(d) p. 50	(i) p. 62
(e) pp. 50–51	(j) p. 64

Critique of Pure Reason

Selection V: The Unity of Understanding

(a) pp. 130–131	(e) p. 136
(b) pp. 131–132	(f) p. 153
(c) p. 133	(g) pp. 156–157
(d) p. 134	

Selection VI: The Schematism of the Understanding

(a) p. 180	(d) pp. 183–184
(b) p. 181	(e) pp. 185–186
(c) p. 183	

Selection VII: The Ideas of Reason

(a) p. 303	(c) pp. 319–320
(b) pp. 318–319	(d) pp. 323–324

Selection VIII: The Idea of Self

(a) p. 377	(b) pp. 377–378

Prolegomena to Any Future Metaphysics

Selection IX: The Idea of the Universe

(a) p. 86	(e) p. 90
(b) pp. 87–88	(f) p. 90
(c) p. 89	(g) pp. 91–93
(d) pp. 89–90	(h) p. 95

Critique of Pure Reason

Selection X: The Idea of God

(a) p. 503	(d) p. 508
(b) pp. 504–505	(e) pp. 519–520
(c) p. 508	(f) pp. 523–524

Immanuel Kant: *Critique of Practical Reason*, translated by Lewis White Beck, copyright © 1956 by The Liberal Arts Press, Inc., reprinted by permission of the Liberal Arts Press Division of The Bobbs-Merrill Company, Inc.

Selection XI: Of Freedom
(a) pp. 97–99
(b) p. 101
(c) p. 108
(d) p. 109

Selection XII: Of Immortality
(a) pp. 126–127

Selection XIII: Of God
(a) pp. 128–129
(b) pp. 129–130
(c) p. 134
(d) p. 134
(e) p. 137

Fundamental Principles of the Metaphysics of Ethics by Immanuel Kant. Translated with an Introduction by Otto Manthey-Zorn. Copyright © 1938 by D. Appleton-Century Company. Reprinted by permission of Appleton-Century-Crofts Division of Meredith Publishing Company.

Selection XIV: The Good Will
(a) p. 8
(b) p. 9
(c) p. 11
(d) p. 12
(e) p. 15
(f) p. 16

Critique of Practical Reason

Selection XIV: The Good Will
(g) pp. 82–83
(h) pp. 83–84

Fundamental Principles of the Metaphysics of Ethics

Selection XIV: The Good Will
(i) p. 19

Selection XV: The Rational Will
(a) p. 29
(b) p. 29

Lectures in Ethics by Immanuel Kant, translated by Louis Infield. Reprinted by permission of Harper and Row Company, copyright © 1963.

Selection XV: The Rational Will
(c) p. 4
(d) pp. 4–5
(e) p. 5

Fundamental Principles of the Metaphysics of Ethics

Selection XV: The Rational Will
(f) p. 38
(g) pp. 18–19
(h) p. 39
(i) p. 38

Selection XVI: The Autonomous Will
(a) p. 45
(b) p. 47
(c) pp. 51–52
(d) p. 53

(e) p. 53   (g) p. 72
(f) p. 56   (h) p. 75

Religion Within the Limits of Reason Alone by Immanuel Kant, translation and introduction by Theodore M. Green and Hoyt H. Hudson. Reprinted by permission of The Open Court Publishing Company, Lasalle, Illinois.

Selection XVII: The Responsible Will
(a) pp. 21–22   (g) p. 30
(b) p. 22   (h) p. 30
(c) pp. 22–23   (i) p. 31
(d) p. 24   (j) pp. 31–32
(e) pp. 24–25   (k) p. 32
(f) p. 30   (l) pp. 32–33

Critique of Judgment by Immanuel Kant, translated by J. H. Bernard, copyright © 1951 by the Hafner Publishing Company.

Selection XVIII: Of Judgment as Mediator
(a) pp. 32–34

Selection XIX: The Beautiful
(a) p. 45   (d) p. 56
(b) p. 44   (e) p. 68
(c) pp. 50–51

Selection XX: The Sublime
(a) pp. 85–86   (d) p. 101
(b) p. 94   (e) p. 105
(c) p. 95

Selection XXI: Art and Genius
(a) pp. 145–146   (f) p. 157
(b) p. 147   (g) p. 196
(c) p. 149   (h) pp. 197–198
(d) p. 150   (i) pp. 198–199
(e) pp. 150–151

Selection XXII: Natural Purpose and Organized Being
(a) p. 206   (d) p. 218
(b) p. 216   (e) pp. 220–221
(c) p. 217   (f) p. 222

Selection XXIII: Of the System of Nature
(a) pp. 251–252   (c) p. 258
(b) pp. 257–258   (d) p. 264

Selection XXIV: On a Purposive Creator
(a) pp. 285–286   (c) pp. 303–304
(b) p. 301

THE WORLDS OF HUME AND KANT

David Hume
1711-1776

INTRODUCTION

The Historical Connections of Hume's Thought

Hume's philosophy is the culmination of eighteenth-century thought. Insofar as he consistently applied to ethics, epistemology, and other areas what he understood to be Newtonian methodology, Hume drew out the full implications of this seminal force in eighteenth-century intellectual life. Both Hume and Newton approached knowledge analytically, both made no hypotheses, and both thought of experience as the final touchstone of truth.[1] Hume supposed further that what is separable in logical analysis is separable in reality, and along with Descartes, the leading philosophical expositor of the seventeenth-century Galilean spirit, attempted to ground his philosophy in *immediate* experience—that is, in experience as it appears independently of any suppositions about a world beyond it. The conclusions of Hume were nonetheless very different from those of Descartes. Beginning with a radical scepticism, Descartes concluded that there are souls, that there is a God, and that nature is a machine governed by God's rational order. Hume, on the other hand, ends with a "mitigated" scepticism. Instead of souls and a rational order of nature, he can find only bundles of

---

[1] Newton writes in the following passage from his *Opticks:* "As in Mathematicks, so in Natural Philosophy, the Investigation of difficult Things by the Method of Analysis, ought ever to precede the Method of Composition. This Analysis consists in making Experiments and Observations, and in drawing general Conclusions from them by Induction, and admitting of no Objections against the Conclusions, but such as are taken from Experiments or other certain Truths. For Hypotheses are not to be regarded in experimental Philosophy." Isaac Newton, *Opticks,* Book III, Part I, Question 31 (New York: Dover, 1952), p. 404.

isolated perceptions standing in need of something more to hold both soul and nature together.

Hume carried forward with greater consistency and scope a task initiated by Locke and Berkeley, philosophers strongly influenced by Newtonian science. Though Locke's epistemology is a somewhat inconsistent amalgam of Newtonian and Aristotelian ideas, his ethics retain a primarily rationalistic character. Berkeley's philosophy is a thorough and clever analysis of nature which denies our knowledge of material substance and effectively pulverizes into a multiplicity of perceptions the Newtonian view of the world as a physical system run by mechanical laws. Referring to these perceptions as "ideas," Berkeley had concluded that the Newtonian world machine was really only a miscellaneous collection of mental entities dependent on the thought cf spiritual beings—that is, human minds and God. It was left to Hume to show that Berkeley's defense of religious notions would not work. Minds, he pointed out, like physical entities, must be subjected to rigorous analysis. Only God escapes analytic disintegration. He escapes, however, at the price of almost losing His worldly relevance, if not His very existence.

A further illustration of Hume's consistent carrying through of eighteenth-century ideas is his empirical approach to ethics in the style of philosophers like Hutcheson. It is here that we find a confluence with Aristotelian empiricism and its attendant emphasis on the role of habit in moral judgment. Since Hume, like Hutcheson, regards taste and sentiment as expressions of human nature common to all men, he holds them capable of serving as an objective standard of moral judgment. It is for this reason that Hume's uncovering of habit and belief as a basic principle of human nature leads him naturally to the thought that habit and belief may be the key to some kind of cognitive standard. In the introduction to the *Treatise* he says:

> 'Tis evident, that all the sciences have a relation, greater or less, to human nature; and that however wide any of them may seem to run from it, they still return back by one passage or another. Even *Mathematics, Natural Philosophy, and Natural Religion,* are in some measure dependent on the science of MAN; since they lie under the cognizance of men and are judged of by their powers and faculties....[2]

[2] *A Treatise of Human Nature,* L.A. Selby-Bigge (ed.) (1st ed.; Oxford: Clarendon Press, 1888), p. xix.

The implications of this passage suggest that Hume anticipated Kant's "Copernican Revolution" in Philosophy [3] and provided a more existential and less intellectualist foundation for it. If the character of the world as man knows it is a product of his interpretation of it through belief and habit and is not simply knowledge he is given and can be certain of, his contribution to the knowing process, rooted in his biological and psychological nature, becomes central.

Because of the divergent philosophical attitudes to which the sceptical approach of Hume and the systematic approach of Kant give expression, it would be easy to think of them as opposed. It is far more useful, however, to regard the philosophies of Hume and Kant as complementary. Although nineteenth-century philosophical developments in Europe are most easily intelligible through Kant's formulation of philosophical problems, a good deal of nineteenth-century British thought is based on Hume's thinking. Hume had a direct effect on Kant. (We have Kant's word that Hume awoke him from his "dogmatic slumber.") [4] In England, he influenced his personal friend Adam Smith, Thomas Reid, and the Scottish Realists, who reacted negatively to Hume's scepticism, and, Bentham and Mill, the Utilitarians who shared both Hume's empiricism and certain features of his approach to ethics. Though such twentieth-century movements as Logical Positivism and Analytic Philosophy have their strongest affinities with Hume, the Philosophy of Science can scarcely be understood without reference to Kant as well as Hume.

Hume's Philosophy and His Life

Hume was born in Scotland of well-to-do but not wealthy parents on April 26, 1711. The fact that his fortune was slender may account for his drive to make a mark in the literary world; he could not support himself otherwise. Hume's earliest efforts were failures. The *Treatise of Human Nature*, his earliest work, published when he was

[3] Kant suggested that the process of knowing can be best understood by assuming that "the objects must conform to our mode of cognition" rather than that "all our knowledge must conform to the objects." He compared this to Copernicus' thought that the spectator rather than the "fixed stars" should be regarded as in motion in attempting to understand the motions of heavenly bodies. Immanuel Kant, *Critique of Pure Reason* from *Kant Selections*, Theodore Meyer Green (ed.) (New York: Charles Scribner's Sons, 1929), p. 14.

[4] Immanuel Kant, *Prolegomena to Any Future Metaphysics* (New York: Bobbs-Merrill, 1950), p. 8 (The Library of Liberal Arts).

twenty-seven, met with scarcely any recognition at all, and early editions of the *Enquiry Concerning Human Understanding*, first published about ten years later, did little better. Only as Hume neared forty did he begin to enjoy some measure of literary success. In his early twenties, while working on the *Treatise*, he had psychological problems serious enough to interfere with the effectiveness of his intellectual work. It is not clear whether his neurosis was due to a personal involvement in the austere scepticism of parts of the *Treatise*, to his inability until then to achieve the literary fame he so much desired, or to other causes. Hume's later characterization of himself, however, does suggest certain conclusions about his relationship to his work.

In a brief autobiographical account,[1] Hume speaks of himself as having always been studious, sober, and industrious. The only real interruption in his studies was a two-year period during which he served as secretary and aide-de-camp to General St. Clair. The following passage from the *Treatise* shows his deep concern with the results of his philosophical analysis:

> I am first affrighted and confounded with that forelorn solitude, in which I am plac'd in my philosophy, and fancy myself some strange uncouth monster, who not being able to mingle and unite in society, has been expell'd all human commerce, and left utterly abandon'd and disconsolate.... When I turn my eye inward, I find nothing but doubt and ignorance. All the world conspires to oppose and contradict me; tho' such is my weakness, that I feel all my opinions loosen and fall of themselves, when unsupported by the approbation of others. Every step I take is with hesitation, and every new reflection makes me dread an error and absurdity in my reasoning.[2]

Luckily he was, as he puts it, "a man of mild dispositions, of command of temper, of an open, social, and cheerful humour, capable of attachment, but little susceptible of enmity, and of great moderation in all ... passions"[3] and found it easy to say of the results of his analytic work:

> Most fortunately it happens, that since reason is incapable of dispelling these clouds, nature herself suffices to that purpose, and cures me

---

[1] David Hume, "My Own Life," autobiographical essay appearing as the first part of a supplement to *Dialogues Concerning Natural Religion*, Norman Kemp Smith (ed.), (New York: Bobbs-Merrill, 1947), p. 233 (The Library of Liberal Arts).

[2] *Treatise*, Book I, Part IV, Section VII, 264–5.

[3] "My Own Life," p. 239.

of this philosophical melancholy and delirium, either by relaxing this
bent of mind, or by some avocation, and lively impression of my senses,
which obliterate all these chimeras. I dine, I play a game of back-
gammon, I converse, and am merry with my friends; and when after
three or four hours' amusement, I wou'd return to these speculations,
they appear so cold, and strain'd, and ridiculous, that I cannot find in
my heart to enter into them any farther.[4]

Yet in the following selection he best expresses the relationship of
his philosophy to his life and also suggests the nature of his sceptical approach to philosophy.

Selection I:
TREATISE OF HUMAN NATURE
Book I, Part IV, Section VII

At the time, therefore, that I am tir'd with amusement and company,
and have indulg'd a *reverie* in my chamber, or in a solitary walk by a
river-side, I feel my mind all collected within itself, and am naturally
inclin'd to carry my view into all those subjects, about which I have met
with so many disputes in the course of my reading and conversation. I
cannot forbear having a curiosity to be acquainted with the principles of
moral good and evil, the nature and foundation of government, and the
cause of those several passions and inclinations, which actuate and
govern me. I am uneasy to think I approve of one object, and disapprove
of another; call one thing beautiful, and another deform'd; decide
concerning truth and falshood, reason and folly, without knowing upon
what principles I proceed. I am concern'd for the condition of the
learned world, which lies under such a deplorable ignorance in all these
particulars. I feel an ambition to arise in me of contributing to the
instruction of mankind, and of acquiring a name by my inventions and
discoveries. These sentiments spring up naturally in my present disposition; and shou'd I endeavour to banish them, by attaching myself
to any other business or diversion, I *feel* I shou'd be a loser in point of
pleasure; and this is the origin of my philosophy.

But even suppose this curiosity and ambition shou'd not transport me
into speculations without the sphere of common life, it wou'd necessarily
happen, that from my very weakness I must be led into such enquiries.
'Tis certain, that superstition is much more bold in its systems and
hypotheses than philosophy; and while the latter contents itself with
assigning new causes and principles to the phaenomena, which appear in

[4] *Treatise*, Book I, Part IV, Section VII, p. 269.

the visible world, the former opens a world of its own, and presents us with scenes, and beings, and objects, which are altogether new. Since therefore 'tis almost impossible for the mind of man to rest, like those of beasts, in that narrow circle of objects, which are the subject of daily conversation and action, we ought only to deliberate concerning the choice of our guide, and ought to prefer that which is safest and most agreeable. And in this respect I make bold to recommend philosophy, and shall not scruple to give it the preference to superstition of every kind or denomination. For as superstition arises naturally and easily from the popular opinions of mankind, it seizes more strongly on the mind, and is often able to disturb us in the conduct of our lives and actions. Philosophy on the contrary, if just, can present us only with mild and moderate sentiments; and if false and extravagant, its opinions are merely the objects of a cold and general speculation, and seldom go so far as to interrupt the course of our natural propensities. The CYNICS[1] are an extraordinary instance of philosophers, who from reasonings purely philosophical ran into as great extravagancies of conduct as any *Monk* or *Dervise* that ever was in the world. Generally speaking, the errors in religion are dangerous; those in philosophy only ridiculous.

I am sensible, that these two cases of the strength and weakness of the mind will not comprehend all mankind, and that there are in *England*, in particular, many honest gentlemen, who being always employ'd in their domestic affairs, or amusing themselves in common recreations, have carried their thoughts very little beyond those objects, which are every day expos'd to their senses. And indeed, of such as these I pretend not to make philosophers, nor do I expect them either to be associates in these researches or auditors of these discoveries. They do well to keep themselves in their present situation; and instead of refining them into philosophers, I wish we cou'd communicate to our founders of systems, a share of this gross earthy mixture, as an ingredient, which they commonly stand much in need of, and which wou'd serve to temper those fiery particles, of which they are compos'd. While a warm imagination is allow'd to enter into philosophy, and hypotheses embrac'd merely for being specious and agreeable, we can never have any steady principles, nor any sentiments, which will suit with common practice and experience. But were these hypotheses once remov'd, we might hope to establish a system or set of opinions, which if not true (for that, perhaps, is too much to be hop'd for) might at least be satisfactory to the human mind, and might stand

[1] The Cynics, noted for their nonconformist behavior, were one of the schools of ancient philosophy after the break up of the Greek world. They claimed affinity with Socrates and offered a practical ethic to the Hellenistic world.

the test of the most critical examination. Nor shou'd we despair of attaining this end, because of the many chimerical systems, which have successively arisen and decay'd away among men, wou'd we consider the shortness of that period, wherein these questions have been the subjects of enquiry and reasoning. Two thousand years with such long interruptions, and under such mighty discouragements are a small space of time to give any tolerable perfection to the sciences; and perhaps we are still in too early an age of the world to discover any principles, which will bear the examination of the latest posterity. For my part, my only hope is, that I may contribute a little to the advancement of knowlege, by giving in some particulars a different turn to the speculation of philosophers, and pointing out to them more distinctly those subjects, where alone they can expect assurance and conviction. Human Nature is the only science of man; and yet has been hitherto the most neglected. 'Twill be sufficient for me, if I can bring it a little more into fashion; and the hope of this serves to compose my temper from that spleen, and invigorate it from that indolence, which sometimes prevail upon me. If the reader finds himself in the same easy disposition, let him follow me in my future speculations. If not, let him follow his inclination, and wait the returns of application and good humour. The conduct of a man, who studies philosophy in this careless manner, is more truly sceptical than that of one, who feeling in himself an inclination to it, is yet so overwhelm'd with doubts and scruples, as totally to reject it. A true sceptic will be diffident of his philosophical doubts, as well as of his philosophical conviction; and will never refuse any innocent satisfaction, which offers itself, upon account of either of them.

Nor is it only proper we shou'd in general indulge our inclination in the most elaborate philosophical researches, notwithstanding our sceptical principles, but also that we shou'd yield to that propensity, which inclines us to be positive and certain in *particular points*, according to the light, in which we survey them in any *particular instant*. 'Tis easier to forbear all examination and enquiry, than to check ourselves in so natural a propensity, and guard against that assurance, which always arises from an exact and full survey of an object. On such an occasion we are apt not only to forget our scepticism, but even our modesty too; and make use of such terms as these, *'tis evident, 'tis certain, 'tis undeniable;* which a due deference to the public ought, perhaps, to prevent. I may have fallen into this fault after the example of others; but I here enter a *caveat* against any objections, which may be offer'd on that head; and declare that such expressions were extorted from me by the present view of the object, and imply no dogmatical spirit, nor conceited idea of my own judgment,

which are sentiments that I am sensible can become no body, and a sceptic
still less than any other.   (a)

This attitude toward philosophy served Hume well throughout his
life. Apparently not only was his life happy and his death peaceful,
but he was well-regarded by almost everyone.

PART I

Two major characteristics of Hume's thought are
1. A critical analytic approach, coming from Newton.
2. A concern for value, stemming from philosophers like Hutcheson, that tended to ground judgment in human nature.

Part I will deal with aspects of Hume's thought associated primarily
with the element of Newtonian analysis in his work. Part II will take
up facets of Hume's philosophy dependent mainly on his theory of
human nature.

Rejection of Cartesian Scepticism, and Aspects of Pyrrhonism

From the Newtonian point of view, sense experience determines
the horizon of knowledge. Hume argues that all attempts to move
beyond this horizon lead only to scepticism. There are several definitions of scepticism. The first, drawn from ordinary language, de-
scribes the sceptic simply as a nonbeliever or agnostic. The second
comes from the period of Greek Scepticism, which extended from the
fourth to the second century B.C. The main characteristic of Greek
Scepticism was the suspension of judgment concerning what might
be known. Pyrrho (c. 360–270 B.C.), the earliest teacher of this
school, differs radically from the two Academic Sceptics,[1] Arcesilaus
(315/14–241/40 B.C.) and Carneades (214/12–129/8 B.C.), when
he emphasizes the importance of belief for the sceptic. Pyrrhonism
is associated with both relativism and detachment: since nothing can
be known, commit yourself to as little as possible, but if you must
act, abide by the laws and conventions of the society in which you
happen to live. Arcesilaus and Carneades were concerned with working out a reasonable basis for justifying action and belief. Carneades

---

[1] Arcesilaus and Carneades are called Academic Sceptics because of their association with the Academy, the school founded by Plato.

even developed a system for "calculating" the probabilities of proposed beliefs. Cicero and Bacon, both of whom Hume admired, were not unsympathetic with Academic Scepticism.[2]

In the following selection Hume first rejects scepticism in still another sense—that is, what he calls Cartesian Scepticism, or the view that reason and experience can seriously be doubted prior to their use. He then goes on to outline a sceptical position which he refers to as a "species of scepticism consequent to science and enquiry," a "species" that really is a variety of Pyrrhonism. The rest of Part I will expand on the Pyrrhonist dilemma into which Hume's Newtonian analysis led him, though it should be kept in mind that Pyrrhonism is a view he later rejects. Part II will explore the consequences of the philosophy Hume reconstructs on the basis of what he calls a "mitigated" or Academic Scepticism, a position he later avows.

The sceptical arguments of the Pyrrhonist's fall into three categories: those based on sense, those having to do with reason, and those dealing with morality. We present here only Hume's treatment of arguments based on sense. In the last two paragraphs of the following selection [3] Hume attacks the notion seemingly implied in Newtonian Physics, that while so-called "secondary" qualities of human experience, such as color, taste, odor, exist only in the mind, "primary" qualities, more intimately associated with material bodies in motion, exist independently of our experience of them. Examples of primary qualities would be weight, figure, volume, size, velocity.

Selection II:
ENQUIRY CONCERNING HUMAN UNDERSTANDING
Section XII, Part I

There is not a greater number of philosophical reasonings, displayed upon any subject, than those, which prove the existence of a Deity, and refute the fallacies of *Atheists;* and yet the most religious philosophers still dispute whether any man can be so blinded as to be a speculative atheist. How shall we reconcile these contradictions? The knights-errant, who wandered about to clear the world of dragons and giants, never entertained the least doubt with regard to the existence of these monsters.

The *Sceptic* is another enemy of religion, who naturally provokes the

[2] Charles W. Hendel, *Studies in the Philosophy of Hume* (New York: Bobbs-Merrill, 1963), p. 41 f. and p. 90 f.
[3] See also pp. 41-43.

indignation of all divines and graver philosophers; though it is certain, that no man ever met with any such absurd creature, or conversed with a man, who had no opinion or principle concerning any subject, either of action or speculation. This begets a very natural question; What is meant by a sceptic? And how far it is possible to push these philosophical principles of doubt and uncertainty?

There is a species of scepticism, *antecedent* to all study and philosophy, which is much inculcated by Des Cartes and others, as a sovereign preservative against error and precipitate judgment. It recommends an universal doubt, not only of all our former opinions and principles, but also of our very faculties; of whose veracity, say they, we must assure ourselves, by a chain of reasoning, deduced from some original principle, which cannot possibly be fallacious or deceitful. But neither is there any such original principle, which has a prerogative above others, that are self-evident and convincing: or if there were, could we advance a step beyond it, but by the use of those very faculties, of which we are supposed to be already diffident. The Cartesian doubt, therefore, were it ever possible to be attained by any human creature (as it plainly is not) would be entirely incurable; and no reasoning could ever bring us to a state of assurance and conviction upon any subject.

It must, however, be confessed, that this species of scepticism, when more moderate, may be understood in a very reasonable sense, and is a necessary preparative to the study of philosophy, by preserving a proper impartiality in our judgements, and weaning our mind from all those prejudices, which we may have imbibed from education or rash opinion. To begin with clear and self-evident principles, to advance by timorous and sure steps, to review frequently our conclusions, and examine accurately all their consequences; though by these means we shall make both a slow and a short progress in our systems; are the only methods, by which we can ever hope to reach truth, and attain a proper stability and certainty in our determinations.

There is another species of scepticism, *consequent* to science and enquiry, when men are supposed to have discovered, either the absolute fallaciousness of their mental faculties, or their unfitness to reach any fixed determination in all those curious subjects of speculation, about which they are commonly employed. Even our very senses are brought into dispute, by a certain species of philosophers; and the maxims of common life are subjected to the same doubt as the most profound principles or conclusions of metaphysics and theology. As these paradoxical tenets (if they may be called tenets) are to be met with in some philosophers, and the refutation of them in several, they naturally excite our curiosity, and make us enquire into the arguments, on which they may be founded.

I need not insist upon the more trite topics, employed by the sceptics in all ages, against the evidence of *sense;* such as those which are derived from the imperfection and fallaciousness of our organs, on numberless occasions; the crooked appearance of an oar in water; the various aspects of objects, according to their different distances; the double images which arise from the pressing one eye; with many other appearances of a like nature. These sceptical topics, indeed, are only sufficient to prove, that the senses alone are not implicitly to be depended on; but that we must correct their evidence by reason, and by considerations, derived from the nature of the medium, the distance of the object, and the disposition of the organ, in order to render them, within their sphere, the proper *criteria* of truth and falsehood. There are other more profound arguments against the senses, which admit not of so easy a solution.

It seems evident, that men are carried, by a natural instinct or prepossession, to repose faith in their senses; and that, without any reasoning, or even almost before the use of reason, we always suppose an external universe, which depends not on our perception, but would exist, though we and every sensible creature were absent or annihilated. Even the animal creation are governed by a like opinion, and preserve this belief of external objects, in all their thoughts, designs, and actions.

It seems also evident, that, when men follow this blind and powerful instinct of nature, they always suppose the very images, presented by the senses, to be the external objects, and never entertain any suspicion, that the one are nothing but representations of the other. This very table, which we see white, and which we feel hard, is believed to exist, independent of our perception, and to be something external to our mind, which perceives it. Our presence bestows not being on it: our absence does not annihilate it. It preserves its existence uniform and entire, independent of the situation of intelligent beings, who perceive or contemplate it.

But this universal and primary opinion of all men is soon destroyed by the slightest philosophy, which teaches us, that nothing can ever be present to the mind but an image or perception, and that the senses are only the inlets, through which these images are conveyed, without being able to produce any immediate intercourse between the mind and the object. The table, which we see, seems to diminish, as we remove farther from it: but the real table, which exists independent of us, suffers no alteration: it was, therefore, nothing but its image, which was present to the mind. These are the obvious dictates of reason; and no man, who reflects, ever doubted, that the existences, which we consider, when we say, *this house* and *that tree*, are nothing but perceptions in the mind, and fleeting copies or representations of other existences, which remain uniform and independent.

So far, then, are we necessitated by reasoning to contradict or depart from the primary instincts of nature, and to embrace a new system with regard to the evidence of our senses. But here philosophy finds herself extremely embarrassed, when she would justify this new system, and obviate the cavils and objections of the sceptics. She can no longer plead the infallible and irresistible instinct of nature: for that led us to a quite different system, which is acknowledged fallible and even erroneous. And to justify this pretended philosophical system, by a chain of clear and convincing argument, or even any appearance of argument, exceeds the power of all human capacity.

By what argument can it be proved, that the perceptions of the mind must be caused by external objects, entirely different from them, though resembling them (if that be possible) and could not arise either from the energy of the mind itself, or from the suggestion of some invisible and unknown spirit, or from some other cause still more unknown to us? It is acknowledged, that, in fact, many of these perceptions arise not from anything external, as in dreams, madness, and other diseases. And nothing can be more inexplicable than the manner, in which body should so operate upon mind as ever to convey an image of itself to a substance, supposed of so different, and even contrary a nature.

It is a question of fact, whether the perceptions of the senses be produced by external objects, resembling them: how shall this question be determined? By experience surely; as all other questions of a like nature. But here experience is, and must be entirely silent. The mind has never anything present to it but the perceptions, and cannot possibly reach any experience of their connexion with objects. The supposition of such a connexion is, therefore, without any foundation in reasoning.

To have recourse to the veracity of the supreme Being, in order to prove the veracity of our senses,[1] is surely making a very unexpected circuit. If his veracity were at all concerned in this matter, our senses would be entirely infallible; because it is not possible that he can ever deceive. Not to mention, that, if the external world be once called in question, we shall be at a loss to find arguments, by which we may prove the existence of that Being or any of his attributes.

This is a topic, therefore, in which the profounder and more philosophical sceptics will always triumph, when they endeavour to introduce an universal doubt into all subjects of human knowledge and enquiry. Do

---

[1] As Descartes had suggested.

you follow the instincts and propensities of nature, may they say, in assenting to the veracity of sense? But these lead you to believe that the very perception or sensible image is the external object. Do you disclaim this principle, in order to embrace a more rational opinion, that the perceptions are only representations of something external? You here depart from your natural propensities and more obvious sentiments; and yet are not able to satisfy your reason, which can never find any convincing argument from experience to prove, that the perceptions are connected with any external objects.

There is another sceptical topic of a like nature, derived from the most profound philosophy; which might merit our attention, were it requisite to dive so deep, in order to discover arguments and reasonings, which can so little serve to any serious purpose. It is universally allowed by modern enquirers, that all the sensible qualities of objects, such as hard, soft, hot, cold, white, black, &c. are merely secondary, and exist not in the objects themselves, but are perceptions of the mind, without any external archetype or model, which they represent. If this be allowed, with regard to secondary qualities, it must also follow, with regard to the supposed primary qualities of extension and solidity; nor can the latter be any more entitled to that denomination than the former. The idea of extension is entirely acquired from the senses of sight and feeling; and if all the qualities, perceived by the senses, be in the mind, not in the object, the same conclusion must reach the idea of extension, which is wholly dependent on the sensible ideas or the ideas of secondary qualities. Nothing can save us from this conclusion, but the asserting, that the ideas of those primary qualities are attained by *Abstraction*, an opinion, which, if we examine it accurately, we shall find to be unintelligible, and even absurd. An extension, that is neither tangible nor visible, cannot possibly be conceived: and a tangible or visible extension, which is neither hard nor soft, black nor white, is equally beyond the reach of human conception. Let any man try to conceive a triangle in general, which is neither *Isosceles* nor *Scalenum*, nor has any particular length or proportion of sides; and he will soon perceive the absurdity of all the scholastic notions with regard to abstraction and general ideas.*

* This argument is drawn from Dr. Berkeley; and indeed most of the writings of that very ingenious author form the best lessons of scepticism, which are to be found either among the ancient or modern philosophers, Bayle not excepted. He professes, however, in his title-page (and undoubtedly with great truth) to have composed his book against the sceptics as well as against the atheists and free-thinkers. But that all his arguments, though otherwise intended, are, in reality, merely sceptical, appears from this, *that they admit of no answer and produce no conviction.* Their only effect is to cause that momentary amazement and irresolution and confusion, which is the result of scepticism.

Thus the first philosophical objection to the evidence of sense or to the opinion of external existence consists in this, that such an opinion, if rested on natural instinct, is contrary to reason, and if referred to reason, is contrary to natural instinct, and at the same time carries no rational evidence with it, to convince an impartial enquirer. The second objection goes farther, and represents this opinion as contrary to reason: at least, if it be a principle of reason, that all sensible qualities are in the mind, not in the object. Bereave matter of all its intelligible qualities, both primary and secondary, you in a manner annihilate it, and leave only a certain unknown, inexplicable *something,* as the cause of our perceptions; a notion so imperfect, that no sceptic will think it worth while to contend against it.   (a)

The Origin of Ideas and a Criterion of Meaning

In Hume's version of Pyrrhonism, experience plays the central role in how we come to know anything. His account of experience sounds simple, but the apparent simplicity is misleading. For example, in the next selection he writes that "all our simple ideas in their first appearance are derived from simple impressions, which are correspondent to them, and which they exactly represent." He refers here both to the origin of our ideas and to their meaning, and consequently involves psychology as well as logic. To say that our simple ideas are first *derived* from simple impressions means for Hume that the relation between impression and idea is one of psychic causation, while to regard ideas as representative of impressions is to assume a theory of meaning. The difficulty is that Hume tends to run together indiscriminately his suggested theory of meaning and his psychology.

In his account of experience Hume also attempts to distinguish between impressions and ideas on the basis of their "degrees of force and liveliness." Elsewhere, a similar criterion is used to distinguish ideas of the memory from those of the imagination (the former regarded as "superior in force and vivacity," or distinguished by a different feeling).[1] Then, in the Appendix to the *Treatise,* Hume explicitly states that two ideas of the same object can differ in feeling not only in their degree of force and vivacity but in other unspecified ways as well,[2] and in still another place, in attempting to distinguish between an idea believed and an idea merely entertained,

[1] *Treatise,* Book I, Part III, Section V, pp. 84–86.
[2] *Ibid.,* Appendix, p. 636.

several references are made to a difference in the way we conceive ideas.[3] Finally, in a footnote to the same section, the term "judgment" is associated with ways of conceiving ideas.[4] The importance of all these hints is that they suggest that Hume may amend his initial account of experience as a collection of impressions and ideas when he considers the varying relations of both impressions and ideas to the experiencing and judging subject. If so, the conclusions he draws from his initial account of experience may also be only provisional.

In addition to the general argument, several points in the following selection are of particular interest:

1. The discrete, "atomic" character of both impressions and ideas.

2. The fact that impressions include passions and emotions as well as sensations.

3. Hume's warning that the term "impression" is not intended to suggest manner of production.

4. Hume's admission that the ability under certain circumstances to come by the idea of a particular shade of color without a previous impression of it might constitute an exception to his view that every idea is derived from an antecedent impression.

Selection III:
TREATISE OF HUMAN NATURE
Book I, Part I, Section I

All the perceptions of the human mind resolve themselves into two distinct kinds, which I shall call IMPRESSIONS and IDEAS. The difference betwixt these consists in the degrees of force and liveliness with which they strike upon the mind, and make their way into our thought or consciousness. Those perceptions, which enter with most force and violence, we may name *impressions;* and under this name I comprehend all our sensations, passions and emotions, as they make their first appearance in the soul. By *ideas* I mean the faint images of these in thinking and reasoning; such as, for instance, are all the perceptions excited by the present discourse, excepting only, those which arise from the sight and touch, and excepting the immediate pleasure or uneasiness it may occasion. I believe it will not be very necessary to employ many words in explaining this distinction. Everyone of himself will readily perceive the

[3] *Ibid.*, Book I, Part III, Section VII, pp. 94–98. (See pp. 58–65 of this text for parallel sections of the *Enquiry.*)

[4] *Ibid.*, see *Note*, pp. 96–97. (See footnote, pp. 51–52 of this text for relevance of this viewpoint to the judgment that "God exists.")

difference betwixt feeling and thinking. The common degrees of these are easily distinguished; tho' it is not impossible but in particular instances they may very nearly approach to each other. Thus in sleep, in a fever, in madness, or in any very violent emotions of soul, our ideas may approach to our impressions: As on the other hand it sometimes happens, that our impressions are so faint and low, that we cannot distinguish them from our ideas. But notwithstanding this near resemblance in a few instances, they are in general so very different, that no-one can make a scruple to rank them under distinct heads, and assign to each a peculiar name to mark the difference.*

There is another division of our perceptions, which it will be convenient to observe, and which extends itself both to our impressions and ideas. This division is into SIMPLE and COMPLEX. Simple perceptions or impressions and ideas are such as admit of no distinction nor separation. The complex are the contrary to these, and may be distinguished into parts. Tho' a particular colour, taste, and smell are qualities all united together in this apple, 'tis easy to perceive they are not the same, but are at least distinguishable from each other.

Having by these divisions given an order and arrangement to our objects, we may now apply ourselves to consider with the more accuracy their qualities and relations. The first circumstance, that strikes my eye, is the great resemblance betwixt our impressions and ideas in every other particular, except their degree of force and vivacity. The one seem to be in a manner the reflexion of the other; so that all the perceptions of the mind are double, and appear both as impressions and ideas. When I shut my eyes and think of my chamber, the ideas I form are exact representations of the impressions I felt; nor is there any circumstance of the one, which is not to be found in the other. In running over my other perceptions, I find still the same resemblance and representation. Ideas and impressions appear always to correspond to each other. This circumstance seems to me remarkable, and engages my attention for a moment.

Upon a more accurate survey I find I have been carried away too far by the first appearance, and that I must make use of the distinction of perceptions into *simple and complex*, to limit this general decision, *that*

---

* I here make use of these terms, *impression and idea*, in a sense different from what is usual, and I hope this liberty will be allowed me. Perhaps I rather restore the word, idea, to its original sense, from which Mr. *Locke* had perverted it, in making it stand for all our perceptions. By the term of impression I would not be understood to express the manner, in which our lively perceptions are produced in the soul, but merely the perceptions themselves; for which there is no particular name either in the *English* or any other language, that I know of.

all our ideas and impressions are resembling. I observe, that many of our complex ideas never had impressions, that corresponded to them, and that many of our complex impressions never are exactly copied in ideas. I can imagine to myself such a city as the *New Jerusalem,* whose pavement is gold and walls are rubies, tho' I never saw any such. I have seen *Paris;* but shall I affirm I can form such an idea of that city, as will perfectly represent all its streets and houses in their real and just proportions?

I perceive, therefore, that tho' there is in general a great resemblance betwixt our *complex* impressions and ideas, yet the rule is not universally true, that they are exact copies of each other. We may next consider how the case stands with our *simple* perceptions. After the most accurate examination, of which I am capable, I venture to affirm, that the rule here holds without any exception, and that every simple idea has a simple impression, which resembles it; and every simple impression a correspondent idea. That idea of red, which we form in the dark, and that impression, which strikes our eyes in sun-shine, differ only in degree, not in nature. That the case is the same with all our simple impressions and ideas, 'tis impossible to prove by a particular enumeration of them. Every one may satisfy himself in this point by running over as many as he pleases. But if any one should deny this universal resemblance, I know no way of convincing him, but by desiring him to shew a simple impression, that has not a correspondent idea, or a simple idea, that has not a correspondent impression. If he does not answer this challenge, as 'tis certain he cannot, we may from his silence and our own observation establish our conclusion.

Thus we find, that all simple ideas and impressions resemble each other; and as the complex are formed from them, we may affirm in general, that these two species of perception are exactly correspondent. Having discover'd this relation, which requires no farther examination, I am curious to find some other of their qualities. Let us consider how they stand with regard to their existence, and which of the impressions and ideas are causes, and which effects.

The *full* examination of this question is the subject of the present treatise; and therefore we shall here content ourselves with establishing one general proposition, *That all our simple ideas in their first appearance are deriv'd from simple impressions, which are correspondent to them, and which they exactly represent.*

In seeking for phænomena to prove this proposition, I find only those of two kinds; but in each kind the phænomena are obvious, numerous, and conclusive. I first make myself certain, by a new review, of what I have already asserted, that every simple impression is attended with a correspondent idea, and every simple idea with a correspondent impression. From this constant conjunction of resembling perceptions I immediately conclude, that there is a great connexion betwixt our correspondent impressions and ideas, and that the existence of the one has a considerable influence upon that of the other. Such a constant conjunction, in such an infinite number of instances, can never arise from chance; but clearly proves a dependence of the impressions on the ideas, or of the ideas on the impressions. That I may know on which side this dependence lies, I consider the order of their *first appearance;* and find by constant experience, that the simple impressions always take the precedence of their correspondent ideas, but never appear in the contrary order. To give a child an idea of scarlet or orange, of sweet or bitter, I present the objects, or in other words, convey to him these impressions; but proceed not so absurdly, as to endeavour to produce the impressions by exciting the ideas. Our ideas upon their appearance produce not their correspondent impressions, nor do we perceive any colour, or feel any sensation merely upon thinking of them. On the other hand we find, that any impressions either of the mind or body is constantly followed by an idea, which resembles it, and is only different in the degrees of force and liveliness. The constant conjunction of our resembling perceptions, is a convincing proof, that the one are the causes of the other; and this priority of the impressions is an equal proof, that our impressions are the causes of our ideas, not our ideas of our impressions.

To confirm this I consider another plain and convincing phænomenon; which is, that where-ever by any accident the faculties, which give rise to any impressions, are obstructed in their operations, as when one is born blind or deaf; not only the impressions are lost, but also their correspondent ideas; so that there never appear in the mind the least traces of either of them. Nor is this only true, where the organs of sensation are entirely destroy'd, but likewise where they have never been put in action to produce a particular impression. We cannot form to ourselves a just idea of the taste of a pine-apple, without having actually tasted it.

There is however one contradictory phænomenon, which may prove, that 'tis not absolutely impossible for ideas to go before their correspondent impressions. I believe it will readily be allow'd, that the several distinct ideas of colours, which enter by the eyes, or those of sounds, which are convey'd by the hearing, are really different from each other, tho' at the same time resembling. Now if this be true of different colours, it must be no less so of the different shades of the same colour, that each of them produces a distinct idea, independent of the rest. For if this shou'd be deny'd, 'tis possible, by the continual gradation of shades, to run a colour insensibly into what is most remote from it; and if you will not allow any of the means to be different, you cannot without absurdity deny the extremes to be the same. Suppose therefore a person to have enjoyed his sight for thirty years, and to have become perfectly well acquainted with colours of all kinds, excepting one particular shade of blue, for instance, which it never has been his fortune to meet with. Let all the different shades of that colour, except that single one, be plac'd before him, descending gradually from the deepest to the lightest; 'tis plain, that he will perceive a blank, where that shade is wanting, and will be sensible, that there is a greater distance in that place betwixt the contiguous colours, than in any other. Now I ask, whether 'tis possible for him, from his own imagination, to supply this deficiency, and raise up to himself the idea of that particular shade, tho' it had never been conveyed to him by his senses? I believe there are few but will be of opinion that he can; and this may serve as a proof, that the simple ideas are not always derived from the correspondent impressions; tho' the instance is so particular and singular, that 'tis scarce worth our observing, and does not merit that for it alone we should alter our general maxim.

But besides this exception, it may not be amiss to remark on this head, that the principle of the priority of impressions to ideas must be understood with another limitation, *viz.* that as our ideas are images of our impressions, so we can form secondary ideas, which are images of the primary; as appears from this very reasoning concerning them. This is not, properly speaking, an exception to the rule so much as an explanation of it. Ideas produce the images of themselves in new ideas; but as the first ideas are supposed to be derived from impressions, it still remains true, that all our simple ideas proceed either mediately or immediately from their correspondent impressions.

This then is the first principle I establish in the science of human nature; nor ought we to despise it because of the simplicity of its appearance. For 'tis remarkable, that the present question concerning the precedency of our impressions or ideas, is the same with what has made so much noise in other terms, when it has been disputed whether there be any *innate ideas,* or whether all ideas be derived from sensation and reflexion. We may observe, that in order to prove the ideas of extension and colour not to be innate, philosophers do nothing but shew, that they are conveyed by our senses. To prove the ideas of passion and desire not to be innate they observe that we have a preceding experience of these emotions in ourselves. Now if we carefully examine these arguments, we shall find that they prove nothing but that ideas are preceded by other more lively perceptions, from which they are derived, and which they represent. I hope this clear stating of the question will remove all disputes concerning it, and will render this principle of more use in our reasonings, than it seems hitherto to have been.   (b)

Abstract Ideas

If an idea is a representation or an image grounded in a particular impression, a problem arises of how to interpret an abstract idea that is of necessity applicable to more than one individual image. For example, how can there be an idea of triangularity applicable indifferently to an individual right triangle and an individual triangle that is not a right triangle if such an idea must be an image of one or the other and cannot be an image of both? Hume's answer is that there is nothing which two or more individual entities classified as similar have in common except the same name. This view is called nominalism.[1]

Selection IV:
TREATISE OF HUMAN NATURE
Book I, Part I, Section VII

... 'tis a principle generally receiv'd in philosophy, that every thing in nature is individual, and that 'tis utterly absurd to suppose a triangle really existent, which has no precise proportion of sides and angles. If this therefore be absurd in *fact and reality*, it must also be absurd *in idea;* since nothing of which we can form a clear and distinct idea is absurd and impossible. But to form the idea of an object, and to form an idea simply is the same thing; the reference of the idea to an object being an extraneous denomination, of which in itself it bears no mark or character. Now as 'tis impossible to form an idea of an object, that is possest of quantity and quality, and yet is possest of no precise degree of either; it follows, that there is an equal impossibility of forming an idea, that is not limited and confin'd in both these particulars. Abstract ideas are therefore in themselves individual, however they may become general in their representation. The image in the mind is only that of a particular object, tho' the application of it in our reasoning be the same, as if it were universal.

[1] Alternative views are conceptualism and realism. In conceptualism, entities are regarded as similar only insofar as they give rise to the same idea, while in realism, it is claimed that there are real similarities in similar things beyond the common name we apply to them and beyond the fact that they may give rise to the same idea.

This application of ideas beyond their nature proceeds from our collecting all their possible degrees of quantity and quality in such an imperfect manner as may serve the purposes of life.... When we have found a resemblance among several objects, that often occur to us, we apply the same name to all of them, whatever differences we may observe in the degrees of their quantity and quality, and whatever other differences may appear among them. After we have acquired a custom of this kind, the hearing of that name revives the idea of one of these objects, and makes the imagination conceive it with all its particular circumstances and proportions. But as the same word is suppos'd to have been frequently applied to other individuals, that are different in many respects from that idea, which is immediately present to the mind; the word not being able to revive the idea of all these individuals, only touches the soul, if I may be allow'd so to speak, and revives that custom, which we have acquir'd by surveying them. They are not really and in fact present to the mind, but only in power; nor do we draw them all out distinctly in the imagination, but keep ourselves in a readiness to survey any of them, as we may be prompted by a present design or necessity. The word raises up an individual idea, along with a certain custom; and that custom produces any other individual one, for which we may have occasion. But as the production of all the ideas, to which the name may be apply'd, is in most cases impossible, we abridge that work by a more partial consideration, and find but few inconveniences to arise in our reasoning from that abridgment. (c)

The Need for a Principle of Association of Ideas

Because ideas, as well as impressions, have a discrete "atomic" character, Hume feels that simple ideas stand in need of principles of association to explain how we are led to combine them into complex ideas of some kinds rather than others. He compares these principles of association to Newton's Law of Universal Gravitation among bodies.

Selection V:

TREATISE OF HUMAN NATURE

Book I, Part I, Section IV

As all simple ideas may be separated by the imagination, and may be united again in what form it pleases, nothing wou'd be more unaccountable than the operations of that faculty, were it not guided by some universal principles, which render it, in some measure, uniform with itself in all times and places. Were ideas entirely loose and unconnected, chance alone wou'd join them; and 'tis impossible the same simple ideas should fall regularly into complex ones (as they commonly do) without some bond of union among them, some associating quality, by which one idea naturally introduces another. This uniting principle among ideas is not to be consider'd as an inseparable connexion; for that has been already excluded from the imagination: nor yet are we to conclude, that without it the mind cannot join two ideas; for nothing is more free than that faculty: but we are only to regard it as a gentle force, which commonly prevails, and is the cause why, among other things, languages so nearly correspond to each other; nature in a manner pointing out to every one those simple ideas, which are most proper to be united into a complex one. The qualities, from which this association arises, and by which the mind is after this manner convey'd from one idea to another, are three, viz. RESEMBLANCE, CONTIGUITY in time or place, and CAUSE and EFFECT.

I believe it will not be very necessary to prove, that these qualities produce an association among ideas, and upon the appearance of one idea naturally introduce another. 'Tis plain, that in the course of our thinking, and in the constant revolution of our ideas, our imagination runs easily from one idea to any other that *resembles* it, and that this quality alone is to the fancy a sufficient bond and association. 'Tis likewise evident, that as the senses, in changing their objects, are necessitated to change them regularly, and take them as they lie *contiguous* to each other, the imagination must by long custom acquire the same method of thinking, and run along the parts of space and time in conceiving its objects. As to the connexion, that is made by the relation of *cause and effect,* we shall have occasion afterwards to examine it to the bottom, and therefore shall not at present insist upon it. 'Tis sufficient to observe, that there is no relation, which produces a stronger connexion in the fancy, and makes one idea more readily recall another, than the relation of cause and effect betwixt their objects.

. . . .

These are therefore the principles of union or cohesion among our simple ideas, and in the imagination supply the place of that inseparable connexion, by which they are united in our memory. Here is a kind of ATTRACTION, which in the mental world will be found to have as extraordinary effects as in the natural, and to shew itself in as many and as various forms. Its effects are every where conspicuous; but as to its causes, they are mostly unknown, and must be resolv'd into *original* qualities of human nature, which I pretend not to explain. Nothing is more requisite for a true philosopher, than to restrain the intemperate desire of searching into causes, and having establish'd any doctrine upon a sufficient number of experiments, rest contented with that, when he sees a farther examination would lead him into obscure and uncertain speculations. In that case his enquiry wou'd be much better employ'd in examining the effects than the causes of his principle.   (d)

The Ideas of Existence and External Existence

Hume's treatment of the idea of existence anticipates both Kant's view that existence is not a predicate and the special treatment that contemporary logicians accord existential statements by use of the existential quantifier.[1] Though his handling of the idea of external existence might first lead one to assume both that Hume denies that we can have any such idea and that each individual is limited to thinking of reality as made up exclusively of his own impressions and ideas (a view called "solipsism"), a more careful reading should dispel both of these misconceptions.

Selection VI:
TREATISE OF HUMAN NATURE
Book I, Part II, Section VI

There is no impression nor idea of any kind, of which we have any consciousness or memory, that is not conceiv'd as existent; and 'tis evident, that from this consciousness the most perfect idea and assurance of *being* is deriv'd. From hence we may form a dilemma, the most clear and conclusive that can be imagin'd, viz. that since we never remember any idea or impression without attributing existence to it, the idea of

---

[1] On this subject Kant says: "Being is obviously not a real predicate; that is, it is not a concept of something which could be added to the concept of a thing. It is merely the positing of a thing, and of certain determinations as existing in themselves." Also, "By whatever and by however many predicates we may think a thing—even if we completely determine it—we do not make the least addition to the thing when we further declare that this thing *is*. Otherwise, it would not be exactly the same thing that exists, but something more than we had thought in the concept; and we could not, therefore, say that the exact object of my concept exists." Immanuel Kant, *Critique of Pure Reason*, Norman Kemp Smith (trans.) (New York: St. Martin's Press, Inc. and London: Macmillan & Co., Ltd.), pp. 504–505.

In contemporary logic, attributions of existence are translated by means of the existential quantifier ($\exists x$) instead of by predicate variables. For example, the sentence "A green man exists" would be translated symbolically ($\exists x$) (Mx. Gx), or in other words: "There exists at least one individual such that he is both a man and green."

existence must either be deriv'd from a distinct impression, conjoin'd with every perception or object of our thought, or must be the very same with the idea of the perception or object.

As this dilemma is an evident consequence of the principle, that every idea arises from a similar impression, so our decision betwixt the propositions of the dilemma is no more doubtful. So far from there being any distinct impression, attending every impression and every idea, that I do not think there are any two distinct impressions, which are inseparably conjoin'd. Tho' certain sensations may at one time be united, we quickly find they admit of a separation, and may be presented apart. And thus, tho' every impression and idea we remember be consider'd as existent, the idea of existence is not deriv'd from any particular impression.

The idea of existence, then, is the very same with the idea of what we conceive to be existent. To reflect on any thing simply, and to reflect on it as existent, are nothing different from each other. That idea, when conjoin'd with the idea of any object, makes no addition to it. Whatever we conceive, we conceive to be existent. Any idea we please to form is the idea of a being; and the idea of a being is any idea we please to form.

Whoever opposes this, must necessarily point out that distinct impression, from which the idea of entity is deriv'd, and must prove, that this impression is inseparable from every perception we believe to be existent. This we may without hesitation conclude to be impossible.

... reasoning concerning the *distinction* of ideas without any real *difference* will not here serve us in any stead. That kind of distinction is founded on the different resemblances, which the same simple idea may have to several different ideas. But no object can be presented resembling some object with respect to its existence, and different from others in the same particular; since every object, that is presented, must necessarily be existent.

A like reasoning will account for the idea of *external existence*. We may observe, that 'tis universally allow'd by philosophers, and is besides pretty obvious of itself, that nothing is ever really present with the mind but its perceptions or impressions and ideas, and that external objects become known to us only by those perceptions they occasion. To hate, to love, to think, to feel, to see; all this is nothing but to perceive.

Now since nothing is ever present to the mind but perceptions, and since all ideas are deriv'd from something antecedently present to the mind; it follows, that 'tis impossible for us so much as to conceive or form an idea of any thing specifically different from ideas and impressions. Let us fix our attention out of ourselves as much as possible: Let us chace our imagination to the heavens, or to the utmost limits of the universe; we never really advance a step beyond ourselves, nor can conceive any kind of existence, but those perceptions, which have appear'd in that narrow compass. This is the universe of the imagination, nor have we any idea but what is there produc'd.

The farthest we can go towards a conception of external objects, when suppos'd *specifically* different from our perceptions, is to form a relative idea of them, without pretending to comprehend the related objects. Generally speaking we do not suppose them specifically different; but only attribute to them different relations, connexions and durations.... (e)

Two Criteria of Truth and the Central Problem of Hume's Theoretical Philosophy

Hume divides objects of knowledge into two kinds: relations among ideas and matters of fact. Explaining the distinction, he then proceeds to formulate the central problem of his theoretical philosophy in the next selection. He asks: "What is the nature of that evidence which assures us of any real existence and matter of fact, beyond the present testimony of our senses, or the records of our memory." The kinds of "real existences and matters of fact" he refers to include

1. The reality in the present of an unobserved situation; for example, my friend is in France.
2. The occurrence in the past of an event previously unknown; for example, men were previously on the desert island I am now visiting for the first time.
3. The occurrence of an event in the future; for example, I will be burned if I put my hand too near a fire.

Hume has already suggested that causation is foremost among the principles leading us to associate one idea with another.[1] But more important is his observation that only the assumption that two events are causally related justifies either our predicting or presupposing the occurrence of one event from the occurrence of the other. It is evident that any conclusions concerning the nature of the relation between cause and effect will have far reaching consequences.

[1] *Treatise*, Book I, Part I, Section IV, p. 11.

Selection VII:
ENQUIRY CONCERNING HUMAN UNDERSTANDING
Section IV, Part I

All the objects of human reason or enquiry may naturally be divided
into two kinds, to wit, *Relations of Ideas,* and *Matters of Fact.* Of the
first kind are the sciences of Geometry, Algebra, and Arithmetic; and in
short, every affirmation which is either intuitively or demonstratively
certain. *That the square of the hypothenuse is equal to the square of the
two sides,* is a proposition which expresses a relation between these figures. *That three times five is equal to the half of thirty,* expresses a relation between these numbers. Propositions of this kind are discoverable
by the mere operation of thought, without dependence on what is anywhere existent in the universe. Though there never were a circle or
triangle in nature, the truths demonstrated by Euclid would for ever
retain their certainty and evidence.[2]

Matters of fact, which are the second objects of human reason, are
not ascertained in the same manner; nor is our evidence of their truth,
however great, of a like nature with the foregoing. The contrary of
every matter of fact is still possible; because it can never imply a contradiction, and is conceived by the mind with the same facility and dis-
tinctness, as if ever so conformable to reality. *That the sun will not rise
to-morrow* is no less intelligible a proposition, and implies no more contradiction than the affirmation, *that it will rise.* We should in vain, therefore,
attempt to demonstrate its falsehood. Were it demonstratively false, it
would imply a contradiction, and could never be distinctly conceived
by the mind.

It may, therefore, be a subject worthy of curiosity, to enquire what
is the nature of that evidence which assures us of any real existence and
matter of fact, beyond the present testimony of our senses, or the records
of our memory. This part of philosophy, it is observable, has been little
cultivated, either by the ancients or moderns; and therefore our doubts

---

[2] In the *Treatise,* Hume distinguishes geometry from algebra and arithmetic.
While the premises of arithmetic and algebra concern numerical relations which we
can know with certainty, those of geometry we cannot know with such certainty,
since, for Hume, they are based on the appearances of things in three dimensional
space. (*Treatise,* Book I, Part III, Section I, p. 71.) Here, however, Hume declares as
certain the truths of Euclid's geometry along with those of algebra and arithmetic.
In fact, uncertainty as to whether anything exists conforming to a given set of
premises or definitions does not call into question the certainty of judgments concerning things conforming to the premises or definitions. Hume remarks that the
truths of Euclidean geometry are not dependent on the existence of Euclidean circles
and triangles in nature.

and errors, in the prosecution of so important an enquiry, may be the more excusable; while we march through such difficult paths without any guide or direction. They may even prove useful, by exciting curiosity, and destroying that implicit faith and security, which is the bane of all reasoning and free enquiry. The discovery of defects in the common philosophy, if any such there be, will not, I presume, be a discouragement, but rather an incitement, as is usual, to attempt something more full and satisfactory than has yet been proposed to the public.

All reasonings concerning matter of fact seem to be founded on the relation of *Cause and Effect*. By means of that relation alone we can go beyond the evidence of our memory and senses. If you were to ask a man, why he believes any matter of fact, which is absent; for instance, that his friend is in the country, or in France; he would give you a reason; and this reason would be some other fact; as a letter received from him, or the knowledge of his former resolutions and promises. A man finding a watch or any other machine in a desert island, would conclude that there had once been men in that island. All our reasonings concerning fact are of the same nature. And here it is constantly supposed that there is a connexion between the present fact and that which is inferred from it. Were there nothing to bind them together, the inference would be entirely precarious. The hearing of an articulate voice and rational discourse in the dark assures us of the presence of some person: Why? because these are the effects of the human make and fabric, and closely connected with it. If we anatomize all the other reasonings of this nature, we shall find that they are founded on the relation of cause and effect, and that this relation is either near or remote, direct or collateral. Heat and light are collateral effects of fire, and the one effect may justly be inferred from the other.

If we would satisy ourselves, therefore, concerning the nature of that evidence, which assures us of matters of fact, we must enquire how we arrive at the knowledge of cause and effect.   (f)

Pyrrhonist Analysis of the Idea of Cause and Effect

Though Hume's analysis of causation can be understood initially in the context of an attempt to determine the truth or falsity of cause and effect judgments, further analysis reveals that the very meaningfulness of the idea of cause and effect is at stake. One of the component ideas of the complex idea of cause and effect is that of necessary connection: cause and effect are necessarily tied to one another. Since Hume cannot find an impression corresponding to the idea of necessary connection, his theory of meaning makes it seem impossible to assign a satisfactory meaning to this idea.

Aspects of the argument to be especially noticed are

1. Its dissection and rejection of the traditional view that "Every effect has a cause" is a self-evident proposition (a cause is *not* always necessary despite the title of the section dealing with this subject).

2. Its criticism of the view that there is at least justification in reason or experience, as Hume has so far interpreted them, for assuming that every effect *probably* has a cause.

3. Its provisional rejection of the meaningfulness of saying that a cause has the "power" to produce its effect.

Selection VIII:
TREATISE OF HUMAN NATURE
Book I, Part III, Sections II & III

'Tis impossible to reason justly, without understanding perfectly the idea concerning which we reason; and 'tis impossible perfectly to understand any idea, without tracing it up to its origin, and examining that primary impression, from which it arises. The examination of the impression bestows a clearness on the idea; and the examination of the idea bestows a like clearness on all our reasoning.

Let us therefore cast our eye on any two objects, which we call cause and effect, and turn them on all sides, in order to find that impression, which produces an idea of such prodigious consequence. At first sight I perceive, that I must not search for it in any of the particular *qualities* of the objects; since, which-ever of these qualities I pitch on, I find some object, that is not possest of it, and yet falls under the denomination of cause or effect. And indeed there is nothing existent, either externally or internally, which is not to be consider'd either as a cause or an effect; tho' 'tis plain there is no one quality, which universally belongs to all beings, and gives them a title to that denomination.

The idea, then, of causation must be deriv'd from some *relation* among objects; and that relation we must now endeavor to discover. I find in the first place, that whatever objects are consider'd as causes or effects are *contiguous*; and that nothing can operate in a time or place, which is ever so little remov'd from those of its existence. Tho' distant objects may sometimes seem productive of each other, they are commonly found upon examination to be link'd by a chain of causes, which are contiguous among themselves, and to the distant objects; and when in any particular instance we cannot discover this connexion, we still presume it to exist. We may therefore consider the relation of CONTIGUITY as essential to that of causation; at least may suppose it such, according to the general opinion, till we can find a more * proper occasion to clear up this matter, by examining what objects are or are not susceptible of juxtaposition and conjunction.

The second relation I shall observe as essential to causes and effects, is not so universally acknowledg'd, but is liable to some controversy. 'Tis that of PRIORITY of time in the cause before the effect. Some pretend that 'tis not absolutely necessary a cause shou'd precede its effect; but that any object or action, in the very first moment of its existence, may exert its productive quality, and give rise to another object or action, perfectly co-temporary with itself. But besides that experience in most instances seems to contradict this opinion, we may establish the relation of priority by a kind of inference or reasoning. 'Tis an establish'd maxim both in natural and moral philosophy, that an object, which exists for any time in its full perfection without producing another, is not its sole cause; but is assisted by some other principle, which pushes it from its state of inactivity, and makes it exert that energy, of which it was secretly possest. Now if any cause may be perfectly co-temporary with its effect, 'tis certain, according to this maxim, that they must all of them be so; since any one of them, which retards its operation for a single moment, exerts not itself at that very individual time, in which it might have operated; and therefore is no proper cause. The consequence of this wou'd be no less than the destruction of that succession of causes, which we observe in the world; and indeed, the utter annihilation of time. For if one cause were co-temporary with its effect, and this effect with *its* effect, and so on, 'tis plain there wou'd be no such thing as succession, and all objects must be co-existent.

If this argument appear satisfactory, 'tis well. If not, I beg the reader to allow me the same liberty, which I have us'd in the preceding case, of supposing it such. For he shall find, that the affair is of no great importance.

Having thus discover'd or suppos'd the two relations of *contiguity* and *succession* to be essential to causes and effects, I find I am stopt short, and can proceed no farther in considering any single instance of cause and effect. Motion in one body is regarded upon impulse as the cause of motion in another. When we consider these objects with the utmost attention, we find only that the one body approaches the other; and that the

* Part IV, Sect. 5.

motion of it precedes that of the other, but without any sensible interval. 'Tis in vain to rack ourselves with *farther* thought and reflexion upon this subject. We can go no *farther* in considering this particular instance.

Shou'd any one leave this instance, and pretend to define a cause, by saying it is something productive of another, 'tis evident he wou'd say nothing. For what does he mean by *production?* Can he give any definition of it, that will not be the same with that of causation? If he can; I desire it may be produc'd. If he cannot; he here runs in a circle, and gives a synonimous term instead of a definition.

Shall we then rest contented with these two relations of contiguity and succession, as affording a compleat idea of causation? By no means. An object may be contiguous and prior to another, without being consider'd as its cause. There is a NECESSARY CONNEXION to be taken into consideration; and that relation is of much greater importance, than any of the other two above-mention'd.

Here again I turn the object on all sides, in order to discover the nature of this necessary connexion, and find the impression, or impressions, from which its idea may be deriv'd. When I cast my eye on the *known qualities* of objects, I immediately discover that the relation of cause and effect depends not in the least on *them.* When I consider their *relations,* I can find none but those of contiguity and succession; which I have already regarded as imperfect and unsatisfactory. Shall the despair of success make me assert, that I am here possest of an idea, which is not preceded by any similar impression? This wou'd be too strong a proof of levity and inconstancy; since the contrary principle has been already so firmly establish'd, as to admit of no farther doubt; at least, till we have more fully examin'd the present difficulty.

We must, therefore, proceed like those, who being in search of any thing that lies conceal'd from them, and not finding it in the place they expected, beat about all the neighbouring fields, without any certain view or design, in hopes their good fortune will at last guide them to what they search for. 'Tis necessary for us to leave the direct survey of this question concerning the nature of that *necessary connexion,* which enters into our idea of cause and effect; and endeavour to find some other questions, the examination of which will perhaps afford a hint, that may serve to clear up the present difficulty. Of these questions there occur two, which I shall proceed to examine, *viz.*

First, For what reason we pronounce it *necessary,* that every thing whose existence has a beginning, shou'd also have a cause?

Secondly, Why we conclude, that such particular causes must *necessarily* have such particular effects; and what is the nature of that *inference* we draw from the one to the other, and of the *belief* we repose in it?

I shall only observe before I proceed any farther, that tho' the ideas of cause and effect be deriv'd from the impressions of reflexion as well as from those of sensation, yet for brevity's sake, I commonly mention only the latter as the origin of these ideas; tho' I desire that whatever I say of them may also extend to the former. Passions are connected with their objects and with one another; no less than external bodies are connected together. The same relation, then, of cause and effect, which belongs to one, must be common to all of them.

Why a cause is always necessary.

'Tis a general maxim in philosophy, that *whatever begins to exist, must have a cause of existence.* This is commonly taken for granted in all reasonings, without any proof given or demanded. 'Tis suppos'd to be founded on intuition, and to be one of those maxims, which tho' they may be deny'd with the lips, 'tis impossible for men in their hearts really to doubt of. But if we examine this maxim by the idea of knowledge above-explain'd, we shall discover in it no mark of any such intuitive certainty; but on the contrary shall find, that 'tis of a nature quite foreign to that species of conviction.

All certainty arises from the comparison of ideas, and from the discovery of such relations as are unalterable, so long as the ideas continue the same. These relations are *resemblance, proportions in quantity and number, degrees of any quality, and contrariety;* none of which are imply'd in this proposition, *Whatever has a beginning has also a cause of existence.* That proposition therefore is not intuitively certain. At least any one, who wou'd assert it to be intuitively certain, must deny these to be the only infallible relations, and must find some other relation of that kind to be imply'd in it; which it will then be time enough to examine.

But here is an argument, which proves at once, that the foregoing proposition is neither intuitively nor demonstrably certain. We can never demonstrate the necessity of a cause to every new existence, or new modification of existence, without shewing at the same time the impossibility there is, that any thing can ever begin to exist without some productive principle; [1] and where the latter proposition cannot be prov'd, we must despair of ever being able to prove the former. Now that the latter proposition is utterly incapable of a demonstrative proof, we may satisfy

[1] This passage appears to conflict with the view that Hume expressed on p. 24: "To reflect on anything simply and to reflect on it as existent are nothing different from each other." For a resolution of the difficulty see the footnote on pp. 51–52. Though the discussion there concerns the existence of God, the conclusions are generally applicable.

ourselves by considering, that as all distinct ideas are separable from each other, and as the ideas of cause and effect are evidently distinct, 'twill be easy for us to conceive any object to be non-existent this moment, and existent the next, without conjoining to it the distinct idea of a cause or productive principle. The separation, therefore, of the idea of a cause from that of a beginning of existence, is plainly possible for the imagination; and consequently the actual separation of these objects is so far possible, that it implies no contradiction nor absurdity; and is therefore incapable of being refuted by any reasoning from mere ideas; without which 'tis impossible to demonstrate the necessity of a cause.

Accordingly we shall find upon examination, that every demonstration, which has been produc'd for the necessity of a cause, is fallacious and sophistical. All the points of time and place, say some philosophers,* in which we can suppose any object to begin to exist, are in themselves equal; and unless there be some cause, which is peculiar to one time and to one place, and which by that means determines and fixes the existence, it must remain in eternal suspence; and the object can never begin to be, for want of something to fix its beginning. But I ask; Is there any more difficulty in supposing the time and place to be fix'd without a cause, than to suppose the existence to be determin'd in that manner? The first question that occurs on this subject is always, *whether* the object shall exist or not: The next, *when* and *where* it shall begin to exist. If the removal of a cause be intuitively absurd in the one case, it must be so in the other: And if that absurdity be not clear without a proof in the one case, it will equally require one in the other. The absurdity, then, of the one supposition can never be a proof of that of the other; since they are both upon the same footing, and must stand or fall by the same reasoning.

The second argument, † which I find us'd on this head, labours under an equal difficulty. Every thing, 'tis said, must have a cause; for if any thing wanted a cause, *it* wou'd produce *itself;* that is, exist before it existed; which is impossible. But this reasoning is plainly unconclusive; because it supposes, that in our denial of a cause we still grant what we expressly deny, *viz.* that there must be a cause; which therefore is taken to be the object itself; and *that,* no doubt, is an evident contradiction. But to say that any thing is produc'd, or to express myself more properly, comes into existence, without a cause, is not to affirm, that 'tis itself its own cause; but on the contrary in excluding all external causes, excludes *a fortiori* the thing itself which is created. An object, that exists absolutely without any cause, certainly is not its own cause; and when you assert,

* Mr. *Hobbes.*
† Dr. *Clarke* and others.

that the one follows from the other, you suppose the very point in question, and take it for granted, that 'tis utterly impossible any thing can ever begin to exist without a cause, but that upon the exclusion of one productive principle, we must still have recourse to another.

'Tis exactly the same case with the * third argument, which has been employ'd to demonstrate the necessity of a cause. Whatever is produc'd without any cause, is produc'd by *nothing*; or in other words, has nothing for its cause. But nothing can never be a cause, no more than it can be something, or equal to two right angles. By the same intuition, that we perceive nothing not to be equal to two right angles, or not to be something, we perceive, that it can never be a cause; and consequently must perceive, that every object has a real cause of its existence.

I believe it will not be necessary to employ many words in shewing the weakness of this argument, after what I have said of the foregoing. They are all of them founded on the same fallacy, and are deriv'd from the same turn of thought. 'Tis sufficient only to observe, that when we exclude all causes we really do exclude them, and neither suppose nothing nor the object itself to be the causes of the existence; and consequently can draw no argument from the absurdity of these suppositions to prove the absurdity of that exclusion. If every thing must have a cause, it follows, that upon the exclusion of other causes we must accept of the object itself or of nothing as causes. But 'tis the very point in question, whether every thing must have a cause or not; and therefore, according to all just reasoning, it ought never to be taken for granted.

They are still more frivolous, who say, that every effect must have a cause, because 'tis imply'd in the very idea of effect. Every effect necessarily pre-supposes a cause; effect being a relative term, of which cause is the correlative. But this does not prove, that every being must be preceded by a cause; no more than it follows, because every husband must have a wife, that therefore every man must be marry'd. The true state of the question is, whether every object, which begins to exist, must owe its existence to a cause; and this I assert neither to be intuitively nor demonstratively certain, and hope to have prov'd it sufficiently by the foregoing arguments.

Since it is not from knowledge or any scientific reasoning, that we derive the opinion of the necessity of a cause to every new production, that opinion must necessarily arise from observation and experience. The next question, then, shou'd naturally be, *how experience gives rise to such a principle?* But as I find it will be more convenient to sink this question in the following, *Why we conclude, that such particular causes must neces-*
* Mr. *Locke.*

sarily have such particular effects, and why we form an inference from one to another? we shall make that the subject of our future enquiry. 'Twill, perhaps, be found in the end, that the same answer will serve for both questions.   (g)

Selection IX:
TREATISE OF HUMAN NATURE
Book I, Part III, Section VI

'Tis easy to observe, that in tracing this relation, the inference we draw from cause to effect, is not deriv'd merely from a survey of these particular objects, and from such a penetration into their essences as may discover the dependance of the one upon the other. There is no object, which implies the existence of any other if we consider these objects in themselves, and never look beyond the ideas which we form of them. Such an inference wou'd amount to knowledge, and wou'd imply the absolute contradiction and impossibility of conceiving any thing different. But as all distinct ideas are separable, 'tis evident there can be no impossibility of that kind. When we pass from a present impression to the idea of any object, we might possibly have separated the idea from the impression, and have substituted any other idea in its room.

'Tis therefore by EXPERIENCE only, that we can infer the existence of one object from that of another. The nature of experience is this. We remember to have had frequent instances of the existence of one species of objects; and also remember, that the individuals of another species of objects have always attended them, and have existed in a regular order of contiguity and succession with regard to them. Thus we remember to have seen that species of object we call *flame,* and to have felt that species of sensation we call *heat.* We likewise call to mind their constant conjunction in all past instances. Without any farther ceremony, we call the one *cause* and the other *effect,* and infer the existence of the one from that of the other. In all those instances, from which we learn the conjunction of particular causes and effects, both the causes and effects have been perceiv'd by the senses, and are remember'd: But in all cases, wherein we reason concerning them, there is only one perceiv'd or remember'd, and the other is supply'd in conformity to our past experience.

Thus in advancing we have insensibly discover'd a new relation betwixt cause and effect, when we least expected it, and were entirely employ'd upon another subject. This relation is their CONSTANT CONJUNCTION. Contiguity and succession are not sufficient to make us pronounce any two objects to be cause and effect, unless we perceive, that these two relations are preserv'd in several instances. We may now see the advantage of quitting the direct survey of this relation, in order to discover the nature of that *necessary connexion*, which makes so essential a part of it. There are hopes, that by this means we may at last arrive at our propos'd end; tho' to tell the truth, this new-discover'd relation of a constant conjunction seems to advance us but very little in our way. For it implies no more than this, that like objects have always been plac'd in like relations of contiguity and succession; and it seems evident, at least at first sight, that by this means we can never discover any new idea, and can only multiply, but not enlarge the objects of our mind. It may be thought, that what we learn not from one object, we can never learn from a hundred, which are all of the same kind, and are perfectly resembling in every circumstance. As our senses shew us in one instance two bodies, or motions, or qualities in certain relations of succession and contiguity; so our memory presents us only with a multitude of instances, wherein we always find like bodies, motions, or qualities in like relations. From the mere repetition of any past impression, even to infinity, there never will arise any new original idea, such as that of a necessary connexion; and the number of impressions has in this case no more effect than if we confin'd ourselves to one only. But tho' this reasoning seems just and obvious; yet as it wou'd be folly to despair too soon, we shall continue the thread of our discourse; and having found, that after the discovery of the constant conjunction of any objects, we always draw an inference from one object to another, we shall now examine the nature of that inference, and of the transition from the impression to the idea. Perhaps 'twill appear in the end, that the necessary connexion depends on the inference, instead of the inference's depending on the necessary connexion.

Since it appears, that the transition from an impression present to the memory or senses to the idea of an object, which we call cause or effect, is founded on past *experience*, and on our remembrance of their *constant conjunction*, the next question is, Whether experience produces the idea by means of the understanding or of the imagination; whether we are determin'd by reason to make the transition, or by a certain association and relation of perceptions. If reason determin'd us, it wou'd proceed upon that principle, *that instances, of which we have had no experience, must resemble those, of which we have had experience, and that the course of nature continues always uniformly the same.* In order therefore to clear up this matter, let us consider all the arguments, upon which such a proposition may be suppos'd to be founded; and as these must be deriv'd either from *knowledge* or *probability*, let us cast our eye on each of these degrees of evidence, and see whether they afford any just conclusion of this nature.

Our foregoing method of reasoning will easily convince us, that there can be no *demonstrative* arguments to prove, *that those instances, of which we have had no experience, resemble those, of which we have had experience.* We can at least conceive a change in the course of nature; which sufficiently proves, that such a change is not absolutely impossible. To form a clear idea of any thing, is an undeniable argument for its possibility, and is alone a refutation of any pretended demonstration against it.

Probability, as it discovers not the relations of ideas, consider'd as such, but only those of objects, must in some respects be founded on the impressions of our memory and senses, and in some respects on our ideas. Were there no mixture of any impression in our probable reasonings, the conclusion wou'd be entirely chimerical: And were there no mixture of ideas, the action of the mind, in observing the relation, wou'd, properly speaking, be sensation, not reasoning. 'Tis therefore necessary, that in all probable reasonings there be something present to the mind, either seen or remember'd; and that from this we infer something connected with it, which is not seen nor remember'd.

The only connexion or relation of objects, which can lead us beyond the immediate impressions of our memory and senses, is that of cause and effect; and that because 'tis the only one, on which we can found a just inference from one object to another. The idea of cause and effect is deriv'd from *experience*, which informs us, that such particular objects, in all past instances, have been constantly conjoin'd with each other: And as an object similar to one of these is suppos'd to be immediately present in its impression, we thence presume on the existence of one similar to its usual attendant. According to this account of things, which is, I think, in every point unquestionable, probability is founded on the presumption of a resemblance betwixt those objects, of which we have had experience, and those, of which we have had none; and therefore 'tis impossible this presumption can arise from probability. The same principle cannot be both the cause and effect of another; and this is, perhaps, the only proposition concerning that relation, which is either intuitively or demonstratively certain.

Shou'd any one think to elude this argument; and without determining whether our reasoning on this subject be deriv'd from demonstration or probability, pretend that all conclusions from causes and effects are built on solid reasoning: I can only desire, that this reasoning may be produc'd, in order to be expos'd to our examination. It may, perhaps, be said, that after experience of the constant conjunction of certain objects, we reason in the following manner. Such an object is always found to produce another. 'Tis impossible it cou'd have this effect, if it was not endow'd with a power of production. The power necessarily implies the effect; and therefore there is a just foundation for drawing a conclusion from the existence of one object to that of its usual attendant. The past production implies a power: The power implies a new production: And the new production is what we infer from the power and the past production.

. . . .

It shall . . . be allow'd for a moment, that the production of one object by another in any one instance implies a power; and that this power is connected with its effect. But it having been already prov'd, that the power lies not in the sensible qualities of the cause; and there being nothing but the sensible qualities present to us; I ask, why in other instances you presume that the same power still exists, merely upon the appearance of these qualities? Your appeal to past experience decides nothing in the present case; and at the utmost can only prove, that that very object, which produc'd any other, was at that very instant endow'd with such a power; but can never prove, that the same power must continue in the same object or collection of sensible qualities; much less, that a like power is always conjoin'd with like sensible qualities. Shou'd it be said, that we have experience, that the same power continues united with the same object, and that like objects are endow'd with like powers, I wou'd renew my question, *why from this experience we form any conclusion beyond those past instances, of which we have had experience.* If you answer this question in the same manner as the preceding, your answer gives still occasion to a new question of the same kind, even *in infinitum;* which clearly proves, that the foregoing reasoning had no just foundation.

Thus not only our reason fails us in the discovery of the *ultimate connexion* of causes and effects, but even after experience has inform'd us of their *constant conjunction,* 'tis impossible for us to satisfy ourselves by our reason, why we shou'd extend that experience beyond those particular instances, which have fallen under our observation. We suppose, but are never able to prove, that there must be a resemblance betwixt those objects, of which we have had experience, and those which lie beyond the reach of our discovery. (h)

Further Consequences of Pyrrhonism

We may examine further consequences of Hume's version of Pyrrhonism under the following headings: (A) Aristotelian Substance and Newtonian Material Substance, (B) Mental Substance and Personal Identity, (C) God, and (D) Miracles.

(A) Aristotelian Substance and Newtonian Material Substance

Hume, using Pyrrhonist arguments, attacks both the Aristotelian notion that there is a common something (or substance) underlying the varying appearances of a single individual and the Newtonian adaptation of this idea which would make that something physical matter. The former is Hume's target when he speaks of "the antient philosophy" in the first of the following selections; the latter is discussed in the second under the heading of "the modern philosophy."

Selection X:
TREATISE OF HUMAN NATURE
Book I, Part IV, Section III

Of the antient philosophy.

Several moralists have recommended it as an excellent method of becoming acquainted with our own hearts, and knowing our progress in virtue, to recollect our dreams in a morning, and examine them with the same rigour, that we wou'd our most serious and most deliberate actions. Our character is the same throughout, say they, and appears best where artifice, fear, and policy have no place, and men can neither be hypocrites with themselves nor others. The generosity, or baseness of our temper, our meekness or cruelty, our courage or pusilanimity, influence the fictions of the imagination with the most unbounded liberty, and discover themselves in the most glaring colours. In like manner, I am persuaded, there might be several useful discoveries made from a criticism of the fictions of the antient philosophy, concerning *substances, and substantial forms, and accidents, and occult qualities;* which, however unreasonable and capricious, have a very intimate connexion with the principles of human nature.

'Tis confest by the most judicious philosophers, that our ideas of bodies are nothing but collections form'd by the mind of the ideas of the several distinct sensible qualities, of which objects are compos'd, and which we find to have a constant union with each other. But however these qualities may in themselves be entirely distinct, 'tis certain we commonly regard the compound, which they form, as ONE thing, and as continuing the SAME under very considerable alterations. The acknowledg'd composition is evidently contrary to this suppos'd *simplicity,* and the variation to the *identity.* It may, therefore, be worth while to consider the *causes,* which make us almost universally fall into such evident contradictions, as well as the *means* by which we endeavour to conceal them.

'Tis evident, that as the ideas of the several distinct *successive* qualities

of objects are united together by a very close relation, the mind, in looking along the succession, must be carry'd from one part of it to another
by an easy transition, and will no more perceive the change, than if it
contemplated the same unchangeable object. This easy transition is the
effect, or rather essence of relation; and as the imagination readily takes
one idea for another, where their influence on the mind is similar; hence
it proceeds, that any such succession of related qualities is readily consider'd as one continu'd object, existing without any variation. The
smooth and uninterrupted progress of the thought, being alike in both
cases, readily deceives the mind, and makes us ascribe an identity to the
changeable succession of connected qualities.

But when we alter our method of considering the succesion, and instead
of tracing it gradually thro' the successive points of time, survey at once
any two distinct periods of its duration, and compare the different conditions of the successive qualities; in that case the variations, which were
insensible when they arose gradually, do now appear of consequence, and
seem entirely to destroy the identity. By this means there arises a kind
of contrariety in our method of thinking, from the different points of view,
in which we survey the object, and from the nearness or remoteness of
those instants of time, which we compare together. When we gradually
follow an object in its successive changes, the smooth progress of the
thought makes us ascribe an identity to the succession; because 'tis by a
similar act of the mind we consider an unchangeable object. When we
compare its situation after a considerable change the progress of the
thought is broke; and consequently we are presented with the idea of
diversity: In order to reconcile which contradictions the imagination is
apt to feign something unknown and invisible, which it supposes to continue the same under all these variations; and this unintelligible something it calls a *substance, or original and first matter.*

We entertain a like notion with regard to the *simplicity* of substances,
and from like causes. Suppose an object perfectly simple and indivisible
to be presented, along with another object, whose *co-existent* parts are
connected together by a strong relation, 'tis evident the actions of the
mind, in considering these two objects, are not very different. The imagination conceives the simple object at once, with facility, by a single effort
of thought, without change or variation. The connexion of parts in the
compound object has almost the same effect, and so unites the object
within itself, that the fancy feels not the transition in passing from one
part to another. Hence the colour, taste, figure, solidity, and other qualities, combin'd in a peach or melon, are conceiv'd to form *one thing;* and
that on account of their close relation, which makes them affect the

thought in the same manner, as if perfectly uncompounded. But the mind rests not here. Whenever it views the object in another light, it finds that all these qualities are different, and distinguishable, and separable from each other; which view of things being destructive of its primary and more natural notions, obliges the imagination to feign an unknown something, or *original* substance and matter, as a principle of union or cohesion among these qualities, and as what may give the compound object a title to be call'd one thing, notwithstanding its diversity and composition.

The peripatetic [1] philosophy asserts the *original* matter to be perfectly homogeneous in all bodies, and considers fire, water, earth, and air,[2] as of the very same substance; on account of their gradual revolutions and changes into each other. At the same time it assigns to each of these species of objects a distinct *substantial form,* which it supposes to be the source of all those different qualities they possess, and to be a new foundation of simplicity and identity to each particular species. All depends on our manner of viewing the objects. When we look along the insensible changes of bodies, we suppose all of them to be of the same substance or essence. When we consider their sensible differences, we attribute to each of them a substantial and essential difference. And in order to indulge ourselves in both these ways of considering our objects, we suppose all bodies to have at once a substance and a substantial form.

The notion of *accidents* is an unavoidable consequence of this method of thinking with regard to substances and substantial forms; nor can we forbear looking upon colours, sounds, tastes, figures, and other properties of bodies, as existences, which cannot subsist apart, but require a subject of inhesion to sustain and support them. For having never discover'd any of these sensible qualities, where, for the reasons above-mention'd, we did not likewise fancy a substance to exist; the same habit, which makes us infer a connexion betwixt cause and effect, makes us here infer a dependance of every quality on the unknown substance. The custom of imagining a dependance has the same effect as the custom of observing it wou'd have. This conceit, however, is no more reasonable than any of the foregoing. Every quality being a distinct thing from another, may be conceiv'd to exist apart, and may exist apart, not only from every other quality, but from that unintelligible chimera of a substance.

But these philosophers carry their fictions still farther in their senti-

---

[1] The word "peripatetic" means "performed or performing while walking," and is said to have been derived from Aristotle's habit of walking with his students while teaching.

[2] The Greeks supposed everything to be made of these four elements in various combinations.

ments concerning *occult qualities,* and both suppose a substance support-
ing, which they do not understand, and an accident supported, of which
they have as imperfect an idea. The whole system, therefore, is entirely
incomprehensible, and yet is deriv'd from principles as natural as any of
these above-explain'd. (i)

Selection XI:
TREATISE OF HUMAN NATURE
Book I, Part IV, Section IV

The opinions of the antient philosophers, their fictions of substance and
accident, and their reasonings concerning substantial forms and occult
qualities, are like the spectres in the dark, and are deriv'd from principles,
which, however common, are neither universal nor unavoidable in human nature. The *modern philosophy* pretends to be entirely free from this
defect, and to arise only from the solid, permanent, and consistent principles of the imagination. Upon what grounds this pretension is founded
must now be the subject of our enquiry.

The fundamental principle of that philosophy is the opinion concerning
colours, sounds, tastes, smells, heat and cold; which it asserts to be nothing
but impressions in the mind, deriv'd from the operation of external objects, and without any resemblance to the qualities of the objects. Upon
examination, I find only one of the reasons commonly produc'd for this
opinion to be satisfactory, *viz.* that deriv'd from the variations of those
impressions, even while the external object, to all appearance, continues
the same. These variations depend upon several circumstances. Upon the
different situations of our health: A man in a malady feels a disagreeable
taste in meats, which before pleas'd him the most. Upon the different com-
plexions and constitutions of men: That seems bitter to one, which is sweet
to another. Upon the difference of their external situation and position:
Colours reflected from the clouds change according to the distance of the
clouds, and according to the angle they make with the eye and luminous
body. Fire also communicates the sensation of pleasure at one distance,
and that of pain at another. Instances of this kind are very numerous and
frequent.

The conclusion drawn from them, is likewise as satisfactory as can possibly be imagin'd. 'Tis certain, that when different impressions of the
same sense arise from any object, every one of these impressions has not
a resembling quality existent in the object. For as the same object cannot, at the same time, be endow'd with different qualities of the same
sense, and as the same quality cannot resemble impressions entirely dif-

ferent; it evidently follows, that many of our impressions have no external model or archetype. Now from like effects we presume like causes. Many of the impressions of colour, sound, &c. are confest to be nothing but internal existences, and to arise from causes, which no ways resemble them. These impressions are in appearance nothing different from the other impressions of colour, sound, &c. We conclude, therefore, that they are, all of them, deriv'd from a like origin.

This principle being once admitted, all the other doctrines of that philosophy seem to follow by an easy consequence. For upon the removal of sounds, colours, heat, cold, and other sensible qualities, from the rank of continu'd independent existences, we are reduc'd merely to what are called primary qualities, as the only *real* ones, of which we have any adequate notion. These primary qualities are extension and solidity, with their different mixtures and modifications; figure, motion, gravity, and cohesion. The generation, encrease, decay, and corruption of animals and vegetables, are nothing but changes of figure and motion; as also the operations of all bodies on each other; of fire, of light, water, air, earth, and of all the elements and powers of nature. One figure and motion produces another figure and motion; nor does there remain in the material universe any other principle, either active or passive, of which we can form the most distant idea.

I believe many objections might be made to this system: But at present I shall confine myself to one, which is in my opinion very decisive. I assert, that instead of explaining the operations of external objects by its means, we utterly annihilate all these objects, and reduce ourselves to the opinions of the most extravagant scepticism concerning them. If colours, sounds, tastes, and smells be merely perceptions, nothing we can conceive is possest of a real, continu'd, and independent existence; not even motion, extension and solidity, which are the primary qualities chiefly insisted on.

To begin with the examination of motion; 'tis evident this is a quality altogether inconceivable alone, and without a reference to some other object. The idea of motion necessarily supposes that of a body moving. Now what is our idea of the moving body, without which motion is incomprehensible? It must resolve itself into the idea of extension or of solidity; and consequently the reality of motion depends upon that of these other qualities.

This opinion, which is universally acknowledg'd concerning motion, I have prov'd to be true with regard to extension; and have shewn that 'tis impossible to conceive extension, but as compos'd of parts, endow'd with colour or solidity. The idea of extension is a compound idea; but as it is not compounded of an infinite number of parts or inferior ideas, it must at least resolve itself into such as are perfectly simple and indivisible. These simple and indivisible parts, not being ideas of extension, must be non-entities, unless conceiv'd as colour'd or solid. Colour is excluded from any real existence. The reality, therefore, of our idea of extension depends upon the reality of that of solidity, nor can the former be just while the latter is chimerical. Let us, then, lend our attention to the examination of the idea of solidity.

The idea of solidity is that of two objects, which being impell'd by the utmost force, cannot penetrate each other; but still maintain a separate and distinct existence. Solidity, therefore, is perfectly incomprehensible alone, and without the conception of some bodies, which are solid, and maintain this separate and distinct existence. Now what idea have we of these bodies? The ideas of colours, sounds, and other secondary qualities are excluded. The idea of motion depends on that of extension, and the idea of extension on that of solidity. 'Tis impossible, therefore, that the idea of solidity can depend on either of them. For that wou'd be to run in a circle, and make one idea depend on another, while at the same time the latter depends on the former. Our modern philosophy, therefore, leaves us no just nor satisfactory idea of solidity; nor consequently of matter.

(j)

(B) Mental Substance and Personal Identity

In addition to discussing the consequences of his Pyrrhonist view of the nature of the mind, Hume gives in the following selection further insight into the metaphysical presuppositions of his Pyrrhonism. Although he obviously did not intend that impressions and ideas be regarded as substances, he argues that this point of view would be valid if we were to accept the definition of a substance as "something which may exist by itself." After rejecting this definition, he finally dismisses as irrelevant the dispute over whether perceptions are material or immaterial.

Selection XII:
TREATISE OF HUMAN NATURE
Book I, Part IV, Section V

As every idea is deriv'd from a precedent impression, had we any idea of the substance of our minds, we must also have an impression of it; which is very difficult, if not impossible, to be conceiv'd. For how can an impression represent a substance, otherwise than by resembling it? And how can an impression resemble a substance, since, according to this philosophy, it is not a substance, and has none of the peculiar qualities or characteristics of a substance?

But leaving the question *of what may or may not be*, for that other *what actually is*, I desire those philosophers, who pretend that we have an idea of the substance of our minds, to point out the impression that produces it, and tell distinctly after what manner that impression operates, and from what object it is deriv'd. Is it an impression of sensation or of reflection? Is it pleasant, or painful, or indifferent? Does it attend us at all times, or does it only return at intervals? If at intervals, at what times principally does it return, and by what causes is it produc'd?

If instead of answering these questions, any one shou'd evade the difficulty, by saying, that the definition of a substance is *something which may exist by itself*; and that this definition ought to satisfy us: Shou'd this be said, I shou'd observe, that this definition agrees to every thing, that can possibly be conceiv'd; and never will serve to distinguish substance from accident, or the soul from its perceptions. For thus I reason. Whatever is clearly conceiv'd may exist; and whatever is clearly conceiv'd, after any manner, may exist after the same manner. This is one principle, which has been already acknowledg'd. Again, every thing, which is different, is distinguishable, and every thing which is distinguishable, is separable by the imagination. This is another principle. My conclusion from both is, that since all our perceptions are different from each other, and from every thing else in the universe, they are also distinct and separable, and may be consider'd as separately existent, and may exist separately, and have no need of any thing else to support their existence. They are, therefore, substances, as far as this definition explains a substance.

Thus neither by considering the first origin of ideas, nor by means of a definition are we able to arrive at any satisfactory notion of substance; which seems to me a sufficient reason for abandoning utterly that dispute concerning the materiality and immateriality of the soul, and makes me absolutely condemn even the question itself. We have no perfect idea of any thing but of a perception. A substance is entirely different from a perception. We have, therefore, no idea of a substance. Inhesion in something is suppos'd to be requisite to support the existence of our perceptions. Nothing appears requisite to support the existence of a perception. We have, therefore, no idea of inhesion. What possibility then of answering that question, *Whether perceptions inhere in a material or immaterial substance*, when we do not so much as understand the meaning of the question? (k)

Closely related to the notion of mental substance is that of personal identity. Hume's examination of personal identity in the following passage includes a striking almost existential image of the mind as a kind of theatre in the middle of nowhere.

Selection XIII:
TREATISE OF HUMAN NATURE
Book I, Part IV, Section VI

There are some philosophers, who imagine we are every moment intimately conscious of what we call our SELF; that we feel its existence and its continuance in existence; and are certain, beyond the evidence of a demonstration, both of its perfect identity and simplicity. The strongest sensation, the most violent passion, say they, instead of distracting us from this view, only fix it the more intensely, and make us consider their influence on *self* either by their pain or pleasure. To attempt a farther proof of this were to weaken its evidence; since no proof can be deriv'd from any fact, of which we are so intimately conscious; nor is there any thing, of which we can be certain, if we doubt of this.

Unluckily all these positive assertions are contrary to that very experience, which is pleaded for them, nor have we any idea of self, after the manner it is here explain'd. For from what impression cou'd this idea be deriv'd? This question 'tis impossible to answer without a manifest contradiction and absurdity; and yet 'tis a question, which must necessarily be answer'd, if we wou'd have the idea of self pass for clear and intelligible. It must be some one impression, that gives rise to every real idea. But self or person is not any one impression but that to which our several impressions and ideas are suppos'd to have a reference. If any impression gives rise to the idea of self, that impression must continue invariably the same, thro' the whole course of our lives; since self is suppos'd to exist after that manner. But there is no impression constant and invariable. Pain and pleasure, grief and joy, passions and sensations succeed each other, and never all exist at the same time. It cannot, therefore, be from any of these impressions, or from any other, that the idea of self is deriv'd; and consequently there is no such idea.

But farther, what must become of all our particular perceptions upon this hypothesis? All these are different, and distinguishable, and separable from each other, and may be separately consider'd, and may exist separately, and have no need of any thing to support their existence. After what manner, therefore, do they belong to self; and how are they connected with it? For my part, when I enter most intimately into what I call *myself*, I always stumble on some particular perception or other, of heat or cold, light or shade, love or hatred, pain or pleasure. I never can catch *myself* at any time without a perception, and never can observe any thing but the perception. When my perceptions are remov'd for any time, as by sound sleep; so long am I insensible of *myself*, and may truly be said not to exist. And were all my perceptions remov'd by death, and cou'd I neither think, nor feel, nor see, nor love, nor hate after the dissolution of my body, I shou'd be entirely annihilated, nor do I conceive what is farther requisite to make me a perfect non-entity. If any one upon serious and unprejudic'd reflexion, thinks he has a different notion of *himself*, I must confess I can reason no longer with him. All I can allow him is, that he may be in the right as well as I, and that we are essentially different in this particular. He may, perhaps, perceive something simple and continu'd, which he calls *himself*; tho' I am certain there is no such principle in me.

But setting aside some metaphysicians of this kind, I may venture to affirm of the rest of mankind, that they are nothing but a bundle of collection of different perceptions, which succeed each other with an inconceivable rapidity, and are in a perpetual flux and movement. Our eyes cannot turn in their sockets without varying our perceptions. Our thought is still more variable than our sight; and all our other senses and faculties contribute to this change; nor is there any single power of the soul, which remains unalterably the same, perhaps for one moment. The mind is a kind of theatre, where several perceptions successively make their appearance; pass, re-pass, glide away, and mingle in an infinite variety of postures and situations. There is properly no *simplicity* in it at one time, nor *identity* in different; whatever natural propension we may have to imagine that simplicity and identity. The comparison of the theatre must not mislead us. They are the successive perceptions only, that constitute the mind; nor have we the most distant notion of the place, where these scenes are represented, or of the materials, of which it is compos'd.   (l)

(C) God

Since Kant, it has become common practice among philosophers to divide attempts to prove the existence of God into three categories: the physico-theological proof, or the proof from design; the cosmological proof; and the ontological proof. The first argues that the existence of order and purposiveness in the world requires the existence of a master order-giver or designer; the second asserts that our experience of particular existents leads us to admit the existence of an absolutely necessary being (one the denial of whose existence would contradict the affirmation that there are particular existents); the third maintains that to assert that God does not exist is itself a contradiction.[1]

Though Hume was of course not familiar with Kant's terminology, in our next selection he summarizes briefly the physico-theological proof in his own terms, and then attempts to refute it by sceptical arguments.

Selection XIV:
ENQUIRY CONCERNING HUMAN UNDERSTANDING
Section XI

... If you saw, for instance, a half-finished building, surrounded with heaps of brick and stone and mortar, and all the instruments of masonry; could you not *infer* from the effect, that it was a work of design and contrivance? And could you not return again, from this inferred cause, to infer new additions to the effect, and conclude, that the building would soon be finished, and receive all the further improvements, which art could bestow upon it? If you saw upon the sea-shore the print of one human foot, you would conclude, that a man had passed that way, and that he had also left the traces of the other foot, though effaced by the rolling of the sands or inundation of the waters. Why then do you refuse to admit the same method of reasoning with regard to the order of nature? Consider the world and the present life only as an imperfect building, from which you can infer a superior intelligence; and arguing from that superior intelligence, which can leave nothing imperfect; why may you not infer a more finished scheme or plan, which will receive its completion in some distant point of space or time? Are not these methods of reasoning exactly similar? And under what pretence can you embrace the one, while you reject the other?

The infinite difference of the subjects, replied he, is a sufficient foundation for this difference in my conclusions. In works of *human* art and contrivance, it is allowable to advance from the effect to the cause, and returning back from the cause, to form new inferences concerning the effect, and examine the alterations, which it has probably undergone, or may still undergo. But what is the foundation of this method of reasoning? Plainly this; that man is a being, whom we know by experience, whose

[1] For further explanation of this threefold division as well as an exposition of Kant's views on the subject, see pp. 136–137 of this volume.

motives and designs we are acquainted with, and whose projects and inclinations have a certain connexion and coherence, according to the laws which nature has established for the government of such a creature. When, therefore, we find, that any work has proceeded from the skill and industry of man; as we are otherwise acquainted with the nature of the animal, we can draw a hundred inferences concerning what may be expected from him; and these inferences will all be founded in experience and observation. But did we know man only from the single work or production which we examine, it were impossible for us to argue in this manner; because our knowledge of all the qualities, which we ascribe to him, being in that case derived from the production, it is impossible they could point to any thing farther, or be the foundation of any new inference. The print of a foot in the sand can only prove, when considered alone, that there was some figure adapted to it, by which it was produced: but the print of a human foot proves likewise, from our other experience, that there was probably another foot, which also left its impression, though effaced by time or other accidents. Here we mount from the effect to the cause; and descending again from the cause, infer alterations in the effect; but this is not a continuation of the same simple chain of reasoning. We comprehend in this case a hundred other experiences and observations, concerning the *usual* figure and members of that species of animal, without which this method of argument must be considered as fallacious and sophistical.

The case is not the same with our reasonings from the works of nature. The Deity is known to us only by his productions, and is a single being in the universe, not comprehended under any species or genus, from whose experienced attributes or qualities, we can, by analogy, infer any attribute or quality in him. As the universe shews wisdom and goodness, we infer wisdom and goodness. As it shews a particular degree of these perfections, we infer a particular degree of them, precisely adapted to the effect which we examine. But farther attributes or farther degrees of the same attributes, we can never be authorised to infer or suppose, by any rules of just reasoning. Now, without some such licence of supposition, it is impossible for us to argue from the cause, or infer any alteration in the effect, beyond what has immediately fallen under our observation. Greater good produced by this Being must still prove a greater degree of goodness: a more impartial distribution of rewards and punishments must proceed from a greater regard to justice and equity. Every supposed addition to the works of nature makes an addition to the attributes of the Author of nature; and consequently, being entirely unsupported by any reason or argument, can never be admitted but as mere conjecture and hypothesis.*

The great source of our mistake in this subject, and of the unbounded licence of conjecture, which we indulge, is, that we tacitly consider ourselves, as in the place of the Supreme Being, and conclude, that he will, on every occasion, observe the same conduct, which we ourselves, in his situation, would have embraced as reasonable and eligible. But, besides that the ordinary course of nature may convince us, that almost everything is regulated by principles and maxims very different from ours; besides this, I say, it must evidently appear contrary to all rules of analogy to reason, from the intentions and projects of men, to those of a Being so different, and so much superior. In human nature, there is a certain experienced coherence of designs and inclinations; so that when, from any fact, we have discovered one intention of any man, it may often be reasonable, from experience, to infer another, and draw a long chain of conclusions concerning his past or future conduct. But this method of reasoning can never have place with regard to a Being, so remote and incomprehensible, who bears much less analogy to any other being in the universe than the sun to a waxen taper, and who discovers himself only by some faint traces or outlines, beyond which we have no authority to ascribe to him any attribute or perfection. What we imagine to be a superior perfection, may really be a defect. Or were it ever so much a perfection, the ascribing of it to the Supreme Being, where it appears not to have been really exerted, to the full, in his works, savours more of flattery and panegyric, than of just reasoning and sound philosophy. All the philosophy, therefore, in the world, and all the religion, which is nothing but a species of philosophy, will never be able to carry us beyond the usual course of experience, or give us measures of conduct and behaviour

---

* In general, it may, I think, be established as a maxim, that where any cause is known only by its particular effects, it must be impossible to infer any new effects from that cause; since the qualities, which are requisite to produce these new effects along with the former, must either be different, or superior, or of more extensive operation, than those which simply produced the effect, whence alone the cause is supposed to be known to us. We can never, therefore, have any reason to suppose the existence of these qualities. To say, that the new effects proceed only from a continuation of the same energy, which is already known from the first effects, will not remove the difficulty. For even granting this to be the case (which can seldom be supposed), the very continuation and exertion of a like energy (for it is impossible it can be absolutely the same), I say, this exertion of a like energy, in a different period of space and time, is a very arbitrary supposition, and what there cannot possibly be any traces of in the effects, from which all our knowledge of the cause is originally derived. Let the *inferred* cause be exactly proportioned (as it should be) to the known effect; and it is impossible that it can possess any qualities, from which new or different effects can be *inferred*.

different from those which are furnished by reflections on common life. No new fact can ever be inferred from the religious hypothesis; no event foreseen or foretold; no reward or punishment expected or dreaded, beyond what is already known by practice and observation.   (m)

In the next selection, from the *Dialogues Concerning Natural Religion,* Hume considers the cosmological proof and attempts to refute it with a line of reasoning applicable equally to the ontological proof. He gives a clue to the relative attitudes of the disputants when he refers to "the rigid inflexible orthodoxy of Demea," "the careless scepticism of Philo," and "the accurate philosophical turn of Cleanthes." [1] Cleanthes sets forth the argument against Demea. Hume thus seems to imply that one doesn't have to be a Pyrrhonist to reject Demea's arguments—that is, the cosmological proof and, by implication, the ontological proof.

Selection XV:
DIALOGUES CONCERNING NATURAL RELIGION
Part IX

But if so many difficulties attend the argument *a posteriori,* said DEMEA; had we not better adhere to that simple and sublime argument *a priori,* which, by offering to us infallible demonstration, cuts off at once all doubt and difficulty? By this argument, too, we may prove the INFINITY of the divine attributes, which, I am afraid, can never be ascertained with certainty from any other topic. For how can an effect, which either is finite, or, for aught we know, may be so; how can such an effect, I say, prove an infinite cause? The unity too of the divine nature, it is very difficult, if not absolutely impossible, to deduce merely from contemplating the works of nature; nor will the uniformity alone of the plan, even were it allowed, give us any assurance of that attribute. Whereas the argument *a priori.* . . .

You seem to reason, DEMEA, interposed CLEANTHES, as if those advantages and conveniences in the abstract argument were full proofs of its solidity. But it is first proper, in my opinion, to determine what argument of this nature you choose to insist on; and we shall afterwards, from itself, better than from its *useful* consequences, endeavour to determine what value we ought to put upon it.

[1] Hume, *Dialogues Concerning Natural Religion,* Norman Kemp Smith (ed.) (New York: Bobbs-Merrill, 1947), p. 128 (The Library of Liberal Arts).

The argument, replied DEMEA, which I would insist on is the common one. Whatever exists must have a cause or reason of its existence; it being absolutely impossible for any thing to produce itself, or be the cause of its own existence. In mounting up, therefore, from effects to causes, we must either go on in tracing an infinite succession, without any ultimate cause at all, or must at last have recourse to some ultimate cause, that is *necessarily* existent: Now that the first supposition is absurd may be thus proved. In the infinite chain or succession of causes and effects, each single effect is determined to exist by the power and efficacy of that cause which immediately preceded; but the whole eternal chain or succession, taken together, is not determined or caused by any thing: And yet it is evident that it requires a cause or reason, as much as any particular object, which begins to exist in time. The question is still reasonable, why this particular succession of causes existed from eternity, and not any other succession, or no succession at all. If there be no necessarily existent Being, any supposition, which can be formed, is equally possible; nor is there any more absurdity in nothing's having existed from eternity, than there is in that succession of causes, which constitutes the universe. What was it, then, which determined something to exist rather than nothing, and bestowed being on a particular possibility, exclusive of the rest? *External causes,* there are supposed to be none. *Chance* is a word without a meaning. Was it *nothing?* But that can never produce any thing. We must, therefore, have recourse to a necessarily existent Being, who carries the REASON of his existence in himself; and who cannot be supposed not to exist without an express contradiction. There is consequently such a Being, that is, there is a Deity.

I shall not leave it to PHILO, said CLEANTHES (though I know that the starting objections is his chief delight), to point out the weakness of this metaphysical reasoning. It seems to me so obviously ill-grounded, and at the same time of so little consequence to the cause of true piety and religion, that I shall myself venture to show the fallacy of it.

I shall begin with observing, that there is an evident absurdity in pretending to demonstrate a matter of fact, or to prove it by any arguments *a priori*. Nothing is demonstrable, unless the contrary implies a contradiction. Nothing, that is distinctly conceivable, implies a contradiction. Whatever we conceive as existent, we can also conceive as non-existent.[2] There

[2] This idea appears to conflict with the one Hume expressed on p. 24: "To reflect on anything simply and to reflect on it as existent are nothing different from each other." In order to resolve the discrepancy, it is necessary to notice that the word "conceive" has at least two meanings. It can mean simply to imagine without involving us in any judgment about what we imagine; or it can mean to make a judgment which presupposes that what we judge we also imagine. Hume's view as it

is no Being, therefore, whose non-existence implies a contradiction. Consequently there is no Being, whose existence is demonstrable. I propose this argument as entirely decisive, and am willing to rest the whole controversy upon it.

It is pretended that the Deity is a necessarily existent Being; and this necessity of his existence is attempted to be explained by asserting, that, if we knew his whole essence or nature, we should perceive it to be as impossible for him not to exist as for twice two not to be four. But it is evident, that this can never happen, while our faculties remain the same as at present. It will still be possible for us, at any time, to conceive the non-existence of what we formerly conceived to exist; nor can the mind ever lie under a necessity of supposing any object to remain always in being; in the same manner as we lie under a necessity of always conceiving twice two to be four. The words, therefore, *necessary existence*, have no meaning; or, which is the same thing, none that is consistent.

But farther; why may not the material universe be the necessarily

---

appears on p. 24 is to be interpreted to mean that there is no difference in the imagination between reflecting on anything simply and reflecting on it as existent. But this does not imply that a judgment declaring something to exist is meaningless or empty. Indeed, Hume presupposes the meaningfulness of the judgment that God exists not only when he says that "whatever we conceive as existent, we can also conceive as non-existent," (interpreting "conceive as" to mean the same as "judge to be") but elsewhere in the *Treatise* where he attempts to relate this point of view with that expressed on p. 24. Here, although the judgment that God exists is regarded as meaningful and supposedly not empty, he also affirms the earlier view. But how is this possible? Hume's answer is to assimilate the judgment that God exists to the belief that he exists, and to interpret the difference between imagining something and believing it to be so as one of feeling or manner of conception. This point of view is brought to bear specifically on the apparent conflict under discussion in the following passage: " 'Tis evident, that all reasonings from causes or effects terminate in conclusions, concerning matter of fact; that is, concerning the existence of objects or of their qualities. 'Tis also evident, that the idea of existence is nothing different from the idea of any object, and that when after the simple conception of any thing we wou'd conceive it as existent, we in reality make no addition to or alteration on our first idea. Thus when we affirm, that God is existent, we simply form the idea of such a being, as he is represented to us: nor is the existence, which we attribute to him, conceiv'd by a particular idea, which we join to the idea of his other qualities, and can again separate and distinguish from them. But I go farther; and not content with asserting, that the conception of the existence of any object is no addition to the simple conception of it, I likewise maintain, that the belief of the existence joins no new ideas to those, which compose the idea of the object. When I think of God, when I think of him as existent, and when I believe him to be existent, my idea of him neither increases nor diminishes. But as 'tis certain there is a great difference betwixt the simple conception of the existence of an object, and the belief of it, and as this difference lies not in the parts or composition of the idea, which we conceive; it follows, that it must lie in the *manner*, in which we conceive it." Hume, *Treatise*, Book I, Part III, Section VII, pp. 94–95.

existent Being, according to this pretending explication of necessity? We dare not affirm that we know all the qualities of matter; and for aught we can determine, it may contain some qualities, which, were they known, would make its non-existence appear as great a contradiction as that twice two is five. I find only one argument employed to prove, that the material world is not the necessarily existent Being; and this argument is derived from the contingency both of the matter and the form of the world. "Any particle of matter," it is said,* "may be *conceived* to be annihilated; and any form may be *conceived* to be altered. Such an annihilation or alteration, therefore, is not impossible." But it seems a great partiality not to perceive, that the same argument extends equally to the Deity, so far as we have any conception of him; and that the mind can at least imagine him to be non-existent, or his attributes to be altered. (n)

(D) Miracles

Another sceptical argument associated with Pyrrhonism is Hume's rejection of the legitimacy of belief in miracles. Hume first points out that the reliability of the testimony of witnesses serving as evidence for belief in a very unusual occurrence must always be weighed against the strength of the evidence responsible for regarding it as unusual (a process often leading to devaluation of the witnesses' testimony). He then argues, in the following selection, that if a miracle is not regarded simply as something very unusual, but rather as "a violation of the laws of nature," the evidence against the supposed miracle must always be stronger than the evidence for it by this very definition.

Selection XVI:
ENQUIRY CONCERNING HUMAN UNDERSTANDING
Section X, Parts I and II

Let us suppose, that the fact, which they [the witnesses] affirm, instead of being only marvellous, is really miraculous; and suppose also, that the testimony considered apart and in itself, amounts to an entire proof; in that case, there is proof against proof, of which the strongest must prevail, but still with a diminution of its force, in proportion to that of its antagonist.

A miracle is a violation of the laws of nature; and as a firm and unalterable experience has established these laws, the proof against a miracle, from the very nature of the fact, is as entire as any argument from experi-

* Dr. Clarke.

ence can possibly be imagined. Why is it more than probable, that all men must die; that lead cannot, of itself, remain suspended in the air; that fire consumes wood, and is extinguished by water; unless it be, that these events are found agreeable to the laws of nature, and there is required a violation of these laws, or in other words, a miracle to prevent them? Nothing is esteemed a miracle, if it ever happen in the common course of nature. It is no miracle that a man, seemingly in good health, should die on a sudden; because such a kind of death, though more unusual than any other, has yet been frequently observed to happen. But it is a miracle, that a dead man should come to life; because that has never been observed in any age or country. There must, therefore, be a uniform experience against every miraculous event, otherwise the event would not merit that appellation. And as a uniform experience amounts to a proof, there is here a direct and full *proof*, from the nature of the fact, against the existence of any miracle; nor can such a proof be destroyed, or the miracle rendered credible, but by an opposite proof, which is superior.*

The plain consequence is (and it is a general maxim worthy of our attention), 'That no testimony is sufficient to establish a miracle, unless the testimony be of such a kind, that its falsehood would be more miraculous, than the fact, which it endeavours to establish; and even in that case there is a mutual destruction of arguments, and the superior only gives us an assurance suitable to that degree of force, which remains, after deducting the inferior.' When anyone tells me, that he saw a dead man restored to life, I immediately consider with myself, whether it be more probable, that this person should either deceive or be deceived, or that the fact, which he relates, should really have happened. I weigh the one miracle against the other; and according to the superiority, which I dis-

---

* Sometimes an event may not, *in itself, seem* to be contrary to the laws of nature, and yet, if it were real, it might, by reason of some circumstances, be denominated a miracle; because, in *fact*, it is contrary to these laws. Thus if a person, claiming a divine authority, should command a sick person to be well, a healthful man to fall down dead, the clouds to pour rain, the winds to blow, in short, should order many natural events, which immediately follow upon his command; these might justly be esteemed miracles, because they are really, in this case, contrary to the laws of nature. For if any suspicion remain, that the event and command concurred by accident, there is no miracle and no transgression of the laws of nature. If this suspicion be removed, there is evidently a miracle, and a transgression of these laws; because nothing can be more contrary to nature than that the voice or command of a man should have such an influence. A miracle may be accurately defined, *a transgression of a law of nature by a particular volition of the Deity, or by the interposition of some invisible agent.* A miracle may either be discoverable by men or not. This alters not its nature and essence. The raising of a house or ship into the air is a visible miracle. The raising of a feather, when the wind wants ever so little of a force requisite for that purpose, is as real a miracle, though not so sensible with regard to us.

cover, I pronounce my decision, and always reject the greater miracle. If the falsehood of his testimony would be more miraculous, than the event which he relates; then, and not till then, can he pretend to command my belief or opinion.

In the foregoing reasoning we have supposed, that the testimony upon which a miracle is founded, may possibly amount to an entire proof, and that the falsehood of that testimony would be a real prodigy: But it is easy to shew, that we have been a great deal too liberal in our concession, and that there never was a miraculous event established on so full an evidence.

(o)

PART II

Rejection of Pyrrhonism and Adoption of a "Mitigated" Scepticism

Hume believed sympathy and moral sentiment as well as self-love to be among the elements of human nature that must be considered in explaining the nature of moral judgment. Sympathy and moral sentiment differ from self-love in their "disinterestedness." All three elements have the capacity for serving as extra-rational criteria of moral judgment in the sense that they are extraneous to the operation of formal reasoning.[1] Both the implicit subordination of formal reasoning to feeling and the necessity to resort to at least moral sentiment to explain moral judgment are ideas Hume owed to Hutcheson. These ideas will be examined in greater detail shortly. In what follows, Hume's handling of sympathy and moral sentiment in the realm of moral judgment is somewhat parallel to his earlier treatment of belief and habit. In both cases, human nature plays a normative role.

In our next selection Hume expressly rejects Pyrrhonism in favor of a "mitigated" or Academic Scepticism. His mitigated scepticism is like the scepticism of Arcesilaus and Carneades in that it retains a healthy respect for the necessities of action.

Selection XVII: ENQUIRY CONCERNING HUMAN UNDERSTANDING Section XII, Parts II and III

The great subverter of *Pyrrhonism* or the excessive principles of scepticism is action, and employment, and the occupations of common life. These

---

[1] "Formal reasoning" is to be distinguished from "experimental reasoning." See pp. 65–68.

principles may flourish and triumph in the schools; where it is, indeed, difficult, if not impossible, to refute them. But as soon as they leave the shade, and by the presence of the real objects, which actuate our passions and sentiments, are put in opposition to the more powerful principles of our nature, they vanish like smoke, and leave the most determined sceptic in the same condition as other mortals.

The sceptic, therefore, had better keep within his proper sphere, and display those *philosophical* objections, which arise from more profound researches. Here he seems to have ample matter of triumph; while he justly insists, that all our evidence for any matter of fact, which lies beyond the testimony of sense or memory, is derived entirely from the relation to cause and effect; that we have no other idea of this relation than that of two objects, which have been frequently *conjoined* together; that we have no argument to convince us, that objects, which have, in our experience, been frequently conjoined, will likewise, in other instances, be conjoined in the same manner; and that nothing leads us to this inference but custom or a certain instinct of our nature; which it is indeed difficult to resist, but which, like other instincts, may be fallacious and deceitful. While the sceptic insists upon these topics, he shows his force, or rather, indeed, his own and our weakness; and seems, for the time at least, to destroy all assurance and conviction. These arguments might be displayed at greater length, if any durable good or benefit to society could ever be expected to result from them.

For here is the chief and most confounding objection to *excessive* scepticism, that no durable good can ever result from it; while it remains in its full force and vigour. We need only ask such a sceptic, *What his meaning is? And what he proposes by all these curious researches?* He is immediately at a loss, and knows not what to answer. A Copernican or Ptolemaic, who supports each his different system of astronomy, may hope to produce a conviction, which will remain constant and durable, with his audience. A Stoic or Epicurean displays principles, which may not be durable, but which have an effect on conduct and behaviour. But a Pyrrhonian cannot expect, that his philosophy will have any constant influence on the mind: or if it had, that its influence would be beneficial to society. On the contrary, he must acknowledge, if he will acknowledge anything, that all human life must perish, were his principles universally and steadily to prevail. All discourse, all action would immediately cease; and men remain in a total lethargy, till the necessities of nature, unsatisfied, put an end to their miserable existence. It is true; so fatal an event is very little to be dreaded. Nature is always too strong for principle. And though a

Pyrrhonian may throw himself or others into a momentary amazement and confusion by his profound reasonings; the first and most trival event in life will put to flight all his doubts and scruples, and leave him the same, in every point of action and speculation, with the philosophers of every other sect, or with those who never concerned themselves in any philosophical researches. When he awakes from his dream, he will be the first to join in the laugh against himself, and to confess, that all his objections are mere amusement, and can have no other tendency than to show the whimsical condition of mankind, who must act and reason and believe; though they are not able, by their most diligent enquiry, to satisfy themselves concerning the foundation of these operations, or to remove the objections, which may be raised against them.

There is, indeed, a more *mitigated* scepticism or *academical* philosophy, which may be both durable and useful, and which may, in part, be the result of this Pyrrhonism, or *excessive* scepticism, when its undistinguished doubts are, in some measure, corrected by common sense and reflection. The greater part of mankind are naturally apt to be affirmative and dog-matical in their opinions; and while they see objects only on one side, and have no idea of any counterpoising argument, they throw themselves precipitately into the principles, to which they are inclined; nor have they any indulgence for those who entertain opposite sentiments. To hesitate or balance perplexes their understanding, checks their passion, and sus-pends their action. They are, therefore, impatient till they escape from a state, which to them is so uneasy: and they think, that they could never remove themselves far enough from it, by the violence of their affirma-tions and obstinacy of their belief. But could such dogmatical reasoners become sensible of the strange infirmities of human understanding, even in its most perfect state, and when most accurate and cautious in its determinations; such a reflection would naturally inspire them with more modesty and reserve, and diminish their fond opinion of themselves, and their prejudice against antagonists. The illiterate may reflect on the dis-position of the learned, who, amidst all the advantages of study and reflec-tion, are commonly still diffident in their determinations: and if any of the learned be inclined, from their natural temper, to haughtiness and obsti-nacy, a small tincture of Pyrrhonism might abate their pride, by showing them, that the few advantages, which they may have attained over their fellows, are but inconsiderable, if compared with the universal perplexity and confusion, which is inherent in human nature. In general, there is a degree of doubt, and caution, and modesty, which, in all kinds of scrutiny and decision, ought for ever to accompany a just reasoner.

Another species of *mitigated* scepticism which may be of advantage to mankind, and which may be the natural result of the Pyrrhonian doubts and scruples, is the limitation of our enquiries to such subjects as are best adapted to the narrow capacity of human understanding. The *imagination* of man is naturally sublime, delighted with whatever is remote and extraordinary, and running, without control, into the most distant parts of space and time in order to avoid the objects, which custom has rendered too familiar to it. A correct *Judgement* observes a contrary method, and avoiding all distant and high enquiries, confines itself to common life, and to such subjects as fall under daily practice and experience; leaving the more sublime topics to the embellishment of poets and orators, or to the arts of priests and politicians. To bring us to so salutary a determination, nothing can be more serviceable, than to be once thoroughly convinced of the force of the Pyrrhonian doubt, and of the impossibility, that anything, but the strong power of natural instinct, could free us from it. Those who have a propensity to philosophy, will still continue their researches; because they reflect, that, besides the immediate pleasure, attending such an occupation, philosophical decisions are nothing but the reflections of common life, methodized and corrected. But they will never be tempted to go beyond common life, so long as they consider the imperfection of those faculties which they employ, their narrow reach, and their inaccurate operations. While we cannot give a satisfactory reason, why we believe, after a thousand experiments, that a stone will fall, or fire burn; can we ever satisfy ourselves concerning any determination, which we may form, with regard to the origin of worlds, and the situation of nature, from, and to eternity?   (a)

Resumption of Earlier Discussion of the Idea of Cause and Effect

There is more than a hint of pragmatism involved when Hume brings his mitigated scepticism to bear on the idea of cause and effect. The following account is to be regarded as a renewal of his earlier discussion of cause and effect (pp. 27–37). In this account, Hume regards "custom" and "habit" as synonomous, and thinks of beliefs as feelings brought about concomitantly with corresponding habits of action, in response to repeated associations of cause with effect. It seems obvious that this account, if accepted, requires reinterpretation of other conclusions based on Pyrrhonism.

The argument resumes with some remarks concerning Academic Scepticism.

Selection XVIII:
ENQUIRY CONCERNING HUMAN UNDERSTANDING
Section V, Parts I & II

Nor need we fear that this philosophy, while it endeavours to limit our enquiries to common life, should ever undermine the reasonings of common life, and carry its doubts so far as to destroy all action, as well as speculation. Nature will always maintain her rights, and prevail in the end over any abstract reasoning whatsoever. Though we should conclude, for instance, as in the foregoing section, that, in all reasonings from experience, there is a step taken by the mind which is not supported by any argument or process of the understanding; there is no danger that these reasonings, on which almost all knowledge depends, will ever be affected by such a discovery. If the mind be not engaged by argument to make this step, it must be induced by some other principle of equal weight and authority; and that principle will preserve its influence as long as human nature remains the same. What that principle is may well be worth the pains of inquiry.

Suppose a person, though endowed with the strongest faculties of reason and reflection, to be brought on a sudden into this world; he would, indeed, immediately observe a continual succession of objects, and one event following another; but he would not be able to discover anything farther. He would not, at first, by any reasoning, be able to reach the idea of cause and effect; since the particular powers, by which all natural operations are performed, never appear to the senses; nor is it reasonable to conclude, merely because one event, in one instance, precedes another, that therefore the one is the cause, the other the effect. Their conjunction may be arbitrary and casual. There may be no reason to infer the existence of one from the appearance of the other. And in a word, such a person, without more experience, could never employ his conjecture or reasoning concerning any matter of fact, or be assured of anything beyond what was immediately present to his memory and senses.

Suppose, again, that he has acquired more experience, and has lived so long in the world as to have observed familiar objects or events to be constantly conjoined together; what is the consequence of this experience? He immediately infers the existence of one object from the appearance of the other. Yet he has not, by all his experience, acquired any idea or knowledge of the secret power by which the one object produces the other; nor is it, by any process of reasoning, he is engaged to draw this inference. But still he finds himself determined to draw it: And though he should be convinced that his understanding has no part in the operation, he would nevertheless continue in the same course of thinking. There is some other principle which determines him to form such a conclusion.

This principle is Custom or Habit. For wherever the repetition of any particular act or operation produces a propensity to renew the same act or operation, without being impelled by any reasoning or process of the understanding, we always say, that this propensity is the effect of *Custom.* By employing that word, we pretend not to have given the ultimate reason of such a propensity. We only point out a principle of human nature, which is universally acknowledged, and which is well known by its effects. Perhaps we can push our enquiries no farther, or pretend to give the cause of this cause; but must rest contented with it as the ultimate principle, which we can assign, of all our conclusions from experience. It is sufficient satisfaction, that we can go so far, without repining at the narrowness of our faculties because they will carry us no farther. And it is certain we here advance a very intelligible proposition at least, if not a true one, when we assert that, after the constant conjunction of two objects—heat and flame, for instance, weight and solidity—we are determined by custom alone to expect the one from the appearance of the other. This hypothesis seems even the only one which explains the difficulty, why we draw, from a thousand instances, an inference which we are not able to draw from one instance, that is, in no respect, different from them. Reason is incapable of any such variation. The conclusions which it draws from considering one circle are the same which it would form upon surveying all the circles in the universe. But no man, having seen only one body moved after being impelled by another, could infer that every other body will move after a like impulse. All inferences from experience, therefore, are effects of custom, not of reasoning.

Custom, then, is the great guide of human life. It is that principle alone which renders our experience useful to us, and makes us expect, for the future, a similar train of events with those which have appeared in the past. Without the influence of custom, we should be entirely ignorant of every matter of fact beyond what is immediately present to the memory and senses. We should never know how to adjust means to ends, or to employ our natural powers in the production of any effect. There would be an end at once of all action, as well as of the chief part of speculation.

But here it may be proper to remark, that though our conclusions from experience carry us beyond our memory and senses, and assures us of matters of fact which happened in the most distant places and most remote ages, yet some fact must always be present to the senses or memory, from which we may first proceed in drawing these conclusions. A man, who should find in a desert country the remains of pompous buildings, would conclude that the country had, in ancient times, been cultivated by civilized inhabitants; but did nothing of this nature occur to him, he could never form such an inference. We learn the events of former ages from history; but then we must peruse the volumes in which this instruction is contained, and thence carry up our inferences from one testimony to another, till we arrive at the eyewitnesses and spectators of these distant events. In a word, if we proceed not upon some fact, present to the memory or senses, our reasonings would be merely hypothetical; and however the particular links might be connected with each other, the whole chain of inferences would have nothing to support it, nor could we ever, by its means, arrive at the knowledge of any real existence. If I ask why you believe any particular matter of fact, which you relate, you must tell me some reason; and this reason will be for some other fact, connected with it. But as you cannot proceed after this manner, *in infinitum*, you must at last terminate in some fact, which is present to your memory or senses; or must allow that your belief is entirely without foundation.

What, then, is the conclusion of the whole matter? A simple one; though, it must be confessed, pretty remote from the common theories of philosophy. All belief of matter of fact or real existence is derived merely from some object, present to the memory or senses, and a customary conjunction between that and some other object. Or in other words; having found, in many instances, that any two kinds of objects—flame and heat, snow and cold—have always been conjoined together; if flame or snow be presented anew to the senses, the mind is carried by custom to expect heat or cold, and to *believe* that such a quality does exist, and will discover itself upon a nearer approach. This belief is the necessary result of placing the mind in such circumstances. It is an operation of the soul, when we are so situated, as unavoidable as to feel the passion of love, when we receive benefits; or hatred, when we meet with injuries. All these operations are a species of natural instincts, which no reasoning or process of the thought and understanding is able either to produce or to prevent.

At this point, it would be very allowable for us to stop our philosophical researches. In most questions we can never make a single step farther; and in all questions we must terminate here at last, after our most restless and curious enquiries. But still our curiosity will be pardonable, perhaps commendable, if it carry us on to still farther researches, and make us examine more accurately the nature of this *belief*, and of the *customary conjunction*, whence it is derived....

Nothing is more free than the imagination of man; and though it cannot exceed that original stock of ideas furnished by the internal and external senses, it has unlimited power of mixing, compounding, separating, and dividing these ideas, in all the varieties of fiction and vision. It can feign a train of events, with all the appearance of reality, ascribe to them a particular time and place, conceive them as existent, and paint them out to itself with every circumstance, that belongs to any historical fact, which it believes with the greatest certainty. Wherein, therefore, consists the difference between such a fiction and belief? It lies not merely in any peculiar idea, which is annexed to such a conception as commands our assent, and which is wanting to every known fiction. For as the mind has authority over all its ideas, it could voluntarily annex this particular idea to any fiction, and consequently be able to believe whatever it pleases; contrary to what we find by daily experience. We can, in our conception, join the head of a man to the body of a horse; but it is not in our power to believe that such an animal has ever really existed.

It follows, therefore, that the difference between *fiction* and *belief* lies in some sentiment or feeling, which is annexed to the latter, not to the former, and which depends not on the will, nor can be commanded at pleasure. It must be excited by nature, like all other sentiments; and must arise from the particular situation, in which the mind is placed at any particular juncture. Whenever any object is presented to the memory or senses, it immediately, by the force of custom, carries the imagination to conceive that object, which is usually conjoined to it; and this conception is attended with a feeling or sentiment, different from the loose reveries of the fancy. In this consists the whole nature of belief. For as there is no matter of fact which we believe so firmly that we cannot conceive the contrary, there would be no difference between the conception assented to and that which is rejected, were it not for some sentiment which distinguishes the one from the other. If I see a billiard-ball moving towards another, on a smooth table, I can easily conceive it to stop upon contact. This conception implies no contradiction; but still it feels very differently from that conception by which I represent to myself the impulse and the communication of motion from one ball to another.

Were we to attempt a *definition* of this sentiment, we should, perhaps, find it a very difficult, if not an impossible task; in the same manner as if we should endeavour to define the feeling of cold or passion of anger, to a creature who never had any experience of these sentiments. Belief is the true and proper name of this feeling; and no one is ever at a loss to know the meaning of that term; because every man is every moment conscious of the sentiment represented by it. It may not, however, be improper to attempt a *description* of this sentiment; in hopes we may, by that means, arrive at some analogies, which may afford a more perfect explication of it. I say, then, that belief is nothing but a more vivid, lively, forcible, firm, steady conception of an object, than what the imagination alone is ever able to attain. This variety of terms, which may seem so unphilosophical, is intended only to express that act of the mind, which renders realities, or what is taken for such, more present to us than fictions, causes them to weigh more in the thought, and gives them a superior influence on the passions and imagination. Provided we agree about the thing, it is needless to dispute about the terms. The imagination has the command over all its ideas, and can join and mix and vary them, in all the ways possible. It may conceive fictitious objects with all the circumstances of place and time. It may set them, in a manner, before our eyes, in their true colours, just as they might have existed. But as it is impossible that this faculty of imagination can ever, of itself, reach belief, it is evident that belief consists not in the peculiar nature or order of ideas, but in the *manner* of their conception, and in their *feeling* to the mind. I confess, that it is impossible perfectly to explain this feeling or manner of conception. We may make use of words which express something near it. But its true and proper name, as we observed before, is *belief;* which is a term that every one sufficiently understands in common life. And in philosophy, we can go no farther than assert, that *belief* is something felt by the mind, which distinguishes the ideas of the judgement from the fictions of the imagination. It gives them more weight and influence; makes them appear of greater importance; enforces them in the mind; and renders them the governing principle of our actions. I hear at present, for instance, a person's voice, with whom I am acquainted; and the sound comes as from the next room. This impression of my senses immediately conveys my thought to the person, together with all the surrounding objects. I paint them out to myself as existing at present, with the same qualities and relations, of which I formerly knew them possessed. These ideas take faster hold of my mind than ideas of an enchanted castle. They are very different to the feeling, and have a much greater influence of every kind, either to give pleasure or pain, joy or sorrow.

Let us, then, take in the whole compass of this doctrine, and allow, that the sentiment of belief is nothing but a conception more intense and steady than what attends the mere fictions of the imagination, and that this *manner* of conception arises from a customary conjunction of the object with something present to the memory or senses: I believe that it will not be difficult, upon these suppositions, to find other operations of the mind analogous to it, and to trace up these phenomena to principles still more general.

We have already observed that nature has established connexions among particular ideas, and that no sooner one idea occurs to our thoughts than it introduces its correlative, and carries our attention towards it, by a gentle and insensible movement. These principles of connexion or association we have reduced to three, namely, *Resemblance, Contiguity* and *Causation*; which are the only bonds that unite our thoughts together, and beget that regular train of reflection or discourse, which, in a greater or less degree, takes place among all mankind. Now here arises a question, on which the solution of the present difficulty will depend. Does it happen, in all these relations, that, when one of the objects is presented to the senses or memory, the mind is not only carried to the conception of the correlative, but reaches a steadier and stronger conception of it than what otherwise it would have been able to attain? This seems to be the case with that belief which arises from the relation of cause and effect. And if the case be the same with the other relations or principles of associations, this may be established as a general law, which takes place in all the operations of the mind.

In immediately succeeding paragraphs not included here, Hume presents evidence to support his view that the case *is* the same with the other relations or principles of associations. He concludes with the following thought.

Here, then is a kind of pre-established harmony between the course of nature and the succession of our ideas; and though the powers and forces, by which the former is governed, be wholly unknown to us; yet our thoughts and conceptions have still, we find, gone on in the same train with the other works of nature. Custom is that principle, by which this correspondence has been effected; so necessary to the subsistence of our species, and the regulation of our conduct, in every circumstance and occurrence of human life. Had not the presence of an object, instantly excited the idea of those objects, commonly conjoined with it, all our knowledge must have been limited to the narrow sphere of our memory and senses; and we should never have been able to adjust means to ends, or employ our natural powers, either to the producing of good, or avoiding of evil. Those, who delight in the discovery and contemplation of *final causes*, have here ample subject to employ their wonder and admiration.

I shall add, for a further confirmation of the foregoing theory, that, as this operation of the mind, by which we infer like effects from like causes, and *vice versa*, is so essential to the subsistence of all human creatures, it is not probable, that it could be trusted to the fallacious deductions of our reason, which is slow in its operations; appears not, in any degree, during the first years of infancy; and at best is, in every age and period of human life, extremely liable to error and mistake. It is more conformable to the ordinary wisdom of nature to secure so necessary an act of the mind, by some instinct or mechanical tendency, which may be infallible in its operations, may discover itself at the first appearance of life and thought, and may be independent of all the laboured deductions of the understanding. As nature has taught us the use of our limbs, without giving us the knowledge of the muscles and nerves, by which they are actuated; so has she implanted in us an instinct, which carries forward the thought in a correspondent course to that which she has established among external objects; though we are ignorant of those powers and forces, on which this regular course and succession of objects totally depends. **(b)**

The Capacity to Reason as an "Instinct," and Alternative Uses of the Terms "Reason" and "Experience"

Hume's naturalism is nowhere more evident than in his comparison of the reasoning capacity of men with that of animals. Although Hume considered both matters of fact and relations among ideas as objects of reason, throughout Part I he generally regards reason as synonomous with the ability to discriminate between relations among ideas. As such, it might be termed "formal reasoning." It is formal reasoning that Hume refers to in the following selection when he denies that the actions of animals, children, and men in their ordinary behavior are guided by reason. Yet he is also led to speak of the capacity for "experimental reasoning" that we share with animals; and, indeed, even formal reasoning, when directed to the determination of matters of fact, becomes a species of experimental reasoning. It is in this context that Hume sets forth a set of criteria against which the relative levels of achievement in the experimental reasoning of men, as well as of animals, can be gauged. He further sees the capacity for experimental reasoning as "instinctive" in both men and animals.

When thinking in a Newtonian analytic vein such as in his preliminary analysis of the idea of cause and effect, Hume has regarded experience as a collection of impressions. Though the collection contains an order within it, an order arising from both temporal sequence and association of various kinds of impressions with others, this order is not regarded as anything beyond the collection itself. Coupled with his empiricism, it is this view of experience that has given rise to the Pyrrhonist difficulties Hume has already encountered. To speak of experimental reasoning, on the other hand, is to speak of something involving reason as well as experience and suggests that the "man of experience," in order to fulfill his capacity for experimental reasoning, must have acquired certain beliefs and habits.

Selection XIX:
ENQUIRY CONCERNING HUMAN UNDERSTANDING
Section IX

Any theory, by which we explain the operations of the understanding, or the origin and connexion of the passions in man, will acquire additional authority, if we find, that the same theory is requisite to explain the same phenomena in all other animals. We shall make trial of this, with regard to the hypothesis, by which we have, in the foregoing discourse, endeavoured to account for all experimental reasonings; and it is hoped, that this new point of view will serve to confirm all our former observations.

First, It seems evident, that animals as well as men learn many things from experience, and infer, that the same events will always follow from the same causes. By this principle they become acquainted with the more obvious properties of external objects, and gradually, from their birth, treasure up a knowledge of the nature of fire, water, earth, stones, heights, depths, &c., and of the effects which result from their operation. The ignorance and inexperience of the young are here plainly distinguishable from the cunning and sagacity of the old, who have learned, by long observation, to avoid what hurt them, and to pursue what gave ease or pleasure. A horse, that has been accustomed to the field, becomes acquainted with the proper height which he can leap, and will never attempt what exceeds his force and ability. An old greyhound will trust the more fatiguing part of the chace to the younger, and will place himself so as to meet the hare in her doubles; nor are the conjectures, which he forms on this occasion, founded in any thing but his observation and experience.

This is still more evident from the effects of discipline and education on animals, who, by the proper application of rewards and punishments, may be taught any course of action, and most contrary to their natural instincts and propensities. Is it not experience, which renders a dog apprehensive of pain, when you menace him, or lift up the whip to beat him? Is it not even experience, which makes him answer to his name, and infer, from such an arbitrary sound, that you mean him rather than any of his fellows, and intend to call him, when you pronounce it in a certain manner, and with a certain tone and accent?

In all these cases, we may observe, that the animal infers some fact beyond what immediately strikes his senses; and that this inference is altogether founded on past experience, while the creature expects from the present object the same consequences, which it has always found in its observation to result from similar objects.

Secondly, It is impossible, that this inference of the animal can be founded on any process of argument or reasoning, by which he concludes, that like events must follow like objects, and that the course of nature will always be regular in its operations. For if there be in reality any arguments of this nature, they surely lie too abstruse for the observation of such imperfect understandings; since it may well employ the utmost care and attention of a philosophic genius to discover and observe them. Animals, therefore, are not guided in these inferences by reasoning: Neither are children: Neither are the generality of mankind, in their ordinary actions and conclusions: Neither are philosophers themselves, who, in all the active parts of life, are, in the main, the same with the vulgar, and are governed by the same maxims. Nature must have provided some other principle, of more ready, and more general use and application; nor can an operation of such immense consequence in life, as that of inferring effects from causes, be trusted to the uncertain process of reasoning and argumentation. Were this doubtful with regard to men, it seems to admit of no question with regard to the brute creation; and the conclusion being once firmly established in the one, we have a strong presumption, from all the rules of analogy, that it ought to be universally admitted, without any exception or reserve. It is custom alone, which engages animals, from every object, that strikes their senses, to infer its usual attendant, and carries their imagination, from the appearance of the one, to conceive the other, in that particular manner, which we denominate *belief*. No other explication can be given of this operation, in all the higher, as well as lower classes of sensitive beings, which fall under our notice and observation.*

* We shall here endeavour briefly to explain the great difference in human understandings: After which the reason of the difference between men and animals will easily be comprehended.

1. When we have lived any time, and have been accustomed to the uniformity of nature, we acquire a general habit, by which we always transfer the known to the unknown, and conceive the latter to resemble the former. By means of this general habitual principle, we regard even one experiment as the foundation of reasoning, and expect a similar event with some degree of certainty, where the experiment has been made accurately, and free from all foreign circumstances. It is therefore considered as a matter of great importance to observe the consequences of things; and

But though animals learn many parts of their knowledge from observation, there are also many parts of it, which they derive from the original hand of nature; which much exceed the share of capacity they possess on ordinary occasions; and in which they improve, little or nothing, by the longest practice and experience. These we denominate Instincts, and are so apt to admire as something very extraordinary, and inexplicable by all the disquisitions of human understanding. But our wonder will, perhaps, cease or diminish, when we consider, that the experimental reasoning itself, which we possess in common with beasts, and on which the whole conduct of life depends, is nothing but a species of instinct or mechanical power, that acts in us unknown to ourselves; and in its chief operations, is not directed by any such relations or comparisons of ideas, as are the proper objects of our intellectual faculties. Though the instinct be different, yet still it is an instinct, which teaches a man to avoid the fire; as much as that, which teaches a bird, with such exactness, the art of incubation, and the whole economy and order of its nursery. (c)

Empirical Approach to Moral Questions

While Hume's sceptical analysis of theoretical questions leads him to regard experience as a touchstone of assurance in action, the values of action serve as a starting point for his moral theory. Hume's em-

---

as one man may very much surpass another in attention and memory and observation, this will make a very great difference in their reasoning.

2. Where there is a complication of causes to produce any effect, one mind may be much larger than another, and better able to comprehend the whole system of objects, and to infer justly their consequences.

3. One man is able to carry on a chain of consequences to a greater length than another.

4. Few men can think long without running into a confusion of ideas, and mistaking one for another; and there are various degress of this infirmity.

5. The circumstance, on which the effect depends, is frequently involved in other circumstances, which are foreign and intrinsic. The separation of it often requires great attention, accuracy, and subtilty.

6. The forming of general maxims from particular observation is a very nice operation; and nothing is more usual, from haste or a narrowness of mind, which sees not on all sides, than to commit mistakes in this particular.

7. When we reason from analogies, the man, who has the greater experience or the greater promptitude of suggesting analogies, will be the better reasoner.

8. Byasses from prejudice, education, passion, party, &c. hang more upon one mind than another.

9. After we have acquired a confidence in human testimony, books and conversation enlarge much more the sphere of one man's experience and thought than those of another.

It would be easy to discover many other circumstances that make a difference in the understandings of men.

pirical approach to moral questions is at once both Aristotelian and Newtonian. It is Aristotelian in using the moral judgments of men to begin a discussion of morality and in recognizing the inexactitude of the subject. It is Newtonian both in its empiricism and in its rejection of empirically unfounded hypotheses.

Selection XX:
ENQUIRY CONCERNING THE PRINCIPLES OF MORALS
Section I

... we shall endeavour to follow a very simple method: we shall analyse that complication of mental qualities, which form what, in common life, we call Personal Merit: we shall consider every attribute of the mind, which renders a man an object either of esteem and affection, or of hatred and contempt; every habit or sentiment or faculty, which, if ascribed to any person, implies either praise or blame, and may enter into any panegyric or satire of his character and manners. The quick sensibility, which, on this head, is so universal among mankind, gives a philosopher sufficient assurance, that he can never be considerably mistaken in framing the catalogue, or incur any danger of misplacing the objects of his contemplation: he needs only enter into his own breast for a moment, and consider whether or not he should desire to have this or that quality ascribed to him, and whether such or such an imputation would proceed from a friend or an enemy. The very nature of language guides us almost infallibly in forming a judgement of this nature; and as every tongue possesses one set of words which are taken in a good sense, and another in the opposite, the least acquaintance with the idiom suffices, without any reasoning, to direct us in collecting and arranging the estimable or blameable qualities of men. The only object of reasoning is to discover the circumstances on both sides, which are common to these qualities; to observe that particular in which the estimable qualities agree on the one hand, and the blameable on the other; and thence to reach the foundation of ethics, and find those universal principles, from which all censure or approbation is ultimately derived. As this is a question of fact, not of abstract science, we can only expect success, by following the experimental method, and deducing general maxims from a comparison of particular instances. The other scientific method, where a general abstract principle is first established, and is afterwards branched out into a variety of inferences and conclusions, may be more perfect in itself, but suits less the imperfection of human nature, and is a common source of illusion and mistake in this as well as in other subjects. Men are now cured of their passion for hypotheses and systems in natural philosophy, and will hearken to no arguments but those which are derived from experience. It is full time they should attempt a like reformation in all moral disquisitions; and reject every system of ethics, however subtle or ingenious, which is not founded on fact and observation.

We shall begin our enquiry on this head by the consideration of the social virtues, Benevolence and Justice. The explication of them will probably give us an opening by which the others may be accounted for.

(d)

The Benevolent Man and the Just Man as Paradigms of Moral Virtue

First among the attributes which render a man an object of moral esteem are benevolence and justice. Hume carries the inquiry further: What is it about benevolence and justice that leads us to judge them as virtuous? He considers benevolence first.

Selection XXI:
ENQUIRY CONCERNING THE PRINCIPLES OF MORALS
Section II, Parts I and II

... it is not my present business to recommend generosity and benevolence, or to paint, in their true colours, all the genuine charms of the social virtues. These, indeed, sufficiently engage every heart, on the first apprehension of them; and it is difficult to abstain from some sally of panegyric, as often as they occur in discourse or reasoning. But our object here being more the speculative, than the practical part of morals, it will suffice to remark (what will readily, I believe, be allowed) that no qualities are more intitled to the general good-will and approbation of mankind than beneficence and humanity, friendship and gratitude, natural affection and public spirit, or whatever proceeds from a tender sympathy with others, and a generous concern for our kind and species. These wherever they appear, seem to transfuse themselves, in a manner, into each beholder, and to call forth, in their own behalf, the same favourable and affectionate sentiments, which they exert on all around.

We may observe that, in displaying the praises of any humane, beneficent man, there is one circumstance which never fails to be amply insisted on, namely the happiness and satisfaction, derived to society from his intercourse and good offices. To his parents, we are apt to say, he endears himself by his pious attachment and duteous care still more than by the connexions of nature. His children never feel his authority, but when employed for their advantage. With him, the ties of love are consolidated by beneficence and friendship. The ties of friendship approach, in a fond observance of each obliging office, to those of love and inclination. His domestics and dependants have in him a sure resource; and no longer dread the power of fortune, but so far as she exercises it over him. From him the hungry receive food, the naked clothing, the ignorant and slothful skill and industry. Like the sun, an inferior minister of providence he cheers, invigorates, and sustains the surrounding world.

If confined to private life, the sphere of his activity is narrower; but his influence is all benign and gentle. If exalted into a higher station, mankind and posterity reap the fruit of his labours.

As these topics of praise never fail to be employed, and with success, where we would inspire esteem for any one; may it not thence be concluded, that the utility, resulting from the social virtues, forms, at least, a *part* of their merit, and is one source of that approbation and regard so universally paid to them?

When we recommend even an animal or a plant as *useful* and *beneficial,* we give it an applause and recommendation suited to its nature. As, on the other hand, reflection on the baneful influence of any of these inferior beings always inspires us with the sentiment of aversion. The eye is pleased with the prospect of corn-fields and loaded vineyards; horses grazing, and flocks pasturing: but flies the view of briars and brambles, affording shelter to wolves and serpents.

A machine, a piece of furniture, a vestment, a house well contrived for use and conveniency, is so far beautiful, and is contemplated with pleasure and approbation. An experienced eye is here sensible to many excellencies, which escape persons ignorant and uninstructed.

Can anything stronger be said in praise of a profession, such as merchandize or manufacture, than to observe the advantages which it procures to society; and is not a monk and inquisitor enraged when we treat his order as useless or pernicious to mankind?

The historian exults in displaying the benefit arising from his labours. The writer of romance alleviates or denies the bad consequences ascribed to his manner of composition.

In general, what praise is implied in the simple epithet *useful!* What reproach in the contrary!

Your Gods, says Cicero,* in opposition to the Epicureans, cannot justly claim any worship or adoration, with whatever imaginary perfections you may suppose them endowed. They are totally useless and inactive. Even the

* De Nat. Deor. lib. i.

Egyptians, whom you so much ridicule, never consecrated any animal but on account of its utility.

The sceptics assert,* though absurdly, that the origin of all religious worship was derived from the utility of inanimate objects, as the sun and moon, to the support and well-being of mankind. This is also the common reason assigned by historians, for the deification of eminent heroes and legislators.†

To plant a tree, to cultivate a field, to beget children; meritorious acts, according to the religion of Zoroaster.

In all determinations of morality, this circumstance of public utility is ever principally in view; and wherever disputes arise, either in philosophy or common life, concerning the bounds of duty, the question cannot, by any means, be decided with greater certainty, than by ascertaining, on any side, the true interest of mankind. If any false opinion, embraced from appearances, has been found to prevail; as soon as farther experience and sounder reasoning have given us juster notions of human affairs, we retract our first sentiment, and adjust anew the boundaries of moral good and evil.

Giving alms to common beggars is naturally praised; because it seems to carry relief to the distressed and indigent: but when we observe the encouragement thence arising to idleness and debauchery, we regard that species of charity rather as a weakness than a virtue.

Tyrannicide, or the assassination of usurpers and oppressive princes, was highly extolled in ancient times; because it both freed mankind from many of these monsters, and seemed to keep the others in awe, whom the sword or poinard could not reach. But history and experience having since convinced us, that this practice increases the jealousy and cruelty of princes, a Timoleon and a Brutus, though treated with indulgence on account of the prejudices of their times, are now considered as very improper models of imitation.

Liberality in princes is regarded as a mark of beneficence, but when it occurs, that the homely bread of the honest and industrious is often thereby converted into delicious cates for the idle and the prodigal, we soon retract our heedless praises. The regrets of a prince, for having lost a day, were noble and generous: but had he intended to have spent it in acts of generosity to his greedy courtiers, it was better lost than misemployed after that manner.

Luxury, or a refinement on the pleasures and conveniencies of life, had not long been supposed the source of every corruption in government, and

* Sext. Emp. adversus Math. lib. viii.
† Diod. Sic. passim.

the immediate cause of faction, sedition, civil wars, and the total loss of liberty. It was, therefore, universally regarded as a vice, and was an object of declamation to all satirists, and severe moralists. Those, who prove, or attempt to prove, that such refinements rather tend to the increase of industry, civility, and arts regulate anew our *moral* as well as *political* sentiments, and represent, as laudable or innocent, what had formerly been regarded as pernicious and blameable.

Upon the whole, then, it seems undeniable, *that* nothing can bestow more merit on any human creature than the sentiment of benevolence in an eminent degree; and *that* a *part*, at least, of its merit arises from its tendency to promote the interests of our species, and bestow happiness on human society. We carry our view into the salutary consequences of such a character and disposition; and whatever has so benign an influence, and forwards so desirable an end, is beheld with complacency and pleasure. The social virtues are never regarded without their beneficial tendencies, nor viewed as barren and unfruitful. The happiness of mankind, the order of society, the harmony of families, the mutual support of friends, are always considered as the result of their gentle dominion over the breasts of men.   (e)

In the following selection Hume not only considers the usefulness of justice in comparison to the usefulness of benevolence but also discusses whether justice is to be regarded as a natural or artificial virtue. That justice is established by "convention" but not by "promise" is Hume's answer to the view, prevalent in his time, that the state came into being through a "social contract."

Selection XXII:
ENQUIRY CONCERNING THE PRINCIPLES OF MORALS
Appendix III

The social virtues of humanity and benevolence exert their influence immediately by a direct tendency or instinct, which chiefly keeps in view the simple object, moving the affections, and comprehends not any scheme or system, nor the consequences resulting from the concurrence, imitation, or example of others. A parent flies to the relief of his child; transported by that natural sympathy which actuates him, and which affords no leisure to reflect on the sentiments or conduct of the rest of mankind in like circumstances. A generous man cheerfully embraces an opportunity of serving his friend; because he then feels himself under the dominion of the beneficent affections, nor is he concerned whether any other person in the universe were ever before actuated by such noble motives, or will ever afterwards prove their influence. In all these cases the social passions have in view a single individual object, and pursue the safety or happiness alone of the person loved and esteemed. With this they are satisfied: in this they acquiesce. And as the good, resulting from their benign influence, is in itself complete and entire, it also excites the moral sentiment of approbation, without any reflection on farther consequences, and without any more enlarged views of the concurrence or imitation of the other members of society. On the contrary, were the generous friend or disinterested patriot to stand alone in the practice of beneficence, this would rather inhance his value in our eyes, and join the praise of rarity and novelty to his other more exalted merits.

The case is not the same with the social virtues of justice and fidelity. They are highly useful, or indeed absolutely necessary to the well-being of mankind: but the benefit resulting from them is not the consequence of every individual single act; but arises from the whole scheme or system concurred in by the whole, or the greater part of the society. General peace and order are the attendants of justice or a general abstinence from the possessions of others; but a particular regard to the particular right of one individual citizen may frequently, considered in itself, be productive of pernicious consequences. The result of the individual acts is here, in many instances, directly opposite to that of the whole system of actions; and the former may be extremely hurtful, while the latter is, to the highest degree, advantageous. Riches, inherited from a parent, are in a bad man's hand, the instrument of mischief. The right of succession may, in one instance, be hurtful. Its benefit arises only from the observance of the general rule; and it is sufficient, if compensation be thereby made for all the ills and inconveniences which flow from particular characters and situations.

Cyrus, young and unexperienced, considered only the individual case before him, and reflected on a limited fitness and convenience, when he assigned the long coat to the tall boy, and the short coat to the other of smaller size. His governor instructed him better, while he pointed out more enlarged views and consequences, and informed his pupil of the general, inflexible rules, necessary to support general peace and order in society.

The happiness and prosperity of mankind, arising from the social virtue of benevolence and its subdivisions, may be compared to a wall, built by many hands, which still rises by each stone that is heaped upon it, and receives increase proportional to the diligence and care of each workman. The same happiness, raised by the social virtue of justice and its sub-

divisions, may be compared to the building of a vault, where each individual stone would, of itself, fall to the ground; nor is the whole fabric
supported but by the mutual assistance and combination of its corresponding parts.

All the laws of nature, which regulate property, as well as all civil
laws, are general, and regard alone some essential circumstances of the
case, without taking into consideration the characters, situations, and connexions of the person concerned, or any particular consequences which may
result from the determination of these laws in any particular case which
offers. They deprive, without scruple, a beneficent man of all his possessions, if acquired by mistake, without a good title; in order to bestow them
on a selfish miser, who has already heaped up immense stores of superfluous riches. Public utility requires that property should be regulated by
general inflexible rules; and though such rules are adopted as best serve
the same end of public utility, it is impossible for them to prevent all particular hardships, or make beneficial consequences result from every individual case. It is sufficient, if the whole plan or scheme be necessary to
the support of civil society, and if the balance of good, in the main, do
thereby preponderate much above that of evil. Even the general laws
of the universe, though planned by infinite wisdom, cannot exclude all evil
or inconvenience in every particular operation.

It has been asserted by some, that justice arises from Human Conventions, and proceeds from the voluntary choice, consent, or combination of
mankind. If by *convention* be here meant a *promise* (which is the most
usual sense of the word) nothing can be more absurd than this position.
The observance of promises is itself one of the most considerable parts of
justice, and we are not surely bound to keep our word because we have
given our word to keep it. But if by convention be meant a sense of common interest; which sense each man feels in his own breast, which he remarks in his fellows, and which carries him, in concurrence with others,
into a general plan or system of actions, which tends to public utility; it
must be owned, that, in this sense, justice arises from human conventions.
For if it be allowed (what is, indeed, evident) that the particular consequences of a particular act of justice may be hurtful to the public as
well as to individuals; it follows that every man, in embracing that virtue,
must have an eye to the whole plan or system, and must expect the concurrence of his fellows in the same conduct and behaviour. Did all his views
terminate in the consequences of each act of his own, his benevolence and
humanity, as well as his self-love, might often prescribe to him measures
of conduct very different from those which are agreeable to the strict rules
of right and justice.

Thus, two men pull the oars of a boat by common convention for common interest, without any promise or contract: thus gold and silver are made the measures of exchange; thus speech and words and language are fixed by human convention and agreement. Whatever is advantageous to two or more persons, if all perform their part; but what loses all advantage if only one perform, can arise from no other principle. There would otherwise be no motive for any one of them to enter into that scheme of conduct.*

The word *natural* is commonly taken in so many senses and is of so loose a signification, that it seems vain to dispute whether justice be natural or not. If self-love, if benevolence be natural to man; if reason and forethought be also natural; then may the same epithet be applied to justice, order, fidelity, property, society. Men's inclination, their necessities, lead them to combine; their understanding and experience tell them that this combination is impossible where each governs himself by no rule, and pays no regard to the possessions of others: and from these passions and reflections conjoined, as soon as we observe like passions and reflections in others, the sentiment of justice, throughout all ages, has infallibly and certainly had place to some degree or other in every individual of the human species. In so sagacious an animal, what necessarily arises from the exertion of his intellectual faculties may justly be esteemed natural.†

(f)

Why Utility Pleases

Hume considers utility (utility to anyone, it will be noted, not just to the person judging) to be primarily responsible for eliciting our moral approval, not only of benevolence and justice but of virtuous characteristics in general. It would be an error, however, to see Hume as a utilitarian in the same sense as Bentham and Mill. While Bentham and Mill define the good as the useful, Hume defines the good instead as what men judge to be so, maintaining, in addition, that men happen to regard the useful as good. The difference in these two views

---

* This theory concerning the origin of property, and consequently of justice, is, in the main, the same with that hinted at and adopted by Grotius....*De jure belli et pacis.* Lib. ii. cap. 2. § 2. art. 4 and 5.

† Natural may be opposed, either to what is *unusual, miraculous,* or *artificial.* In the two former senses, justice and property are undoubtedly natural. But as they suppose reason, forethought, design, and a social union and confederacy among men, perhaps that epithet cannot strictly, in the last sense, be applied to them. Had men lived without society, property had never been known, and neither justice nor injustice had ever existed. But society among human creatures had been impossible without reason and forethought. Inferior animals, that unite, are guided by instinct, which supplies the place of reason. But all these disputes are merely verbal.

is that while for Bentham and Mill the good is *necessarily* the useful, for Hume, the equation of the good with the useful is contingent upon human judgment.

Hume's view raises the additional question of why utility pleases—even in situations opposed or indifferent to our own interest. His answer is to be found in the two principles of human nature he calls respectively "sympathy" or the "sentiment of humanity" and "moral sentiment." In the following selection he attempts to establish both that our moral approval or disapproval of the "social virtues" of benevolence and justice is elicited independently of our own self interest, and that sympathy or the sentiment of humanity is a psychological principle capable of accounting for such approval or disapproval.

Selection XXIII:
ENQUIRY CONCERNING THE PRINCIPLES OF MORALS
Section V, Parts I and II

From the apparent usefulness of the social virtues, it has readily been inferred by sceptics, both ancient and modern, that all moral distinctions arise from education, and were, at first, invented, and afterwards encouraged, by the art of politicians, in order to render men tractable, and subdue their natural ferocity and selfishness, which incapacitated them for society. This principle, indeed, of precept and education, must so far be owned to have a powerful influence, that it may frequently increase or diminish, beyond their natural standard, the sentiments of approbation or dislike; and may even, in particular instances, create, without any natural principle, a new sentiment of this kind; as is evident in all superstitious practices and observances: But that *all* moral affection or dislike arises from this origin, will never surely be allowed by any judicious enquirer. Had nature made no such distinction, founded on the original constitution of the mind, the words, *honourable* and *shameful, lovely* and *odious, noble* and *despicable,* had never had place in any language; nor could politicians, had they invented these terms, ever have been able to render them intelligible, or make them convey any idea to the audience. So that nothing can be more superficial than this paradox of the sceptics; and it were well, if, in the abstruser studies of logic and metaphysics, we could as easily obviate the cavils of that sect, as in the practical and more intelligible sciences of politics and morals.

The social virtues must, therefore, be allowed to have a natural beauty and amiableness, which, at first, antecedent to all precept or education, recommends them to the esteem of uninstructed mankind, and engages their affections. And as the public utility of these virtues is the chief circumstance, whence they derive their merit, it follows, that the end, which they have a tendency to promote, must be some way agreeable to us, and take hold of some natural affection. It must please, either from considerations of self-interest, or from more generous motives and regards.

It has often been asserted, that, as every man has a strong connexion with society, and perceives the impossibility of his solitary subsistence, he becomes, on that account, favourable to all those habits or principles, which promote order in society, and insure to him the quiet possession of so inestimable a blessing. As much as we value our own happiness and welfare, as much must we applaud the practice of justice and humanity, by which alone the social confederacy can be maintained, and every man reap the fruits of mutual protection and assistance.

This deduction of morals from self-love, or a regard to private interest, is an obvious thought, and has not arisen wholly from the wanton sallies and sportive assaults of the sceptics . . . . yet . . . the voice of nature and experience seems plainly to oppose the selfish theory.

We frequently bestow praise on virtuous actions, performed in very distant ages and remote countries; where the utmost subtilty of imagination would not discover any appearance of self-interest, or find any connexion of our present happiness and security with events so widely separated from us.

A generous, a brave, a noble deed, performed by an adversary, commands our approbation; while in its consequences it may be acknowledged prejudicial to our particular interest.

Where private advantage concurs with general affection for virtue, we readily perceive and avow the mixture of these distinct sentiments, which have a very different feeling and influence on the mind. We praise, perhaps, with more alacrity, where the generous humane action contributes to our particular interest: But the topics of praise, which we insist on, are very wide of this circumstance. And we may attempt to bring over others to our sentiments, without endeavouring to convince them, that they reap any advantage from the actions which we recommend to their approbation and applause.

Frame the model of a praiseworthy character, consisting of all the most amiable moral virtues: Give instances, in which these display themselves after an eminent and extraordinary manner: You readily engage the esteem and approbation of all your audience, who never so much as enquire in what age and country the person lived, who possessed these

noble qualities: A circumstance, however, of all others, the most material
to self-love, or a concern for our own individual happiness.

Once on a time, a statesman, in the shock and contest of parties, prevailed so far as to procure, by his eloquence, the banishment of an able
adversary; whom he secretly followed, offering him money for his support
during his exile, and soothing him with topics of consolation in his misfortunes. *Alas!* cries the banished statesman, *with what regret must I leave
my friends in this city, where even enemies are so generous!* Virtue,
though in an enemy, here pleased him: And we also give it the just tribute
of praise and approbation; nor do we retract these sentiments, when we
hear, that the action passed at Athens, about two thousand years ago, and
that the persons names were Eschines and Demosthenes.... We have
found instances, in which private interest was separate from public; in
which it was even contrary: And yet we observed the moral sentiment to
continue, notwithstanding this disjunction of interests. And wherever
these distinct interests sensibly concurred, we always found a sensible increase of the sentiment, and a more warm affection to virtue, and detestation of vice, or what we properly call, *gratitude* and *revenge*. Compelled by
these instances, we must renounce the theory, which accounts for every
moral sentiment by the principle of self-love. We must adopt a more public
affection, and allow, that the interests of society are not, even on their own
account, entirely indifferent to us. Usefulness is only a tendency to a certain end; and it is a contradiction in terms, that anything pleases as means
to an end, where the end itself no wise affects us. If usefulness, therefore, be a source of moral sentiment, and if this usefulness be not always considered with a reference to self; it follows, that everything, which
contributes to the happiness of society, recommends itself directly to our
approbation and good-will. Here is a principle, which accounts, in great
part, for the origin of morality: And what need we seek for abstruse and
remote systems, when there occurs one so obvious and natural? *   (g)

---

* It is needless to push our researches so far as to ask, why we have humanity [here
synonomous with sympathy rather than with moral sentiment] or a fellow-feeling
with others. It is sufficient, that this is experienced to be a principle in human nature.
We must stop somewhere in our examination of causes; and there are, in every
science, some general principles, beyond which we cannot hope to find any principle
more general. No man is absolutely indifferent to the happiness and misery of others.
The first has a natural tendency to give pleasure; the second, pain. This every one
may find in himself. It is not probable, that these principles can be resolved into
principles more simple and universal, whatever attempts may have been made to
that purpose. But if it were possible, it belongs not to the present subject; and
we may here safely consider these principles as original: happy, if we can render
all the consequences sufficiently plain and perspicuous!

Other Virtues

Utility is not only the distinguishing mark of the social virtues, but of anything of moral value whatever. Virtues other than the social virtues fall under the heading of qualities either useful or agreeable to the person possessing them or to others. The next selection includes Hume's enumeration of these virtues, as well as a discussion of how they fit into his overall moral theory.

Selection XXIV:
ENQUIRY CONCERNING THE PRINCIPLES OF MORALS
Section IX, Part I

It may justly appear surprising that any man in so late an age, should find it requisite to prove, by elaborate reasoning, that Personal Merit consists altogether in the possession of mental qualities, *useful* or *agreeable* to the *person himself* or to *others*. It might be expected that this principle would have occurred even to the first rude, unpractised enquirers concerning morals, and been received from its own evidence, without any argument or disputation. Whatever is valuable in any kind, so naturally classes itself under the division of *useful* or *agreeable* the *utile* or the *dulce*, that it is not easy to imagine why we should ever seek further, or consider the question as a matter of nice research or inquiry. And as every thing useful or agreeable must possess these qualities with regard either to the *person himself* or to *others*, the complete delineation or description of merit seems to be performed as naturally as a shadow is cast by the sun, or an image is reflected upon water. If the ground, on which the shadow is cast, be not broken and uneven; nor the surface from which the image is reflected, disturbed and confused; a just figure is immediately presented, without any art or attention. And it seems a reasonable presumption, that systems and hypotheses have perverted our natural understanding, when a theory, so simple and obvious, could so long have escaped the most elaborate examination.

But however the case may have fared with philosophy, in common life these principles are still implicitly maintained; nor is any other topic of praise or blame ever recurred to, when we employ any panegyric or satire, any applause or censure of human action and behaviour. If we observe men, in every intercourse of business or pleasure, in every discourse and conversation, we shall find them nowhere, except in the schools, at any loss upon this subject. What so natural, for instance, as the following dialogue? You are very happy, we shall suppose one to say, addressing himself to another, that you have given your daughter to Cleanthes. He is a man of honour and humanity. Every one, who has any intercourse with him, is sure of *fair* and *kind* treatment.* I congratulate you too, says another, on the promising expectations of this son-in-law; whose assiduous application to the study of the laws, whose quick penetration and early knowledge both of men and business, prognosticate the greatest honours and advancement.† You surprise me, replies a third, when you talk of Cleanthes as a man of business and application. I met him lately in a circle of the gayest company, and he was the very life and soul of our conversation: so much wit with good manners; so much gallantry without affectation; so much ingenious knowledge so genteelly delivered, I have never before observed in any one.‡ You would admire him still more, says a fourth, if you knew him more familiarly. That cheerfulness, which you might remark in him, is not a sudden flash struck out by company: it runs through the whole tenor of his life, and preserves a perpetual serenity on his countenance, and tranquillity in his soul. He has met with severe trials, misfortunes as well as dangers; and by his greatness of mind, was still superior to all of them.** The image, gentlemen, which you have here delineated of Cleanthes, cried I, is that of accomplished merit. Each of you has given a stroke of the pencil to his figure; and you have unawares exceeded all the pictures drawn by Gratian or Castiglione. A philosopher might select this character as a model of perfect virture.

And as every quality which is useful or agreeable to ourselves or others is, in common life, allowed to be a part of personal merit; so no other will ever be received, where men judge of things by their natural, unprejudiced reason, without the delusive glosses of superstition and false religion. Celibacy, fasting, penance, mortification, self-denial, humility, silence, solitude, and the whole train of monkish virtues; for what reason are they everywhere rejected by men of sense, but because they serve to no manner of purpose; neither advance a man's fortune in the world, nor render him a more valuable member of society; neither qualify him for the entertainment of company, nor increase his power of self-enjoyment? We observe, on the contrary, that they cross all these desirable ends; stupify the understanding and harden the heart, obscure the fancy and sour the temper. We justly, therefore, transfer them to the opposite column, and place them in the catalogue of vices; nor has any superstition force sufficient among men of the world, to pervert entirely these natural sentiments. A gloomy, hair-brained enthusiast, after his death, may have a place in

---

* Qualities useful to others.
† Qualities useful to the person himself.
‡ Qualities immediately agreeable to others.
** Qualities immediately agreeable to the person himself.

the calendar; but will scarcely ever be admitted, when alive, into intimacy and society, except by those who are as delirious and dismal as himself.

(h)

The Roles of Reason and Feeling in Moral Judgment

Having established that utility is the trigger of moral sentiment and having examined the psychological framework out of which it operates, Hume now directs his attention to the nature of moral sentiment and its manner of operation, particularly in relation to reason. Moral sentiment gives rise to feelings of moral approval or disapproval. Though formal reasoning has an important function in moral judgment, Hume, as does Hutcheson, clearly subordinates its role to that of feeling, and makes an attack on rationalism in ethics. Such a position is a natural consequence of his linking philosophy with practice and its associated notions of habit and belief. Mention of practice, however, underscores an equally important point: Hume's subordination of formal reasoning to feeling does not imply that he subordinates experimental reasoning to feeling. Insofar as experimental reasoning determines practice, practice (and hence feeling), though manifesting varying degrees of rationality, can never itself be completely devoid of reason. Hume is no irrationalist.

Selection XXV:
ENQUIRY CONCERNING THE PRINCIPLES OF MORALS
Appendix I

One principal foundation of moral praise being supposed to lie in the usefulness of any quality or action, it is evident that *reason* must enter for a considerable share in all decisions of this kind; since nothing but that faculty can instruct us in the tendency of qualities and actions, and point out their beneficial consequences to society and to their possessor. In many cases this is an affair liable to great controversy: doubts may arise; opposite interests may occur; and a preference must be given to one side, from very nice views, and a small overbalance of utility. This is particularly remarkable in questions with regard to justice; as is, indeed, natural to suppose, from that species of utility which attends this virtue. Were every single instance of justice, like that of benevolence, useful to society; this would be a more simple state of the case, and seldom liable to great controversy. But as single instances of justice are often pernicious in their first and immediate tendency, and as the advantage to society results only from the observance of the general rule, and from the concurrence and combination of several persons in the same equitable conduct; the case here becomes more intricate and involved. The various circumstances of society; the various consequences of any practice; the various interests which may be proposed; these, on many occasions, are doubtful, and subject to great discussion and inquiry. The object of municipal laws is to fix all the questions with regard to justice: the debates of civilians; the reflections of politicians; the precedents of history and public records, are all directed to the same purpose. And a very accurate *reason* or *judgement* is often requisite, to give the true determination, amidst such intricate doubts arising from obscure or opposite utilities.

But though reason, when fully assisted and improved, be sufficient to instruct us in the pernicious or useful tendency of qualities and actions; it it not alone sufficient to produce any moral blame or approbation. Utility is only a tendency to a certain end; and were the end totally indifferent to us, we should feel the same indifference towards the means. It is requisite a *sentiment* should here display itself, in order to give a preference to the useful above the pernicious tendencies. This sentiment can be no other than a feeling for the happiness of mankind, and a resentment of their misery; since these are the different ends which virtue and vice have a tendency to promote. Here therefore *reason* instructs us in the several tendencies of actions, and *humanity* makes a distinction in favour of those which are useful and beneficial.

This partition between the faculties of understanding and sentiment, in all moral decisions, seems clear from the preceding hypothesis. But I shall suppose that hypothesis false: it will then be requisite to look out for some other theory that may be satisfactory; and I dare venture to affirm that none such will ever be found, so long as we suppose reason to be the sole source of morals. To prove this, it will be proper to weigh the five following considerations.

I. It is easy for a false hypothesis to maintain some appearance of truth, while it keeps wholly in generals, makes use of undefined terms, and employs comparisons, instead of instances. This is particularly remarkable in that philosophy, which ascribes the discernment of all moral distinctions to reason alone, without the concurrence of sentiment. It is impossible that, in any particular instance, this hypothesis can so much as be rendered intelligible, whatever specious figure it may make in general declamations and discourses. Examine the crime of *ingratitude*, for instance; which has place, wherever we observe good-will, expressed and known, together with good-offices performed, on the one side, and a return of ill-will or indifference, with ill-offices or neglect on the other: anatomize all these circumstances, and examine, by your reason alone, in what consists the demerit or blame. You never will come to any issue or conclusion.

Reason judges either of *matter of fact* or of *relations*. Enquire then, *first*, where is that matter of fact which we here call *crime*; point it out; determine the time of its existence; describe its essence or nature; explain the sense or faculty to which it discovers itself. It resides in the mind of the person who is ungrateful. He must, therefore, feel it, and be conscious of it. But nothing is there, except the passion of ill will or absolute indifference. You cannot say that these, of themselves, always, and in all circumstances, are crimes. No, they are ony crimes when directed towards persons who have before expressed and displayed good-will towards us. Consequently, we may infer, that the crime of ingratitude is not any particular individual *fact*; but arises from a complication of circumstances, which, being presented to the spectator, excites the *sentiment* of blame, by the particular structure and fabric of his mind.

This representation, you say, is false. Crime, indeed, consists not in a particular *fact*, of whose reality we are assured by *reason*; but it consists in certain *moral relations*, discovered by reason, in the same manner as we discover by reason the truths of geometry or algebra. But what are the relations, I ask, of which you here talk? In the case stated above, I see first good-will and good-offices in one person; then ill-will and ill-offices in the other. Between these, there is a relation of *contrariety*. Does the crime consist in that relation? But suppose a person bore me ill-will or did me ill-offices; and I, in return, were indifferent towards him, or did him good-offices. Here is the same relation of *contrariety*; and yet my conduct is often highly laudable. Twist and turn this matter as much as you will, you can never rest the morality on relation; but must have recourse to the decisions of sentiment.

When it is affirmed that two and three are equal to the half of ten, this relation of equality I understand perfectly. I conceive, that if ten be divided into two parts, of which one has as many units as the other; and if any of these parts be compared to two added to three, it will contain as many units as that compound number. But when you draw thence a comparison to moral relations, I own that I am altogether at a loss to understand you. A moral action, a crime, such as ingratitude, is a complicated object. Does the morality consist in the relation of its parts to each other? How? After what manner? Specify the relation: be more particular and explicit in your propositions, and you will easily see their falsehood.

No, say you, the morality consists in the relation of actions to the rule of right; and they are denominated good or ill, according as they agree or disagree with it. What then is this rule of right? In what does it consist? How is it determined? By reason, you say, which examines the moral relations of actions. So that moral relations are determined by the comparison of action to a rule. And that rule is determined by considering the moral relations of objects. Is not this fine reasoning?

All this is metaphysics, you cry. That is enough; there needs nothing more to give a strong presumption of falsehood. Yes, reply I, here are metaphysics surely; but they are all on your side, who advance an abstruse hypothesis, which can never be made intelligible, nor quadrate with any particular instance or illustration. The hypothesis which we embrace is plain. It maintains that morality is determined by sentiment. It defines virtue to be *whatever mental action or quality gives to a spectator the pleasing sentiment of approbation;* and vice the contrary. We then proceed to examine a plain matter of fact, to wit, what actions have this influence. We consider all the circumstances in which these actions agree, and thence endeavour to extract some general observations with regard to these sentiments. If you call this metaphysics, and find anything abstruse here, you need only conclude that your turn of mind is not suited to the moral sciences.

II. When a man, at any time, deliberates concerning his own conduct (as, whether he had better, in a particular emergence, assist a brother or a benefactor), he must consider these separate relations, with all the circumstances and situations of the persons, in order to determine the superior duty and obligation; and in order to determine the proportion of lines in any triangle, it is necessary to examine the nature of that figure, and the relation which its several parts bear to each other. But notwithstanding this appearing similarity in the two cases, there is, at bottom, an extreme difference between them. A speculative reasoner concerning triangles or circles considers the several known and given relations of the parts of these figures, and thence infers some unknown relation, which is dependent on the former. But in moral deliberations we must be acquainted beforehand with all the objects, and all their relations to each other; and from a comparison of the whole, fix our choice or approbation. No new fact to be ascertained; no new relation to be discovered. All the circumstances of the case are supposed to be laid before us, ere we can fix any sentence of blame or approbation. If any material circumstance be yet unknown or doubtful, we must first employ our inquiry or intellectual faculties to assure us of it; and must suspend for a time all moral decision or sentiment. While we are ignorant whether a man were aggressor or not, how can we determine whether the person who killed him be criminal or innocent? But after every circumstance, every relation is known, the understanding has no further room to operate, nor any object on which it could employ itself. The approbation or blame which then ensues, cannot be the work of the judgement, but of the heart; and is not a speculative proposition or affirmation, but an active feeling or sentiment. In the disquisitions of the understanding, from known circumstances and relations, we infer some new and unknown. In moral decisions, all the circumstances and relations must be previously known; and the mind, from the contemplation of the whole, feels some new impression of affection or disgust, esteem or contempt, approbation or blame.

Hence the great difference between a mistake of *fact* and one of *right*; and hence the reason why the one is commonly criminal and not the other. When Oedipus killed Laius, he was ignorant of the relation, and from circumstances, innocent and involuntary, formed erroneous opinions concerning the action which he committed. But when Nero killed Agrippina, all the relations between himself and the person, and all the circumstances of the fact, were previously known to him; but the motive of revenge, or fear, or interest, prevailed in his savage heart over the sentiments of duty and humanity. And when we express that detestation against him to which he himself, in a little time, became insensible, it is not that we see any relations, of which he was ignorant; but that, for the rectitude of our disposition, we feel sentiments against which he was hardened from flattery and a long perseverance in the most enormous crimes. In these sentiments then, not in a discovery of relations of any kind, do all moral determinations consist. Before we can pretend to form any decision of this kind, everything must be known and ascertained on the side of the object or action. Nothing remains but to feel, on our part, some sentiment of blame or approbation; whence we pronounce the action criminal or virtuous.

III. This doctrine will become still more evident, if we compare moral beauty with natural, to which in many particulars it bears so near a resemblance. It is on the proportion, relation, and position of parts, that all natural beauty depends; but it would be absurd thence to infer, that the perception of beauty, like that of truth in geometrical problems, consists wholly in the perception of relations, and was performed entirely by the understanding or intellectual faculties. In all the sciences, our mind from the known relations investigates the unknown. But in all decisions of taste or external beauty, all the relations are beforehand obvious to the eye; and we thence proceed to feel a sentiment of complacency or disgust, according to the nature of the object, and disposition of our organs.

Euclid has fully explained all the qualities of the circle; but has not in any proposition said a word of its beauty. The reason is evident. The beauty is not a quality of the circle. It lies not in any part of the line, whose parts are equally distant from a common centre. It is only the effect

which that figure produces upon the mind, whose peculiar fabric of structure renders it susceptible of such sentiments. In vain would you look for
it in the circle, or seek it, either by your senses or by mathematical reasoning, in all the properties of that figure.

Attend to Palladio and Perrault, while they explain all the parts and
proportions of a pillar. They talk of the cornice, and frieze, and base, and
entablature, and shaft and architrave; and give the description and position of each of these members. But should you ask the description and
position of its beauty, they would readily reply, that the beauty is not in
any of the parts or members of a pillar, but results from the whole, when
that complicated figure is presented to an intelligent mind, susceptible to
those finer sensations. Till such a spectator appear, there is nothing but
a figure of such particular dimensions and proportions: from his sentiments alone arise its elegance and beauty.

Again; attend to Cicero, while he paints the crimes of a Verres or a
Catiline. You must acknowledge that the moral turpitude results, in the
same manner, from the contemplation of the whole, when presented to a
being whose organs have such a particular structure and formation. The
orator may paint rage, insolence, barbarity on the one side; meekness,
suffering, sorrow, innocence on the other. But if you feel no indignation
or compassion arise in you from this complication of circumstances, you
would in vain ask him, in what consists the crime or villainy, which he so
vehemently exclaims against? At what time, or on what subject it first
began to exist? And what has a few months afterwards become of it,
when every disposition and thought of all the actors is totally altered or
annihilated? No satisfactory answer can be given to any of these questions, upon the abstract hypothesis of morals; and we must at last acknowledge, that the crime or immorality is no particular fact or relation, which
can be the object of the understanding, but arises entirely from the sentiment of disapprobation, which, by the structure of human nature, we
unavoidably feel on the apprehension of barbarity or treachery.

IV. Inanimate objects may bear to each other all the same relations
which we observe in moral agents; though the former can never be the
object of love or hatred, nor are consequently susceptible of merit or
iniquity. A young tree, which over-tops and destroys its parent, stands in
all the same relations with Nero, when he murdered Agrippina; and if
morality consisted merely in relations, would no doubt be equally
criminal.

V. It appears evident that the ultimate ends of human actions can
never, in any case, be accounted for by *reason*, but recommend themselves entirely to the sentiments and affections of mankind, without any
dependance on the intellectual faculties. Ask a man *why he uses exercise;*

he will answer, *because he desires to keep his health.* If you then enquire, *why he desires health,* he will readily reply, *because sickness is painful.* If you push your enquiries farther, and desire a reason *why he hates pain,* it is impossible he can ever give any. This is an ultimate end, and is never referred to any other object.

Perhaps to your second question, *why he desires health,* he may also reply, that *it is necessary for the exercise of his calling.* If you ask, *why he is anxious on that head,* he will answer, *because he desires to get money.* If you demand *Why? It is the instrument of pleasure,* says he. And beyond this it is an absurdity to ask for a reason. It is impossible there can be a progress *in infinitum;* and that one thing can always be a reason why another is desired. Something must be desirable on its own account, and because of its immediate accord or agreement with human sentiment and affection.

Now as virtue is an end, and is desirable on its own account, without fee and reward, merely for the immediate satisfaction which it conveys; it is requisite that there should be some sentiment which it touches, some internal taste or feeling, or whatever you may please to call it, which distinguishes moral good and evil, and which embraces the one and rejects the other.

Thus the distinct boundaries and offices of *reason* and of *taste* are easily ascertained. The former conveys the knowledge of truth and falsehood: the latter gives the sentiment of beauty and deformity, vice and virtue. The one discovers objects as they really stand in nature, without addition or diminution: the other has a productive faculty, and gilding or staining all natural objects with the colours, borrowed from internal sentiment, raises in a manner a new creation. Reason being cool and disengaged, is no motive to action, and directs only the impulse received from appetite or inclination, by showing us the means of attaining happiness or avoiding misery: Taste, as it gives pleasure or pain, and thereby constitutes happiness or misery, becomes a motive to action, and is the first spring or impulse to desire and volition. From circumstances and relations, known or supposed, the former leads us to the discovery of the concealed and unknown: after all circumstances and relations are laid before us, the latter makes us feel from the whole a new sentiment of blame or approbation. The standard of the one, being founded on the nature of things, is eternal and inflexible, even by the will of the Supreme Being: the standard of the other, arising from the eternal frame and constitution of animals, is ultimately derived from that Supreme Will, which bestowed on each being its peculiar nature, and arranged the several classes and orders of existence. (i)

PROBLEMS

1. Discuss and evaluate Hume's view of the status of universals.
2. Kant maintains that there is no difference in thought between an existing $100 and an imaginary $100. Explain Kant's contention in the light of what Hume says about the idea of existence.
3. A metaphysical solipsist is one who believes that the whole of reality is dependent on the existence of his individual self. Is Hume a metaphysical solipsist?
4. A metaphysical idealist is one who believes that everything real other than minds is dependent on the existence of minds. Is Hume a metaphysical idealist?
5. Discuss the legitimacy of Hume's contention that all objects of human reason may be divided into two kinds—relations of ideas and matters of fact.
6. Discuss Hume's views concerning
   a. the meaningfulness of the idea of cause and effect.
   b. the possibility of knowing particular cause and effect judgments to be true or false.
7. Discuss the role in Hume's philosophy of his analysis of the idea of cause and effect.
8. Outline Hume's argument that we can have no certain or probable knowledge of the future course of experience. Do you regard his conclusion as warranted? Why or why not?
9. Discuss and evaluate Hume's Pyrrhonist criticism of the traditional (Aristotelian) notion of substance.
10. Discuss and evaluate Hume's Pyrrhonist criticism of the Newtonian notion of material substance.
11. Evaluate Hume's Pyrrhonist principle that what is separable in analysis is separable in reality.
12. Discuss the adequacy of Hume's Pyrrhonist view of the self as a bundle of perceptions.
13. Discuss and evaluate Hume's refutation of the *a priori* and *a posteriori* arguments for God's existence.
14. Discuss the proposition that Hume's thinking about miracles must be faulty because it would keep us from acknowledging the existence of miracles even if they are assumed to exist.
15. To what extent does Hume's epistemology confuse logic with psychology? How serious a threat is this confusion to the soundness of Hume's conclusions?
16. Explain what is meant by Hume's "atomism." Discuss its validity. To what extent are Hume's conclusions dependent on his atomism?
17. Discuss the extent to which Hume's Pyrrhonist conclusions are dependent on his nominalism. (See p. 20 for a definition of nominalism.)

18. What does Hume mean by
    a. instinct.
    b. belief.
    c. custom and habit.
    How does each operate in his philosophy?
19. Suggest ways in which one might try to "refute" Hume, indicating whether or not you feel these attempts might succeed.
20. Discuss in what sense Hume may or may not be called a sceptic.
21. Discuss the value of the idea that one of Hume's major contributions to philosophy is his concept that man's apprehension of reality lies not simply in his acceptance of something given, but in his interpretation of the given as well.
22. Discuss the view that Hume's philosophy does not make adequate provision for the role of the hypothesis in science.
23. Evaluate the criticism commonly made of Hume that his Pyrrhonist analysis of the principle of cause and effect, as well as his recourse to habit and belief as a solution of difficulties arising from his analysis, presuppose this very principle.
24. Explicate Hume's conception of the nature of reason.
25. Discuss Hume's conception of the nature of experience.
26. At one point Hume denies that we can know anything of "real existence and matter of fact beyond the present testimony of our senses, or the records of our memory" by either reason or experience. Yet he claims elsewhere that reason is "a wonderful and unintelligible instinct in our souls," and that we learn through experience grounded in this instinct. Resolve the apparent contradiction.
27. Discuss the truth or falsity of each of the following statements:
    a. The conclusions to which Hume's philosophical position leads are surely absurd.
    b. Hume's notions of habit and belief imply that we "make believe" what we know isn't true.
    c. One of Hume's major contributions to philosophy consists in his depriving reason of its "magical halo."
    d. Hume has an abiding faith in the power of human reason.
28. In what respects does Hume regard justice as a natural virtue? In what respects as an artificial virtue? Be sure to define your terms.
29. Hume argues that justice is established by "convention" and not by promise. Explain.
30. What does Hume mean by
    a. moral sentiment.
    b. sympathy.
    c. self-love.
    d. benevolence.
31. Discuss the relation between moral sentiment and sympathy in Hume's moral theory.

32. To what extent does Hume's moral theory presuppose unchanging moral standards? In what sense is his position consistent with relativism?
33. Discuss Hume's likening of moral sentiment to aesthetic taste, and its implications.
34. It may be argued that though Hume may have adequately explained moral approval and disapproval, he has not given a satisfactory account of moral obligation. Explain. What defense could Hume offer?
35. Paint a character portrait of a man fitting Hume's moral ideal, and compare it with that of a man fitting the Christian moral idea.
36. To what extent may Hume properly be accused of dogmatism?
37. Discuss the charge that Hume is an irrationalist.
38. Discuss the question of whether scepticism in philosophy has any special relation to radical, liberal, conservative, or reactionary tendencies in politics.
39. Reason, defined as the capacity to learn by experience, seems to have given rise, at least in part, to the notion of "the reasonable man" in law. Reason in this sense makes man's capacity for forming habits and expectations able to serve as a standard of "justifiable" beliefs. Yet it is obvious that men can form "bad" as well as "good" habits—that they can acquire superstitious or insane beliefs as well as justifiable ones. Do you feel that reason in the sense defined is any criterion of justifiable beliefs? If not, why not? If so, to what extent?
40. What is Hume's conception of human nature, and what is its role in his philosophy?
41. A theory of meaning to the effect that the meaning of an idea should be defined by reference to its practical consequences would be accepted by all pragmatists. A theory of truth to the effect that an idea is true if action based on it works, would be accepted by some pragmatists. Discuss the pragmatic aspects of Hume's philosophy.
42. Characteristic of existentialism is the belief that reality is beyond comprehension by any system of rational concepts and the accompanying notion that reality is accessible only through immediate experience for which the individual must take personal responsibility. Discuss possible existentialist implications of Hume's philosophy.

RECOMMENDED READING

Editions of Hume's Works

The Philosophical Works of David Hume, in 4 vols. T. H. Green and T. H. Grose (eds.). London: Longmans, Green, 1898.

The standard edition of the complete works. The introduction has been historically influential in perpetuating the interpretation of Hume as exclusively within the tradition of Locke and Berkeley.

A Treatise of Human Nature. L. A. Selby-Bigge (ed.). Oxford: The Clarendon Press, 1964 (reprinted from the 1888 edition).

   The best easily available edition. Contains a detailed analytical index.

A Treatise of Human Nature. Garden City, New York: Doubleday, 1961 (Dolphin Books).

   An inexpensive edition of the complete work.

Enquiries Concerning the Human Understanding and Concerning the Principles of Morals. L. A. Selby-Bigge (ed.). Oxford: The Clarendon Press, 1963 impression of the second edition of 1902.

   The best easily available edition of the two *Enquiries.* Also contains Hume's "A Dialogue" (an interesting essay bearing on the relativity of moral values), and a detailed comparative table of contents of the *Treatise* and *Enquiries.*

An Inquiry Concerning Human Understanding. Charles W. Hendel (ed.). New York: Bobbs-Merrill, 1956 (The Library of Liberal Arts).

   An inexpensive standard edition which also contains Hume's own *An Abstract of a Treatise of Human Nature.*

An Inquiry Concerning the Principles of Morals. Charles W. Hendel (ed.). New York: Bobbs-Merrill, 1957 (The Library of Liberal Arts).

   An inexpensive standard edition which also contains Hume's "A Dialogue."

Dialogues Concerning Natural Religion. Norman Kemp Smith (ed.). New York: Bobbs-Merrill, 1947 (The Library of Liberal Arts).

   The standard edition with an excellent introduction and extensive appendices and supplements including Hume's autobiographical essay "My Own Life."

Hume's Moral and Political Philosophy. Henry D. Aiken (ed.). New York: Hafner, 1959 (reprint of 1948 edition).

   A wide selection of Hume's writings from the *Treatise, Enquiry Concerning the Principles of Morals,* and *Essays, Moral and Political.*

David Hume's Political Essays. Charles W. Hendel (ed.). New York: Bobbs-Merrill, 1953 (The Library of Liberal Arts).

   A selection of essays from Hume's *Essays, Moral, Political and Literary.*

The Natural History of Religion. H. Chadwick (ed.) with an introduction by H. E. Root. London, 1956.

Hume Selections. Charles W. Hendel (ed.). New York: Charles Scribner's Sons, 1927.

   A standard book of selections from the *Treatise, Enquiries, Dialogues Concerning Natural Religion,* and *The Natural History of Religion.*

Of Standard of Taste and Other Essays. John W. Lenz (ed.). New York: Bobbs-Merrill, 1965 (The Library of Liberal Arts).

The Letters of David Hume. J. Y. T. Greig (ed.). Oxford: The Clarendon Press, 1932.

The New Letters of David Hume. R. Klibansky and E. C. Mossner (eds.). Oxford: The Clarendon Press, 1952.

Selected Works on Hume

Basson, A. H. *David Hume.* London: Penguin, 1958.
An exposition and crtical appraisal of Hume's philosophy.
Brunius, Teddy. *David Hume on Criticism.* Almquist & Wiksell, 1954.
Broad, C. D. *Five Types of Ethical Theory.* Paterson, New Jersey: Littlefield, Adams, 1959 (reprint of 1930 edition published by Routledge & Kegan Paul, Ltd., London). Chapter IV.
A good short examination of Hume's moral theory included in a study also concerned with four other ethical thinkers: Spinoza, Butler, Kant and Sidgwick.
Church, Ralph W. *Hume's Theory of the Understanding.* Ithaca, New York: Cornell University Press, 1935.
A clear account of Hume's theoretical philosophy.
Copleston, Frederick, S. J. *A History of Philosophy.* Garden City, New York: Doubleday, 1964 (Image Books). Vol. 5, Part III, Chapters 14–18.
An excellent, balanced exposition of Hume's philosophy.
Flew, Anthony. *Hume's Philosophy of Belief: A Study of His First Inquiry.* New York: Humanities Press, 1961.
An important study of the part of Hume's philosophy that is of greatest contemporary relevance.
Glanthe, Alfred B. *Hume's Theory of the Passion and of Morals.* Berkeley: University of California Press, 1950.
A detailed textual analysis of Hume's moral theory at variance with the Kemp Smith-Hendel interpretation that holds Hutcheson's influence to be dominant.
Hendel, Charles W. *Studies in the Philosophy of David Hume.* New York: Bobbs-Merrill, 1963 (The Library of Liberal Arts).
Perhaps the most comprehensive study of Hume's philosophy by one who along with Norman Kemp Smith held that the influence of Hutcheson was dominant in the shaping of Hume's theoretical as well as his moral philosophy. Contains a valuable review of Hume scholarship since 1925 and a supplement on Hume's atomism.
Laing, B. M. *David Hume.* London: Benn, 1932.
An interpretation of Hume at variance with the Kemp Smith-Hendel interpretation.
Laird, John. *Hume's Philosophy of Human Nature.* London: Methuen, 1932.
Another alternative interpretation of Hume.
Mossner, Ernest C. *The Life of David Hume.* Edinburgh: Nelson, 1954.
An excellent biography.
Passmore, John A. *Hume's Intentions.* Cambridge: Cambridge University Press, 1952.
An interesting discussion of various strands in Hume's thought.
Price, Henry H. *Hume's Theory of the External World.* Oxford: The Clarendon Press, 1940.

A somewhat technical but readable and suggestive examination of the implications of Hume's theories of perception and the external world.

Smith, Norman Kemp. *The Philosophy of David Hume*. London: Macmillan, 1949 (reprint of the 1941 edition).

A classic in Hume scholarship by a leading proponent if not originator of the view that Hutcheson's influence was dominant in Hume's theoretical as well as in his moral philosophy.

Additional Works on Hume

Anderson, Robert Fendel. *Hume's First Principles*. Lincoln: University of Nebraska Press, 1966.

Ayer, A.J. *Hume*. New York: Hill & Wang, 1980.

Beck, Lewis White. *Essays on Kant & Hume*. New Haven: Yale University Press, 1978.

Chappell, V.C. (ed.) *Hume*. Garden City, New York: Doubleday, 1966 (Anchor Books). A collection of reprinted papers on a wide range of topics.

Gaskin, J.C.A. *Hume's Philosophy of Religion*. New York: Barnes & Noble, 1978.

Harrison, Jonathan. *Hume's Moral Epistemology*. Oxford: Clarendon Press, 1976.

Livingston, Donald W. & King, James T. (eds.) *Hume: A Re-evaluation*. New York: Fordham University Press, 1976. Contains nineteen papers by eighteen authors on a broad variety of subjects, and including reprints of four articles by Wolin 1954, Adair 1957, Flew 1967, and Walton 1974.

Mackie, J.L. *Hume's Moral Theory*. Boston: Routledge & Kegan Paul, 1980.

Merrill, K.R. & Shahan R.W. (eds.) *David Hume, Many-sided Genius*. Norman, Oklahoma: University of Oklahoma Press, 1976. A collection of nine independent essays, including a translation by J.N. Mohanty of a 1908 article by Adolph Reinach: "Kant's Interpretation of Hume's Problem."

Murphy, Richard T. *Hume and Husserl: Towards Radical Subjectivism*. Hingham, Massachusetts: Kluwer Boston, 1980.

Pears, D.F. *David Hume: A Symposium*. London: Macmillan & Co., 1963. A collection of essays on major themes.

Penelhum, Terence. *Hume*. New York: St. Martin's Press, 1975.

Price, John Valdimir, *The Ironic Hume*. Austin, Texas: University of Texas Press, 1965.

Sesonske, Alexander & Fleming, Noel (eds.). *Human Understanding: Studies in the Philosophy of David Hume*. Belmont, California: Wadsworth, 1965.

Stove, D.C. *Probability & Hume's Inductive Scepticism*. Oxford at the Clarendon Press, 1973. A clearly written examination of Hume's inductive scepticism along with an assessment of its present influence.

Immanuel Kant
1724-1804

INTRODUCTION

To indicate the outlines of Kant's thought, we shall center our attention on three conceptions: (a) Nature and Freedom, (b) the Creativity of Human Reason, and (c) the contribution of Human Reason.

Nature and Freedom

In the conclusion of the *Critique of Practical Reason,* Kant writes: "Two things fill the mind with ever new and increasing admiration and awe, the oftener and more steadily we reflect on them: the starry heavens above me and the moral law within me." This expresses the basic division in the world of Kant, the realm of Nature and the realm of Morality—the salient feature of which is Freedom. That contemporary man finds his world divided between the realm of Fact and the realm of Value reflects not only Kant's influence, but also his relevance. For man is concerned with and indeed belongs to both realms and it is in their nature and interrelation that Kant is primarily interested.

Our first selection is from an unusual essay, written in 1786, entitled "Conjectural Beginnings of Human History." In a preliminary way it sets forth Kant's understanding of the human situation as participation in and concern for nature and morality. Kant interprets the myth of the Garden of Eden and the Fall as the emergence of man from the guidance of natural instinct to the uses of reason and the reality of choice.

Selection I:
THE NATURE OF MAN

Because I here venture on a mere pleasure trip, I may hope to be favored with the permission to use, as a map for my trip, a sacred document; and also to fancy that my trip—undertaken on the wings of the imagination, albeit not without a clue rationally derived from experience—may take the very route sketched out in that document. Let the reader consult it (Gen. 2–6) and check at every point whether the road which philosophy takes with the help of concepts coincides with the story told in Holy Writ.

Unless one is to indulge in irresponsible conjectures, one must start out with something which human reason cannot derive from prior natural causes—in the present case, the existence of man. Moreover, it must be man as an adult, because he must get along without the help of a mother; it must be a pair, in order that he may perpetuate his kind; and it must be a single pair. . . .   (a)

What is still more, I begin with this pair, not in the natural state with all its crudeness, but rather after it has already taken mighty steps in the skillful use of its powers. For if I were to attempt to fill this gap—which presumably encompasses a great space of time—there might be for the reader too many conjectures and too few probabilities. The first man, then, was able to stand and walk; he could speak (2:20) and even discourse, i.e., speak according to coherent concepts (2:23), and hence think. These are all skills which he had to acquire for himself (for if he were created with them, he would also pass them on through heredity; but this contradicts experience). But I take him as already in possession of these skills. For my sole purpose is to consider the development of manners and morals [des Sittlichen] in his way of life, and these already presuppose the skills referred to.

In the beginning, the novice must have been guided by instinct alone, that voice of God which is obeyed by all animals. . . .   (b)

So long as inexperienced man obeyed this call of nature all was well with him. But soon reason began to stir. A sense different from that to which instinct was tied—the sense, say, of sight—presented other food than that normally consumed as similar to it; and reason, instituting a comparison, sought to enlarge its knowledge of foodstuffs beyond the bounds of instinctual knowledge (3:6). This experiment might, with good luck, have ended well, even though instinct did not advise it, so long as it was at least not contrary to instinct. But reason has this peculiarity that, aided by the imagination, it can create artificial desires which are not only unsupported by natural instinct but actually contrary to it.

These desires, in the beginning called concupiscence, gradually generate a whole host of unnecessary and indeed unnatural inclinations called luxuriousness. The original occasion for deserting natural instinct may have been trifling. But this was man's first attempt to become conscious of his reason as a power which can extend itself beyond the limits to which all animals are confined. As such its effect was very important and indeed decisive for his future way of life. Thus the occasion may have been merely the external appearance of a fruit which tempted because of its similarity to tasty fruits of which man had already partaken. In addition there may have been the example of an animal which consumed it because, for it, it was naturally fit for consumption, while on the contrary, being harmful for man, it was consequently resisted by man's instinct. Even so, this was a sufficient occasion for reason to do violence to the voice of nature (3:1) and, its protest notwithstanding, to make the first attempt at a free choice; an attempt which, being the first, probably did not have the expected result. But however insignificant the damage done, it sufficed to open man's eyes (3:7). He discovered in himself a power of choosing for himself a way of life, of not being bound without alternative to a single way, like the animals. Perhaps the discovery of this advantage created a moment of delight. But of necessity, anxiety and alarm as to how he was to deal with this newly discovered power quickly followed; for man was a being who did not yet know either the secret properties or the remote effects of anything. He stood, as it were, at the brink of an abyss. Until that moment instinct had directed him toward specific objects of desire. But from these there now opened up an infinity of such objects, and he did not yet know how to choose between them. On the other hand, it was impossible for him to return to the state of servitude (i.e., subjection to instinct) from the state of freedom, once he had tasted the latter.

Next to the instinct for food, by means of which nature preserves the individual, the greatest prominence belongs to the sexual instinct, by means of which she preserves the species. Reason, once aroused, did not delay in demonstrating its influence here as well. In the case of animals, sexual attraction is merely a matter of transient, mostly periodic impulse. But man soon discovered that for him this attraction can be prolonged and even increased by means of the imagination—a power which carries on its business, to be sure, the more moderately, but at once also the more constantly and uniformly, the more its object is removed from the senses. By means of the imagination, he discovered, the surfeit was avoided which goes with the satisfaction of mere animal desire. The fig leaf (3:7), then, was a far greater manifestation of reason than that shown in the earlier stage of development. For the one shows merely a power to choose the extent to which to serve impulse; but the other—rendering an inclination more inward [*inniglich*] and constant by removing its object from the senses—already reflects consciousness of a certain degree of mastery of reason over impulse. Refusal was that feat which brought about the passage from merely sensual [*empfundenen*] to spiritual [*idealischen*] attractions, from mere animal desire gradually to love, and along with this from the feeling of the merely agreeable to a taste for beauty, at first only for beauty in man but at length for beauty in nature as well. In addition, there came a first hint at the development of man as a moral creature. This came from the sense of decency [*Sittsamkeit*], which is an inclination to inspire others to respect by proper manners, i.e., by concealing all that which might arouse low esteem. Here, incidentally, lies the real basis of all true sociability [*Geselligkeit*].

This may be a small beginning. But if it gives a wholly new direction to thought, such a beginning is epoch-making. It is then more important than the whole immeasurable series of expansions of culture which subsequently spring from it.

After having thus insinuated itself into the first immediately felt needs, reason took its third step. This was the conscious *expectation of the future*. This capacity for facing up in the present to the often very distant future, instead of being wholly absorbed by the enjoyment of the present, is the most decisive mark of the human's advantage. It enables man to prepare himself for distant aims according to his role as a human being. But at the same time it is also the most inexhaustible source of cares and troubles, aroused by the uncertainty of his future—cares and troubles of which animals are altogether free (3:13–19). Man, compelled to support himself, his wife and his future children, foresaw the ever-increasing hardships of labor. Woman foresaw the troubles to which nature had subjected her sex, and those additional ones to which man, a being stronger than she, would subject her. Both foresaw with fear—in the background of the picture and at the end of a troublesome life—that which, to be sure, inexorably strikes all animals without, however, causing them care, namely, death. And they apparently foreswore and decried as a crime the use of reason, which had been the cause of all these ills. Perhaps their sole comfort was the prospect of living through their children who might enjoy a better fortune, or else the hope that these latter members of their family might alleviate their burden (3:16-20).

But there was yet a fourth and final step which reason took, and this raised man altogether above community with animals. He came to understand, however obscurely, that he is the true end of nature, and that nothing that lives on earth can compete with him in this regard. The first time he ever said to the sheep, "Nature has given you the skin you wear for my use, not for yours"; the first time he ever took that skin and put it upon himself (3:21)—that time he became aware of the way in which his nature privileged and raised him above all animals. And from then on he looked upon them, no longer as fellow creatures, but as mere means and tools to whatever ends he pleased. This idea entails (obscurely, to be sure) the idea of contrast, that what he may say to an animal he may not say to a fellow human; that he must rather consider the latter as an equal participant in the gifts of nature. This idea was the first preparation of all those restraints in his relations with his fellow men which reason would in due course impose on man's will, restraints which are far more essential for the establishment of a civil society than inclination and love.

Thus man had entered into a relation of equality with all rational beings, whatever their rank (3:22), with respect to the claim of being an end in himself, respected as such by everyone, a being which no one might treat as a mere means to ulterior ends. So far as natural gifts are concerned, other beings may surpass man beyond all comparison. Nevertheless, man is without qualification equal even to higher beings in that none has the right to use him according to pleasure. This is because of his reason—reason considered not insofar as it is a tool to the satisfaction of his inclinations, but insofar as it makes him an end in himself. Hence this last step of reason is at the same time man's *release* from the womb of nature, an alteration of condition which is honorable, to be sure, but also fraught with danger. For nature had now driven him from the safe and harmless state of childhood—a garden, as it were, which looked after his needs without any trouble on his part (3:23)—into the wide world, where so many cares, troubles, and unforeseen ills awaited him. In the future, the wretchedness of his condition would often arouse in him the wish for a paradise, the creation of his imagination, where he could dream or while away his existence in quiet inactivity and permanent peace. But between him and that imagined place of bliss, restless reason would interpose itself, irresistibly impelling him to develop the faculties implanted within him. It would not permit him to return to that crude and simple state from which it had driven him to begin with (3:24). It would make him take up patiently the toil which he yet hates, and pursue the frippery which he despises. It would make him forget even death itself which he dreads, because of all those trifles which he is even more afraid to lose.

Remark

From this account of original human history we may conclude: man's departure from that paradise which his reason represents as the first abode of his species was nothing but the transition from an uncultured, merely animal condition to the state of humanity, from bondage to instinct to rational control—in a word, from the tutelage of nature to the state of freedom. Whether man has won or lost in this change is no longer an open question, if one considers the destiny of his species. This consists in nothing less than progress toward perfection, be the first attempts toward that aim, or even the first long series of attempts, ever so faulty.

However, while for the species the direction of this road may be from worse to better, this is not true for the individual. Before reason awoke, there was as yet neither commandment nor prohibition and hence also no violation of either. But when reason began to set about its business, it came, in all its pristine weakness, into conflict with animality, with all its power. Inevitably evils sprang up, and (which is worse) along with the cultivation of reason also vices, such as had been wholly alien to the state of ignorance and innocence. Morally, the first step from this latter state was therefore a fall; physically, it was a punishment, for a whole host of formerly unknown ills were a consequence of this fall. The history of nature therefore begins with good, for it is the work of God, while the history of freedom begins with wickedness, for it is the work of man. For the individual, who in the use of his freedom is concerned only with himself, this whole change was a loss; for nature, whose purpose with man concerns the species, it was a gain. Hence the individual must consider as his own fault, not only every act of wickedness which he commits, but also all the evils which he suffers; and yet at the same time, insofar as he is a member of a whole (a species), he must admire and praise the wisdom and purposiveness of the whole arrangement. . . .   (c)

Now here it must be seen that all evils which express human life, and all vices which dishonor it, spring from this unresolved conflict.* This

---

* I will mention the following, by way of giving a few examples of this conflict between man's striving toward the fulfillment of his moral destiny, on the one hand, and, on the other, his unalterable subjection to laws fit for the uncivilized and animal state.

When he is about sixteen or seventeen years old, nature makes man come of age; that is, she gives him both the desire and the power to reproduce his kind. In the uncivilized state of nature, a youth literally becomes a man at that age. He is then able to look after himself, to reproduce his kind, and to take care of both a wife and children. This is easy because his needs are simple. But in order to discharge the responsibilities of manhood in the civilized state, one needs means and skills, as well as fortunate external circumstances. Hence a youth acquires the civil aspect of manhood on the average only about ten years later. But as society increases in complexity nature does not alter the age of sexual maturity. She stubbornly pereeveres in her law, which aims at the perpetuation of man as an animal species. Hence manners and morals, and the aim of nature, inevitably come to interfere with each other. For as a natural being a person is already a man at an age when conflict is in fact altogether unresolved, because culture, considered as the genuine education of man as man and citizen, has perhaps not even begun properly, much less been completed. Sometimes a natural impulse toward vice is mistakenly identified as the ultimate cause of these evils. But in itself and as a natural disposition, impulse serves a good purpose. The real trouble is that, on the one hand, culture progressively interferes with its natural function, by altering the conditions to which it was suited;

---

a civil being (who yet does not cease to be a natural being as well) he is still a a youth or even a child. For thus one may well call a person unable, in the civil state, to provide for himself, let alone for others of his kind. Yet he has the urge and capacity to reproduce his kind. What is more, he also has the nature-given vocation to do so. For surely nature has not endowed living beings with instincts and capacities in order that they should fight and suppress them. The disposition in question, then, did not intend the civilized state, but merely the preservation of man as an animal species. And the civilized state comes into inevitable conflict with that disposition. This conflict only a perfect civil constitution could end, and indeed such a constitution is the ultimate end at which all culture aims. But the space of time during which there is still conflict is as a rule filled with vices and their consequences—the various kinds of human misery.

This, then, is one example to prove that nature has given us two different dispositions for two different purposes, the one for man as an animal, the other for him as a moral species. Another example is the *ars longa, vita brevis* of Hippocrates. A single man of talent, who had reached mature judgment through long practice and acquisition of knowledge, could further the arts and sciences far more than whole generations of scholars, if only he could live, mentally alert, for the length of their life-spans added together. But nature has apparently disposed concerning the length of human life with ends other than the furtherance of the sciences in view. For just when the luckiest of thinkers is on the verge of the greatest discoveries which his trained intellect and experience entitle him to hope for, just then old age sets in. His mind becomes dull, and he must leave to another generation the task of adding a step in the progress of culture; and that generation must once more begin with the ABC, and once more travel the whole road which that thinker had already traversed. Hence the road of the human species toward its destined goal appears to be subject to ceaseless interruptions, and mankind in perpetual danger of lapsing into ancient savagery. Not entirely without reason does the Greek philosopher complain: it is a pity that one must die when one has just begun to learn how one should have lived.

Human inequality may serve as our third example, not inequality as regards natural talent or worldly good fortune, but with regard to universal human rights. There is much truth in Rousseau's complaint about this inequality. At the same time, it is inseparable from culture, so long as the latter progresses without plan, as it were; and this too is for a long time inevitable. Surely nature did not intend this inequality, for she gave man freedom and along with it reason, by which to limit this freedom through nothing other than its own inherent conformity to law, a universal and external lawfulness which is called *civil right*. Man was meant to rise by his own labors above the crudeness of his natural dispositions, and yet in so doing to take care lest he do violence to them. But he can expect to acquire the skill for this only at a late date and after many abortive attempts. In the meantime, mankind groans under the burden of evils which, in its inexperience, it inflicts on itself.

while on the other hand, natural impulse interferes with culture until such time as finally art will be strong and perfect enough to become a second nature. This indeed is the ultimate moral end of the human species."   (d)

Two ideas stand out in this selection. The first is the contrast between man's moral nature as a rational being and his sensuous nature as an animal, a contrast that runs throughout Kant's ethical writings. This basic split in human nature is indicative of the more general dichotomy, in Kant's thought, that exists between the realm of Freedom to which man belongs as moral being and the realm of Nature to which he belongs as animal, but which he is able to know through science and reason.

The second idea is that Nature and Freedom, although distinct and in opposition to each other, are to be reconciled. This will occur when the realm of Freedom and its product, culture, shall become second nature to man through the mediation of art.

The first and second of Kant's three *Critiques* of human reason deal with the concepts and principles of Nature and Freedom respectively, and in the introduction to the third *Critique*, Kant speaks of this mediating function.

> Now even if an immeasurable gulf is fixed between the sensible realm of the concept of nature and the supersensible realm of the concept of freedom, so that no transition is possible from the first to the second (by means of the theoretical use of reason), just as if they were two different worlds of which the first could have no influence upon the second, yet the second is *meant* to have an influence upon the first. The concept of freedom is meant to actualize in the world of sense the purpose proposed by its laws, and consequently nature must be so thought that the conformity to law of its form at least harmonizes with the possibility of the purposes to be effected in it according to laws of freedom.[1]

The Creativity of Human Reason

The distinction between man's nature as animal and his human nature conveys the idea that through his human nature man is creatively engaged in making not only his culture but himself as a

[1] *Critique of Judgement*, J. H. Bernard (trans.) (New York: Hafner, 1951), p. 12. See pp. 165ff for consideration of Reason's mediating function.

human being. In the Third Thesis from his *Idea for a Universal History*, Kant writes:

> Nature has willed that man should, by himself, produce everything that goes beyond the mechanical ordering of his animal existence, and that he should partake of no other happiness or perfection than that which he himself, independently of instinct, has created by his own reason.[2]

Individual man is unique in that he creatively and rationally participates in his world; in a measure he creates it as an intelligible world through an act of interpretation.

There are several ways in which man's mind has been thought to be related to what it knows: (1) It may be understood as passive in the receipt of its materials from an external world conceived as sensible and/or intelligible; (2) It may be understood as active in combining and rearranging these materials (so that the whole equals the sum of the parts involved) ; (3) It may be understood as active in contributing to the formation and development of these materials by a creative act of synthesis (so that the whole is more than the sum of the parts involved) ; (4) It may be understood as active in creating these materials and producing something where before there was nothing.

It is in criticism of (1) and (2) above that Kant develops his Critical Philosophy. Number (4) is inappropriate for Kant's conception of human reason and is reserved for God.

Human reason is creative in sense (3), as an act of synthesis, the product of which reflects not only the materials synthesized but also the act of synthesis itself. The Critical Philosophy is concerned to discover (not create) the ways in which reason carries out this act of synthesis. Strictly speaking, it is incorrect to suppose that at every level and use of reason its activity can be understood only by reference to an act of synthesis. At times, Kant sees reason either as the ability to combine and rearrange or as the power to create, as God. But generally speaking, he refers to the creativity of human reason as an act of synthesis.

While Nature and Freedom constitute a basic dichotomy in Kant's thought, his works are ordered after his understanding of the kinds

[2] From *Immanuel Kant: On History*, edited by Lewis White Beck, copyright © 1957 by the Liberal Arts Press, Inc., © 1963, reprinted by permission of the Liberal Arts Press Division of the Bobbs-Merrill Company, Inc.

of human activity—knowing, willing (or desiring), and feeling. Philosophy is concerned with knowing, and since Kant is particularly interested in the creative contribution that man, as rational creature, makes to knowledge, he conceives of the cognitive capacities of human reason as composed of Understanding, Reason, and Judgment.

Just how the capacities of Understanding, Reason, and Judgment are involved in the activities of knowing, willing, and feeling and in what ways they are related to the realms of Nature and Freedom is exactly what Kant's philosophy is all about.

Although we will treat Kant in the usual order of knowing, willing, and feeling, the order of the three *Critiques*, we will do so from the point of view of the three cognitive faculties: Understanding, Reason, and Judgment. They are the source of man's contribution and, taken together, they constitute unified human activity.

The Contribution of Human Reason

If the world we know is partly a function of our minds, then the structures of our experience must reflect the nature of the contribution we make to it. To discover the contribution of human reason, Kant starts with man's experience of a meaningful world and from it infers the principles underlying his participation in and contribution to this experience. When he refers to the "concept of nature" and the "concept of freedom," he is speaking of the principles of human nature and activity that man brings to his world, principles without which our experience of that world would not be the way, in fact, it is.

Such principles Kant calls *a priori*, because they are not derived from experience. And he calls them "true" because, once we know these principles, we know something about the character of any possible future experience in which man may participate.

Prior to this quest for the principles that mind contributes, we must ask: What made Kant suppose there were any such *a priori* principles? Kant held with the rationalistic tradition that knowledge, to *be* knowledge, must be certain and beyond doubt. Further, he believed that we possess such certain knowledge in the form of Euclidean geometry and Newtonian physics, sciences that tell us something about the world. The postulate of parallel lines in geometry tells us something absolutely certain about the relations in space that pertain between a given line and another line, drawn through a point, parallel to the given line. And the law of gravity tells us something absolutely certain about the force of attraction between two bodies in relation to their mass and their distance apart. It was generally supposed that scientists were able to arrive at such principles because they experimented and observed in order to discover relationships between things. It was, of course, the analysis of David Hume that flatly denied that any amount of observation could ever establish for us matter of fact knowledge of any such relationships at all. While Hume tended to relegate all knowledge of matters of fact to the limbo of custom and habit, Kant read Hume's scepticism as the result of our misunderstanding the nature of experience as the source of knowledge. If Euclidean geometry and Newtonian physics constitute real knowledge, and if conceiving of experience through perceptual observation alone makes this knowledge impossible to explain, then so much the worse for that conception of experience. If the certainty of our knowledge of the experienced world cannot be found in perception, then the only other source available is the mind for which it is an experience. The certainty that obtains between ideas in the logical realm must in some way be applicable to the perceptual content of experience in order to produce our certain knowledge of space and physical laws. And Kant sets out to explain how such an application is possible.

Kant uses four terms to express his problem: *analytical* (analytic), *synthetical* (synthetic), *a priori*, and *a posteriori*.

There are judgments concerning the relations between ideas of which we are certain. For example, "All bachelors are unmarried men." Kant calls this kind of judgment analytical because the predicate, "unmarried men," tells nothing new about the subject, "bachelors." The judgment is true absolutely in that the predicate merely makes explicit something already contained in the subject. In addition, its truth in no way depends on the existence of bachelors. Hence, the judgment is "*a priori* analytic." For Kant the marks of the *a priori* are universality and necessity.

There are judgments concerning relations between ideas which are derived from experience. For example, "Water runs down hill." Kant calls these judgments synthetical because the predicate, "runs down hill," extends our knowledge of the subject beyond that which we could derive from the idea of "water" alone. About synthetic judgments there is no certainty, and their truth depends on experience. They are *a posteriori*. But, says Kant, the systems of Euclid and Newton give us judgments that extend our knowledge about the external world of experience and therefore are synthetic and at the same time universal and necessary—that is, true *a priori*. Such judgments are possible only if reason participates creatively in our understanding of experience. Kant expresses his problem, with scholastic precision, in logical form: "How are synthetic judgments *a priori* possible?"

The problem of the *a priori* element in knowledge is as old as Plato, but the particular form Kant gives it has exercised the modern mind considerably. Kant's assertion that the propositions of mathematics are "synthetic *a priori*" goes directly against our contemporary understanding that follows Hume in considering them analytic. It is not at all clear, however, that Kant is wrong, and the whole matter deserves further thought.

Selection II:
SYNTHETIC JUDGMENTS A PRIORI

Concerning the Kind of Knowledge
Which Can Alone Be Called Metaphysical

a. ON THE DISTINCTION BETWEEN ANALYTICAL AND SYNTHETICAL JUDGMENTS IN GENERAL. The peculiarity of its sources demands that metaphysical knowledge must consist of nothing but *a priori* judgments. But whatever be their origin or their logical form, there is a distinction in judgments, as to their content, according to which they are either merely *explicative*, adding nothing to the content of knowledge, or *expansive*, increasing the given knowledge. The former may be called *analytical*, the latter *synthetical*, judgments.

Analytical judgments express nothing in the predicate but what has been already actually thought in the concept of the subject, though not so distinctly or with the same (full) consciousness. When I say: "All bodies are extended," I have not amplified in the least my concept of body, but have only analyzed it, as extension was really thought to belong to that concept before the judgment was made, though it was not expressed. This judgment is therefore analytical. On the contrary, this judgment, "All bodies have weight," contains in its predicate something not actually thought in the universal concept of body; it amplifies my knowledge by adding something to my concept, and must therefore be called synthetical.

b. THE COMMON PRINCIPLE OF ALL ANALYTICAL JUDGMENTS IS THE LAW OF CONTRADICTION. All analytical judgments depend wholly on the law of contradiction, and are in their nature *a priori* cognitions, whether the concepts that supply them with matter be empirical or not. For the predicate of an affirmative analytical judgment is already contained in the concept of the subject, of which it cannot be denied without contradiction. In the same way its opposite is necessarily denied of the subject in an analytical, but negative, judgment, by the same law of contradiction. Such is the nature of the judgments: "All bodies are extended," and "No bodies are unextended (that is, simple)."

For this very reason all analytical judgments are *a priori* even when the concepts are empirical, as, for example, "Gold is a yellow metal"; for to know this I require no experience beyond my concept of gold as a yellow metal. It is, in fact, the very concept, and I need only analyze it without looking beyond it.

c. SYNTHETICAL JUDGMENTS REQUIRE A DIFFERENT PRINCIPLE FROM THE LAW OF CONTRADICTION. There are synthetical *a posteriori* judgments of empirical origin; but there are also others which are certain *a priori*, and which spring from pure understanding and reason. Yet they both agree in this, that they cannot possibly spring from the principle of analysis, namely, the law of contradiction, alone. They require a quite different principle from which they may be deduced, subject, of course, always to the law of contradiction, which must never be violated, even though everything cannot be deduced from it. I shall first classify synthetical judgments.

1. *Judgments of Experience* are always synthetical. For it would be absurd to base an analytical judgment on experience, as our concept suffices for the purpose without requiring any testimony from experience. That body is extended is a judgment established *a priori*, and not an empirical judgment. For before appealing to experience, we already have all the conditions of the judgment in the concept, from which we have but to elicit the predicate according to the law of contradiction, and thereby to become conscious of the necessity of the judgment, which experience could not in the least teach us.

2. *Mathematical Judgments* are all synthetical. This fact seems hitherto to have altogether escaped the observation of those who have analyzed human reason; it even seems directly opposed to all their conjectures, though it is incontestably certain and most important in its consequences. For as it was found that the conclusions of mathematicians all proceed according to the law of contradiction (as is demanded by all apodictic certainty), men persuaded themselves that the fundamental principles were known from the same law. This was a great mistake, for a synthetical proposition can indeed be established by the law of contradiction, but

only by presupposing another synthetical proposition from which it follows, but never by that law alone.

First of all, we must observe that all strictly mathematical judgments are *a priori*, and not empirical, because they carry with them necessity, which cannot be obtained from experience. But if this be not conceded to me, very good; I shall confine my assertion to *pure mathematics*, the very notion of which implies that it contains pure *a priori* and not empirical knowledge.

It must at first be thought that the proposition $7 + 5 = 12$ is a mere analytical judgment, following from the concept of the sum of seven and five, according to the law of contradiction. But on closer examination it appears that the concept of the sum of $7 + 5$ contains merely their union in a single number, without its being at all thought what the particular number is that unites them. The concept of twelve is by no means thought by merely thinking of the combination of seven and five; and, analyze this possible sum as we may, we shall not discover twelve in the concept. We must go beyond these concepts, by calling to our aid some intuition which corresponds to one of the concepts—that is, either our five fingers or five points (as Segner has it in his *Arithmetic*)—and we must add successively the units of the five given in the intuition to the concept of seven. Hence our concept is really amplified by the proposition $7 + 5 = 12$, and we add to the first concept a second concept not thought in it. Arithmetical judgments are therefore synthetical, and the more plainly according as we take larger numbers; for in such cases it is clear that, however closely we analyze our concepts without calling intuition [1] to our aid, we can never find the sum by such mere dissection.

Just as little is any principle of geometry analytical. That a straight line is the shortest path between two points is a synthetical proposition. For my concept of straight contains nothing of quantity, but only a quality. The concept "shortest" is therefore altogether additional and cannot be obtained by any analysis of the concept "straight line." Here, too, intuition must come to aid us. It alone makes the synthesis possible. What usually makes us believe that the predicate of such apodictic judgments is already contained in our concept, and that the judgment is therefore analytical, is the duplicity of the expression. We must think a certain predicate as attached to a given concept, and necessity indeed belongs to the concepts. But the question is not what we must join in thought to the given concept, but what we actually think together with and in it, though obscurely; and so it appears that the predicate belongs

---

[1] Later on in this *Critique* and also in the *Critique of Judgment* Kant includes in his concept of "intuition" the results of imagination as an act of synthesis.

to this concept necessarily indeed, yet not directly but indirectly by means of an intuition which must be present. (a)

The essential and distinguishing feature of pure mathematical knowledge among all other *a priori* knowledge is that it cannot at all proceed from concepts, but only by means of the construction of concepts.[2] As therefore in its propositions it must proceed beyond the concept to that which its corresponding intuition contains, these propositions neither can, nor ought to, arise analytically, by dissection of the concept, but are all synthetical. (b)

PART I:
Of Reason in Knowing (Theoretical Reason)

The three *Critiques*—of *Pure Reason,* of *Practical Reason* and of *Judgment*—are concerned with the *a priori* principles of thinking, willing, and feeling. While only the first of these, thinking, involves knowledge of objects, all three involve *a priori* principles and ideas that must be thought yet cannot be known. This is Kant's way of stating the necessity of the ideal. In the broadest sense, Kant holds that conscious human activity is by its very nature purposive; it is goal-directed activity. And here we come on perhaps the root problem in Kant's thought. In the area of theoretical science, where man's activity is directed towards knowing his world, the world he knows is partly a function of his own activity. The science of Kant's day consisted of the geometry of Euclid and the mechanics of Newton, neither of which has anything to say about purposes or goal-directed activity. The question might be put this way: How can the activity of thinking, which is essentially purposive, participate creatively in the scientific enterprise of knowing and produce a world that must be understood in a mechanical and nonpurposive fashion?

Kant's answer is to distinguish between two types of *a priori* principles. In the *Critique of Pure Reason,* he distinguishes between the constitutive and the regulative principles of reason. The former actually participate in the character and structure of the world of science as it is known. The latter serve as guides, goals, and limits for the human activity of science as knowing. The difference lies in conceiving of knowing as a purposive activity and conceiving of it as what is known, the result of the activity. This distinction is more important to the realm of Nature than to the realm of Freedom.

[2] Synthesis is prior to analysis and must be based on intuition.

While the *a priori* principles of the system of Nature that come under the cognitive faculty of Understanding are constitutive, the *a priori* principles of the system of Nature that come under the cognitive faculty of Reason are regulative. The *a priori* principles of Freedom come under Reason also, but Reason conceived of as Practical Reason rather than the Speculative Reason of the system of Nature.

The world as known, the realm of Nature, is the deterministic world of Newtonian mechanics; Kant calls it the "phenomenal" world. The world as lived is the purposive world of Freedom; he calls it the "noumenal" world. Kant's works can be seen as the attempt to reconcile these two worlds. This polarity can be expressed as determinism and freedom, science and morality, theoretical and practical, and mechanism and organism. Both the nature of knowledge and the nature of activity are separate facts for Kant, and, ultimately, the facts of activity are prior to the facts of knowledge because knowing is an activity.

Kant works out the problem of knowing on the basis of Hume's analysis of causality. Hume had said that necessary connection is a creature of thought, a characteristic of ideas, and that under no circumstances can we apply with certainty such necessary connection to the empirical world of things. Quite so, says Kant. We can never apply it, yet Euclid's geometry and Newton's physics both do, and very successfully. How is this application possible? It is possible only if we consider the world of things, as we know it, as partly a product of man's ways of thinking. As we have seen, from the logical point of view this is the problem of explaining the possibility of "synthetic judgments *a priori*."

Mind contributes to knowing constitutively on three levels: Intuition, Understanding, and Imagination. This is realized through acts of synthesis on each level. We shall consider each of these and then turn to the regulative function of Speculative Reason.

The Synthesis of Intuition

The level of Intuition is the basic stage in knowledge at which man is directly confronted by the outer world. Intuition in its broadest sense refers to the act of perceiving or apprehending what is directly presented, to what is immediately known, rather than what is inferred. To open one's eyes is to see, to intuit directly, what is there.

From a common sense point of view, man intuits objects as spatially related and events as temporally related. These spatial relations are indicated by such expressions as "next to," "behind," and "south of." Events are temporally related by such words as "before," "after," and "at the same time as." The question now becomes: Where do these spatial and temporal relationships found in intuition originate? Common sense would say that this network of relationships is just as much a part of the external world as the things that are related. But Kant is not concerned with whether things in themselves are related. He would say that we cannot know this. His question is: How do we come to know them as being so related? From direct perception? No. From your perception of St. Louis, would you know that it is south of Chicago? From your perception of a certain building, would you know that it is between Eighteenth and Nineteenth on Chestnut Street? No. To determine the spatial relations of a given object, you must have a frame of reference that goes beyond the object and is brought to your experience of the object. Kant's point is rather simple, and a good one. If this frame of reference is a part of every experience, and its source cannot be traced to perception, then it must be a contribution of mind.

On the basis of the four ways of thinking about the relation of mind to its materials, it is clear from the following selection that Kant conceives of the activity of mind as an act of creative synthesis. There are no perceptions that are not ordered spatially and temporally. They constitute the possibility of perception. We shall return to the intuitional or perceptual level, the level of direct contact with the world of experience, over and over again in Kant's works because on its character rests the possibility of synthetic *a priori* judgments in all areas. In this selection, however, he is concerned primarily with intuition as it involves the *a priori* forms of space and time.

Selection III:
THE FORMS OF SENSIBILITY

If our intuition were of such a nature as to represent things as they are in themselves, there would not be any intuition *a priori*, but intuition would be always empirical. For I can only know what is contained in the object in itself if it is present and given to me. It is indeed even then incomprehensible how the intuition of a present thing should make me know this thing as it is in itself, as its properities cannot migrate into my faculty of representation. But even granting this possibility, an intuition of that sort would not take place *a priori*, that is, before the object were presented to me; for without this latter fact no ground of a relation between my representation and the object can be imagined, unless it depend upon a direct implantation.

Therefore in one way only can my intuition anticipate the actuality of the object, and be a cognition *a priori*, namely: *if my intuition contains nothing but the form of sensibility, antedating in my mind all the actual impressions through which I am affected by objects.* (a)

In the transcendental aesthetic we shall, therefore, first *isolate* sensibility, by taking away from it everything which the understanding thinks through its concepts, so that nothing may be left save empirical intuition. Secondly, we shall also separate off from it everything which belongs to sensation, so that nothing may remain save pure intuition and the mere form of appearances, which is all that sensibility can supply *a priori*. In the course of this investigation it will be found that there are two pure forms of sensible intuition, serving as principles of *a priori* knowledge, namely, space and time. To the consideration of these we shall now proceed. (b)

Of Space

By means of outer sense, a property of our mind, we represent to ourselves objects as outside us, and all without exception in space. In space their shape, magnitude, and relation to one another are determined or determinable. Inner sense, by means of which the mind intuits itself or its inner state, yields indeed no intuition of the soul itself as an object; but there is nevertheless a determinate form [namely, time] in which alone the intuition of inner states is possible, and everything which belongs to inner determinations is therefore represented in relations of time. Time cannot be outwardly intuited, any more than space can be intuited as something in us. What, then, are space and time? Are they real existences? Are they only determinations or relations of things, yet such as would belong to things even if they were not intuited? Or are space and time such that they belong only to the form of intuition, and therefore to the subjective constitution of our mind, apart from which they could not be ascribed to anything whatsoever? In order to obtain light upon these questions, let us first give an exposition of the concept of space. (c)

1. Space is not an empirical concept which has been derived from outer experiences. For in order that certain sensations be referred to something outside me (that is, to something in another region of space from that in which I find myself), and similarly in order that I may be

able to represent them as outside and alongside one another, and accordingly as not only different but as in different places, the representation of space must be presupposed. The representation of space cannot, therefore, be empirically obtained from the relations of outer appearance. On the contrary, this outer experience is itself possible at all only through that representation.

2. Space is a necessary *a priori* representation, which underlies all outer intuitions. We can never represent to ourselves the absence of space, though we can quite well think it as empty of objects. It must therefore be regarded as the condition of the possibility of appearances, and not as a determination dependent upon them. It is an *a priori* representation, which necessarily underlies outer appearances. (d)

CONCLUSIONS FROM THE ABOVE CONCEPTS. (a) Space does not represent any property of things in themselves, nor does it represent them in their relation to one another. That is to say, space does not represent any determination that attaches to the objects themselves, and which remains even when abstraction has been made of all the subjective conditions of intuition. For no determinations, whether absolute or relative, can be intuited prior to the existence of the things to which they belong, and none, therefore, can be intuited *a priori*.

(b) Space is nothing but the form of all appearances of outer sense. It is the subjective condition of sensibility, under which alone outer intuition is possible for us. Since, then, the receptivity of the subject, its capacity to be affected by objects, must necessarily precede all intuitions of these objects, it can readily be understood how the form of all appearances can be given prior to all actual perceptions, and so exist in the mind *a priori*, and how, as a pure intuition, in which all objects must be determined, it can contain, prior to all experience, principles which determine the relations of these objects. (e)

Of Time

1. Time is not an empirical concept that has been derived from any experience. For neither coexistence nor succession would ever come within our perception, if the representation of time were not presupposed as underlying them *a priori*. Only on the presupposition of time can we represent to ourselves a number of things as existing at one and the same time (simultaneously) or at different times (successively).

2. Time is a necessary representation that underlies all intuitions. We cannot, in respect of appearances in general, remove time itself, though we can quite well think time as void of appearances. Time is, therefore,

given *a priori*. In it alone is actuality of appearances possible at all. Appearances may, one and all, vanish; but time (as the universal condition of their possibility) cannot itself be removed.

3. The possibility of apodeictic principles concerning the relations of time, or of axioms of time in general, is also grounded upon this *a priori* necessity. Time has only one dimension; different times are not simultaneous but successive (just as different spaces are not successive but simultaneous). These principles cannot be derived from experience, for experience would give neither strict universality nor apodeictic certainty. We should only be able to say that common experience teaches us that it is so; not that it must be so. These principles are valid as rules under which alone experiences are possible; and they instruct us in regard to the experiences, not by means of them.   (f)

CONCLUSIONS FROM THESE CONCEPTS. (a) Time is not something which exists of itself, or which inheres in things as an objective determination, and it does not, therefore, remain when abstraction is made of all subjective conditions of its intuition.   (g)

(b) Time is nothing but the form of inner sense, that is, of the intuition of ourselves and of our inner state. It cannot be a determination of outer appearances; it has to do neither with shape nor position, but with the relation of representations in our inner state. And just because this inner intuition yields no shape, we endeavour to make up for this want by analogies. We represent the time-sequence by a line progressing to infinity, in which the manifold constitutes a series of one dimension only; and we reason from the properties of this line to all the properties of time, with this one exception, that while the parts of the line are simultaneous the parts of time are always successive. From this fact also, that all the relations of time allow of being expressed in an outer intuition, it is evident that the representation is itself an intuition.

(c) Time is the formal *a priori* condition of all appearances whatsoever. Space, as the pure form of all *outer* intuition, is so far limited; it serves as the *a priori* condition only of outer appearances. But since all representations, whether they have for their objects outer things or not, belong, in themselves, as determinations of the mind, to our inner state; and since this inner state stands under the formal condition of inner intuition, and so belongs to time, time is an *a priori* condition of all appearance whatsoever. ...   (h)

It has objective validity only in respect of appearances, these being things which we take *as objects of our senses*. It is no longer objective, if we abstract from the sensibility of our intuition, that is, from that mode of representation which is peculiar to us, and speak of *things in general*. Time is therefore a purely subjective condition of our (human) intuition (which is always sensible, that is, so far as we are affected by objects), and in itself, apart from the subject, is nothing. Nevertheless, in respect of all appearances, and therefore of all the things which can enter into our experience, it is necessarily objective.   (i)

Mind contributes the pattern of spatial and temporal relations found in our experience of the phenomenal world. Kant says that space and time are "phenomenally real, but transcendentally ideal." Often this theory is labeled "subjective," but for Kant what is "objective" is permanent, no matter what its origin. What is "subjective" is impermanent, relative, and transitory, no matter what its origin. Space and time are an objectively real pattern of permanent relations brought to experience by the interpreting mind. Space and time are the *a priori* forms of sensibility. There is no possibility of a perception that does not come under these forms.

The first level of synthesis, then, produces the perceptual aspect of theoretical knowledge in which the manifold of sensory impressions is ordered by the forms of sensibility.

The Synthesis of Understanding

The question here again is how a pure (*a priori*) science of nature is possible.

The answer for Kant is found in the universal *a priori* conditions of any possible experience. These conditions can be known *a priori* as the categories of the Understanding. These categories are not things; rather, they are ways of knowing or interpreting the perceptions produced at the first level of synthesis. They are the rules of understanding in the application of which the perceptual level is synthesized into an experience of a connected world of interrelated objects and events. One of the more interesting consequences of this view is that it sheds light on our understanding of what "reality" may mean. According to Kant, to be real—that is, to be an object in a known context of experiences—is to be amenable to a rule. To be real then, it is not enough just to exist. A thing must be part of the intelligible pattern of the phenomenal world, a product of the synthesis of the categories.

In the next selection Kant discusses first the function of the Under-

standing and its foundations in the ways in which we make judgments. This Table of Judgments presupposes the Table of Categories
of the mind, which enables us to make judgments. It is important to
ask here, what made Kant suppose that the category is prior to the
judgment? If mind is creatively active, why would the act of judging not come first and the concept follow? It would seem that Kant,
like Descartes in the *cogito*,[1] cannot conceive of an activity without
seeing it depend on something with the capacity to carry out that
activity.[2]

For Kant the categories represent the structure of mind antecedent
to its operation. This structure makes it possible to make the kinds
of judgments we find in our experience. Here Kant seems to be
talking as if the categories are rules for thinking which we apply to
the perceptual level. As we shall see later on, Kant has second
thoughts on this matter that more nearly approximate our characterization of the activity of the mind as creative synthesis.

Having explained the origin of our categories, Kant goes on to
show that they are an answer to Hume's skepticism. It is important
to see the sense in which Kant's answer is "complete" and the sense
in which it is not.

Selection IV:
THE CATEGORIES

Empirical judgments, so far as they have objective validity, are *judgments of experience*, but those which are only subjectively valid I name
mere *judgments of perception*. The latter require no pure concept of the
understanding, but only the logical connection of perception in a thinking subject. But the former always require, besides the representation of
the sensuous intuition, special *concepts originally begotten in the understanding*, which make possible the objective validity of the judgment of
experience.   (a)

We must consequently analyze experience in general in order to see
what is contained in this product of the senses and of the understanding,
and how the judgment of experience itself is possible. The foundation is
the intuition of which I become conscious, that is, perception (*per-*

---

[1] See page 130 for Kant's consideration of this matter.

[2] The point of this very old problem is whether "activity" is prior to substantive
"thinghood." I see a tree growing. Is the tree only that particular pattern of growing, that activity, or is it a thing that acts in a certain way? In ethical theory the
question may be expressed thus: Am I the sum total of my behavior (activity), or
is there such a thing as a person who does the behaving and is something in himself?

ceptio), which pertains merely to the senses. But in the next place, there is judging (which belongs only to the understanding). (b)

Before, therefore, a judgment of perception can become a judgment of experience, it is requisite that the perception should be subsumed under some concept of the understanding. . . .* (c)

To prove, then, the possibility of experience so far as it rests upon pure concepts of the understanding *a priori*, we must first represent what belongs to judging in general and the various functions of the understanding in a complete table. (d)

LOGICAL TABLE OF JUDGMENTS

1 *As to Quantity*	2 *As to Quality*
Universal	Affirmative
Particular	Negative
Singular	Infinite

3 *As to Relation*	4 *As to Modality*
Categorical	Problematic
Hypothetical	Assertoric
Disjunctive	Apodictic

TRANSCENDENTAL TABLE OF THE CONCEPTS OF THE UNDERSTANDING

1 *As to Quantity*	2 *As to Quality*
Unity (Measure)	Reality
Plurality (Magnitude)	Negation
Totality (Whole)	Limitation

3 *As to Relation*	4 *As to Modality*
Substance	Possibility
Cause	Existence
Community	Necessity	(e)

* As an easier example, we may take the following: "When the sun shines on the stone, it grows warm." This judgment, however often I and others may have perceived it, is a mere judgment of perception and contains no necessity; perceptions are only usually conjoined in this manner. But if I say, "The sun warms the stone," I add to the perception a concept of the understanding, namely, that of cause which necessarily connects with the concept of sunshine that of heat, and the synthetical judgment becomes of necessity universally valid, namely, objective, and is converted from a perception into experience.

The sum of the matter is this: the business of the senses is to intuit, that of the understanding is to think. But thinking is uniting representations in one consciousness. This union originates either merely relative to the subject and is accidental and subjective, or takes place absolutely and is necessary or objective. The union of representations in one consciousness is judgment. Thinking, therefore, is the same as judging or referring representations to judgments in general. Hence judgments are either merely subjective, when representations are referred to a consciousness in one subject only and united in it, or objective, when they are united in consciousness in general, that is, necessarily. The logical functions of all judgments are but various modes of uniting representations in consciousness. (f)

Judgments, when considered merely as the condition of the union of given representations in a consciousness, are rules. These rules so far as they represent the union as necessary, are rules *a priori* and, insofar as they cannot be deduced from higher rules, are principles. But in regard to the possibility of all experience, merely in relation to the form of thinking in it, no conditions of judgments of experience are higher than those which bring the appearances, according to the various form of their intuition, under pure concepts of the understanding, which render the empirical judgment objectively valid. These are therefore the *a priori* principles of possible experience.

The principles of possible experience are then at the same time universal laws of nature, which can be known *a priori*. And thus the problem of our second question, "How is the pure science of nature possible?" is solved. For the system which is required for the form of a science is to be met with in perfection here, because, beyond the above-mentioned formal conditions of all judgments in general (and hence of all rules in general) offered in logic, no others are possible, and these constitute a logical system. The concepts grounded thereupon, which contain the *a priori* conditions of all synthetical and necessary judgments, accordingly constitute a transcendental system. Finally the principles, by means of which all phenomena are subsumed under these concepts, constitute a physical system, that is, a system of nature, which precedes all empirical knowledge of nature, and makes it possible. It may in strictness be denominated the universal and pure science of nature.... (g)

This complete (though to its originator unexpected) solution of Hume's problem rescues for the pure concepts of the understanding their *a priori* origin and for the universal laws of nature their validity as laws of the understanding, yet in such a way as to limit their use to experience, because their possibility depends solely on the reference of the understanding to experience, but with a completely reversed mode of connection which never occurred to Hume—they do not derive from experience, but experience derives from them.

This is, therefore, the result of all our foregoing inquiries: "All synthetical principles *a priori* are nothing more than principles of possible experience" and can never be referred to things in themselves, but to appearances as objects of experience.... (h)

There is indeed something seductive in our pure concepts of the understanding which tempts us to a transcendent use—a use which transcends all possible experience. Not only are our concept of substance, of power, of action, or reality, and others, quite independent of experience, containing nothing of sense appearance, and so apparently applicable to things in themselves (*noumena*), but what strengthens this conjecture, they contain a necessity of determination in themselves, which experience never attains. The concept of cause implies a rule according to which one state follows another necessarily; but experience can only show us that one state of things often or, at most, commonly follows another, and therefore affords neither strict universality nor necessity. (i)

... Our understanding is not a faculty of intuition, but of the connection of given intuitions in one experience. Experience must therefore contain all the objects for our concepts; but beyond it no concepts have any significance, as there is no intuition that might offer them a foundation.

(j)

Kant put great stock in his "deduction" of these categories. Perhaps it is the weakest part of the whole *Critique*, but the general conviction that a system of concepts is necessary for interpretation is a major insight. To acquire an adequate idea of what Kant tried to convey, we shall consider the third category, Relation.

To determine the categories, Kant asked: "What types of judgment do we make about experience?" Under the general type called relational judgments we find those judgments that attribute relative permanence and independence to some aspects of our experience. Formulated logically, such a judgment is contained in the categorical proposition "All men are mortal." We also find that we attribute dependence and transcience to some aspects, as expressed logically in the hypothetical proposition "If it rains, I will get wet." These first two subcategories are antithetical to each other. They mark out separately what is permanent and independent and what is transient and dependent, not absolutely but relatively. The third subcategory, the disjunctive, synthesizes the other two. The result is that we get an experienced world of relatively substantial entities in reciprocal causal relationships—in short, a world of things in connected process. This result is expressed logically in the disjunctive proposition "Either A or B, and possibly both."

At the very end of the last selection Kant speaks of how the categories tend to become objects for their own interpretation, and points out that much of what has passed for traditional metaphysics comes about because of this misapplication of the categories. Only in conjunction with the synthesis of perceptual intuition can they produce knowledge. Synthetic *a priori* judgments in mathematics and the physical sciences are possible, but they are not possible in metaphysics because here they lack grounding in experience. The activity of human reason, as the faculty of Understanding, is able to know when its categories are grounded in perception. However, human reason by itself, as the cognitive faculty of Reason, produces no knowledge. Metaphysics, in the traditional sense of knowledge derived through Reason, has never recovered from this Kantian body blow.[1]

The Synthesis of Imagination

In the next two selections Kant discusses how we apply concepts to percepts. He asserts that we apply them in an orderly fashion. Every time I look out of my office window I experience very much the same thing. Kant supposes that this experience can be the result neither of the percepts themselves nor of the categories conceived by themselves, but must be a function of the act of interpreting. In the first of the two selections Kant explains that the application of the categories is the function of a single unified perspective, the "transcendental unity of apperception." Such a function accounts for the unity and consistency of our experience. It is spontaneity, the creative character of the mind, that accounts for our sense of a whole that is greater than the sum of its parts. Knowledge would be impossible without both receptivity and spontaneity. An example of this knowledge is the relation between a generalization and the instances of which it is a generalization. Such a generalization relates instances by a reference to them, in fact, it helps us determine them as instances as well as go creatively beyond them. Without this going be-

[1] See the Synthesis of Reason, p. 127ff.

yond there would be no immanent character of the instances to be known. Kant distinguishes three aspects of this synthetic act: (1) the survey that expresses a temporal sequence in a single representation; (2) the reproduction through memory of the earlier elements in a sequence that allows them to participate in the unity; and (3) the act of self-consciousness that takes into account this whole process as happening "for a mind." "For a mind" may not be an adequate phrase, because there is a sense in which this threefold act of synthesis is mind itself.

Selection V:
THE UNITY OF UNDERSTANDING

If each representation were completely foreign to every other, standing apart in isolation, no such thing as knowledge would ever arise. For knowledge is [essentially] a whole in which representations stand compared and connected. As sense contains a manifold in its intuition, I ascribe to it a synopsis. But to such synopsis a synthesis must always correspond; receptivity can make knowledge possible only when combined with spontaneity. Now this spontaneity is the ground of a three-fold synthesis which must necessarily be found in all knowledge; namely, the *apprehension* of representations as modifications of the mind in intuition, their *reproduction* in imagination, and their *recognition* in a concept. These point to three subjective sources of knowledge which make possible the understanding itself—and consequently all experience as its empirical product. (a)

Synthesis of Apprehension in Intuition

All our knowledge is subject to time, the formal condition of inner sense. In it they must all be ordered, connected, and brought into relation. This is a general observation which, throughout what follows, must be borne in mind as being quite fundamental.

Every intuition contains in itself a manifold which can be represented as a manifold only in so far as the mind distinguishes the time in the sequence of one impression upon another; for each representation, *in so far as it is contained in a single moment,* can never be anything but absolute unity. In order that unity of intuition may arise out of this manifold (as is required in the representation of space) it must first be run through, and held together. This act I name the *synthesis of apprehension,* because it is directed upon intuition, which does indeed offer a manifold, but a manifold which can never be represented as a manifold, and as contained *in a single representation,* save in virtue of such a synthesis.

This synthesis of apprehension must also be exercised *a priori,* that is, in respect of representations which are not empirical. (b)

The Synthesis of Reproduction in Imagination

When I seek to draw a line in thought, or to think of the time from one noon to another, or even to represent to myself some particular number, obviously the various manifold representations that are involved must be apprehended by me in thought one after the other. But if I were always to drop out of thought the preceding representations (the first parts of the line, the antecedent parts of the time period, or the units in the order represented), and did not reproduce them while advancing to those that follow, a complete representation would never be obtained: none of the above-mentioned thoughts, not even the purest and most elementary representations of space and time, could arise.

The synthesis of apprehension is thus inseparably bound up with the synthesis of reproduction. And as the former constitutes the transcendental ground of the possibility of all modes of knowledge whatsoever—of those that are pure *a priori* no less than of those that are empirical—the reproductive synthesis of the imagination is to be counted among the transcendental acts of the mind. We shall therefore entitle this faculty the transcendental faculty of imagination.

The Synthesis of Recognition in a Concept

If we were not conscious that what we think is the same as what we thought a moment before, all reproduction in the series of representations would be useless. . . . (c)

The word "concept" might of itself suggest this remark. For this unitary consciousness is what combines the manifold, successively intuited, and thereupon also reproduced, into one representation. . . . (d)

There can be in us no modes of knowledge, no connection or unity of one mode of knowledge with another, without that unity of consciousness which precedes all data of intuitions, and by relation to which representation of objects is alone possible. This pure original unchangeable consciousness I shall name *transcendental apperception.* (e)

All the manifold of intuition has, therefore, a necessary relation to the "I think" in the same subject in which this manifold is found. But this representation is an act of spontaneity, that is, it cannot be regarded as belonging to sensibility. (f)

The first pure knowledge of understanding, then, upon which all the rest of its employment is based, and which also at the same time is completely independent of all conditions of sensible intuition, is the principle of the original *synthetic* unity of apperception. Thus the mere form of outer sensible intuition, space, is not yet [by itself] knowledge; it supplies only the manifold of *a priori* intuition for a possible knowledge. To know anything in space (for instance, a line), I must *draw* it, and thus synthetically bring into being a determinate combination of the given manifold, so that the unity of this act is at the same time the unity of consciousness (as in the concept of a line); and it is through this unity of consciousness that an object (a determinate space) is first known. The synthetic unity of consciousness is, therefore, an objective condition of all knowledge. It is not merely a condition that I myself require in knowing an object, but is a condition under which every intuition must stand in order *to become an object for me.* For otherwise, in the absence of this synthesis, the manifold would *not* be united in one consciousness.

(g)

The Transcendental Unity of Understanding accounts for the order and regularity of our experience, but the question of how categories are to be applied to the perceptual level remains. Just as in the synthesis of the imagination the syntheses of apprehension and memory are required to produce a unity for consciousness, so they are also required to produce the possibility of representations to which categories could be applied. The common ground needed to make this application possible lies in the *a priori* condition of the inner sense, Time. Since Time is both *a priori* and the general condition of all representation, it qualifies as mediator between concepts and percepts. As each category is translated into temporal terms, it becomes easier to see how they are all applicable at once, and not as disconnected, separate elements. For instance, the schema of the subcategory of Causality is expressed by temporal succession. Temporal succession is, of course, the perceptual fact. By virtue of the categorial rule of intelligibility, such succession is experienced as causal connection.

Selection VI:
THE SCHEMATISM OF THE UNDERSTANDING

In all subsumptions of an object under a concept the representation of the object must be *homogeneous* with the concept; in other words, the concept must contain something which is represented in the object that is to be subsumed under it. This, in fact, is what is meant by the expression, "an object is contained under a concept." Thus the empirical concept of a *plate* is homogeneous with the pure geometrical concept of a *circle.* The roundness which is thought in the latter can be intuited in the former.

But pure concepts of understanding being quite heterogeneous from empirical intuitions, and indeed from all sensible intuitions, can never be met with in any intuition. For no one will say that a category, such as that of causality, can be intuited through sense and is itself contained in appearance. How, then, is the *subsumption* of intuitions under pure concepts, the *application* of a category to appearances, possible? A transcendental doctrine of judgment is necessary just because of this natural and important question. We must be able to show how pure concepts can be applicable to appearances. (a)

Obviously there must be some third thing, which is homogeneous on the one hand with the category, and on the other hand with the appearance, and which thus makes the application of the former to the latter possible. This mediating representation must be pure, that is, void of all empirical content, and yet at the same time, while it must in one respect be *intellectual,* it must in another be sensible. Such a representation is the *transcendental schema.*

The concept of understanding contains pure synthetic unity of the manifold in general. Time, as the formal condition of the manifold of inner sense, and therefore of the connection of all representations, contains an *a priori* manifold in pure intuition. Now a transcendental determination of time is so far homogeneous with the category, which constitutes its unity, in that it is universal and rests upon an *a priori* rule. But, on the other hand, it is so far homogeneous with appearance, in that time is contained in every empirical representation of the manifold. Thus an application of the category to appearances becomes possible by means of the transcendental determination of time, which, as the schema of the concepts of understanding, mediates the subsumption of the appearances under the category. (b)

This schematism of our understanding, in its application to appearances and their mere form, is an art concealed in the depths of the human soul, whose real modes of activity nature is hardly likely ever to allow us to discover, and to have open to our gaze. This much only we can assert: the *image* is a product of the empirical faculty of reproductive imagination; the *schema* of sensible concepts, such as of figures in space, is a product and, as it were, a monogram, of pure *a priori* imagination, through which, and in accordance with which, images themselves first become possible. These images can be connected with the concept only by means of the schema to which they belong. In themselves they are never completely at one with the concept. On the other hand, the schema of a *pure* concept of understanding can never be reduced to any image whatsoever. It is simply the pure synthesis, determined by a rule of that unity, in accordance with concepts, to which the category gives expression. It is a transcendental product of imagination, a product which concerns the determination of inner sense in general according to conditions of its form (time), in respect of all representations, so far as these representations are to be connected *a priori* in one concept in conformity with the unity of apperception. (c)

The pure image of all magnitudes (*quantorum*) for outer sense is space; that of all objects of the senses in general is time. But the pure *schema* of magnitude (*quantitatis*), as a concept of the understanding, is *number*, a representation which comprises the successive addition of homogeneous units. Number is therefore simply the unity of the synthesis of the manifold of a homogeneous intuition in general, a unity due to my generating time itself in the apprehension of the intuition.

Reality, in the pure concept of understanding, is that which corresponds to a sensation in general; it is that, therefore, the concept of which in itself points to being (in time). Negation is that the concept of which represents not-being (in time). The opposition of these two thus rests upon the distinction of one and the same time as filled and as empty. Since time is merely the form of intuition, and so of objects as appearances, that in the objects which corresponds to sensation is not the transcendental matter of all objects as things in themselves (thinghood, reality). Now every sensation has a degree or magnitude whereby, in respect of its representation of an object otherwise remaining the same, it can fill out one and the same time, that is, occupy inner sense more or less completely, down to its cessation in nothingness ($= 0 =$ negatio). There therefore exists a relation and connection between reality and negation, or rather a transition from the one to the other, which makes every reality representable as a quantum. The schema of a reality, as the quantity of something in so far as it fills time, is just this continuous and uniform production of that reality in time as we successively descend from a sensation which has a certain degree of its vanishing point, or progressively ascend from its negation to some magnitude of it.

The schema of substance is permanence of the real in time, that is, the representation of the real as a substrate of empirical determination of time in general, and so as abiding while all else changes. ... (d)

The schema of cause, and of the causality of a thing in general, is the real upon which, whenever posited, something else always follows. It consists, therefore, in the succession of the manifold, in so far as that succession is subject to a rule.

The schema of community or reciprocity, the reciprocal causality of substances in respect of their accidents, is the coexistence, according to a universal rule, of the determinations of the one substance with those of the other.

The schema of possibility is the agreement of the synthesis of different representations with the conditions of time in general. Opposites, for instance, cannot exist in the same thing at the same time, but only the one after the other. The schema is therefore the determination of the representation of a thing at any time whatsoever.

The schema of actuality is existence in some determinate time.

The schema of necessity is existence of an object at all times.

We thus find that the schema of each category contains and makes capable of representation only a determination of time. The schema of magnitude is the generation (synthesis) of time itself in the successive apprehension of an object. The schema of quality is the synthesis of sensation or perception with the representation of time; it is the filling of time. The schema of relation is the connection of perceptions with one another at all times according to a rule of time-determination. Finally the schema of modality and of its categories is time itself as the correlate of the determination whether and how an object belongs to time. The schemata are thus nothing but *a priori* determinations of time in accordance with rules. These rules relate in the order of the categories to the *time-series*, the *time-content*, the *time-order*, and lastly to the *scope of time* in respect of all possible objects.

It is evident, therefore, that what the schematism of understanding effects by means of the transcendental synthesis of imagination is simply the unity of all the manifold of intuition in inner sense, and so indirectly the unity of apperception which as a function corresponds to the receptivity of inner sense. The schemata of the pure concepts of understanding are thus the true and sole conditions under which these concepts obtain relation to objects and so possess *significance*. In the end, therefore, the categories have no other possible employment than the empirical. As the grounds of an *a priori* necessary unity that has its source in the necessary combination of all consciousness in one original apperception, they serve only to subordinate appearances to universal rules of synthesis, and thus to fit them for thoroughgoing connection in one experience. (e)

The schemata of the understanding may be conceived in various ways: (1) The schemata are rules expressed temporally for the application of the categories to perception, (2) The schemata are temporal expressions of the categories, (3) The categories are generalized ways of expressing the multiple *a priori* time determinations in experience, (4) Just as the synthesis of "apprehension," "reproduction," and "recognition" constitute the "unity of understanding" and are grounded in "spontaneity," so the schemata constitute the "multiplicity of the understanding" and are grounded in that same spontaneity. When the compatability of all of these elements is grasped, it is possible to raise a question.

There seems little doubt that Kant conceived of our experience of the phenomenal world as a product of an external environment in interaction with the apparatus of human reason or mind. As we read his descriptions of how this product is effected, the grounds for assuming the existence of a separate external environment are quickly undercut. All sense of "objectivity" and "regularity out there" seem to be a function of the apparatus of human reason. But then on closer look at passages such as the last and the next, it appears that we have no grounds for the prior assumption of a separate human apparatus of reason or mind. The environment, as well as the apparatus, appears to be the result of a spontaneous creative reciprocity in experience. It cannot be said that Kant held this view, but these considerations do suggest that his thinking had gone beyond the dualistic confines of the modern mind.

The Synthesis of Reason (Speculative Reason)

The "constitutive" principles make possible the direct contribution that the mind makes to the world as known. In this section we shall consider the "regulative" principles, which do not participate in what is known but which Kant feels are necessary to the guidance of the activity of knowing itself.

Even though the categories of the understanding are consistently applied in the interpretive act, the fact that experience is strung out along a temporal line and proceeds from a past which is no longer to a future which is not yet—this fact lends incompleteness and fragmentation to experience and to the task of Reason. Because of this openendness, Reason has need of what Kant called the "ideas of Reason." There are three such ideas: Self, Universe, and God. These ideas are not necessary for Nature conceived as a system of objective truth, but are necessary for the guidance and regulation of knowing through which man consistently attempts to complete such a system. Although these ideas are expressive of the completeness of possible experience, their goal lies beyond possible experience since experience is always partial. However, from a practical point of view there are some ideas that must necessarily be thought as a basis for the knowing activity, even though they cannot be known.

Kant thus expresses the primacy of the practical over the theoretical, but he also implies that without the speculative activity of reason there can be no theoretical knowledge. He regards metaphysics as an indispensable speculative activity, the goal of which is to display the structure of what must be thought, not only for the sake of knowing but also for doing and feeling. These beings of thought constitute the "noumenal" world. Nonetheless and of equal import, Kant concludes that it is not possible to have synthetic *a priori* judgments based on the activity of Speculative Reason and that traditional metaphysics, resting as it does upon the misuse of Speculative Reason, produces no knowledge.

Selection VII:
THE IDEAS OF REASON

Understanding may be regarded as a faculty which secures the unity of appearances by means of rules, and reason as being the faculty which secures the unity of the rules of understanding under principles. Accordingly, reason never applies itself directly to experience or to any object, but to understanding, in order to give to the manifold knowledge of the latter an *a priori* unity by means of concepts, a unity which may be called the unity of reason, and which is quite different in kind from any unity that can be accomplished by the understanding.

This is the universal concept of the faculty of reason in so far as it has been possible to make it clear in the total absence of examples. These will be given in the course of our argument.   (a)

I understand by idea a necessary concept of reason to which no corresponding object can be given in sense-experience. Thus the pure concepts of reason, now under consideration, are *transcendental ideas*. They are concepts of pure reason, in that they view all knowledge gained in experience as being determined through an absolute totality of conditions. They are not arbitrarily invented; they are imposed by the very nature of reason itself, and therefore stand in necessary relation to the whole employment of understanding. Finally, they are transcendent and overstep the limits of all experience; no object adequate to the transcendental idea can ever be found within experience.   (b)

Although we must say of the transcendental concepts of reason that *they are only ideas,* this is not by any means to be taken as signifying that they are superfluous and void. For even if they cannot determine any object, they may yet, in a fundamental and unobserved fashion, be of service to the understanding as a canon for its extended and consistent employment.... (c)

Now all pure concepts in general are concerned with the synthetic unity of representations, but [those of them which are] concepts of pure reason (transcendental ideas) are concerned with the unconditioned synthetic unity of all conditions in general. All transcendental ideas can therefore be arranged in three classes, the *first* containing the absolute (unconditioned) *unity* of the *thinking subject,* the second the absolute *unity of the series of conditions of appearance,* the *third* the absolute *unity of the condition of all objects of thought in general.*

The thinking subject is the object of *psychology,* the sum-total of all appearances (the world) is the object of *cosmology,* and the thing which contains the highest condition of the possibility of all that can be thought (the being of all beings) the object of *theology.* Pure reason thus furnishes the idea for a transcendental doctrine of the soul (*psychologia rationalis*) for a transcendental science of the world (*cosmologia-rationalis*), and, finally, for a transcendental knowledge of God (*theologia transzendentalis*). The understanding is not in a position to yield even the mere project of any one of these sciences, not even though it be supported by the highest logical employment of reason, that is, by all the conceivable inferences through which we seek to advance from one of its objects (appearance) to all others, up to the most remote members of the empirical synthesis; each of these sciences is an altogether pure and genuine product, or problem, of pure reason.   (d)

Rational Psychology

The idea of Self expresses the sum total of the conditions of the inner reality of man. Our experience of the Self is always phenomenal; that is, it is expressed always on the basis of the categories.

And yet, it is never complete because the self that is aware is never an item in our awareness. We can express the problem in grammatical form. I only know the "me," never the "I." Yet it is necessary to think the "I" in order to organize the fragmentary sequence of experienced "me's."

Selection VIII:
THE IDEA OF SELF

Rational psychology exists not as *doctrine,* furnishing an addition to our knowledge of the self, but only as *discipline.* It sets impassable limits to speculative reason in this field, and thus keeps us, on the one hand, from throwing ourselves into the arms of a soulless materialism, or, on the other hand, from losing ourselves in a spiritualism which must be quite unfounded so long as we remain in this present life.   (a)

From all this it is evident that rational psychology owes its origin simply to misunderstanding. The unity of consciousness, which underlies the categories, is here mistaken for an intuition of the subject as object, and the category of substance is then applied to it. But this unity is only unity in *thought,* by which alone no object is given, and to which, therefore, the category of substance, which always presupposes a given *intuition,* cannot be applied. Consequently, this subject cannot be known. The subject of the categories cannot by thinking the categories acquire a concept of itself as an object of the categories. For in order to think them, its pure self-consciousness, which is what was to be explained, must itself be presupposed. Similarly, the subject, in which the representation of time has its original ground, cannot thereby determine its own existence in time. And if this latter is impossible, the former, as a determination of the self (as a thinking being in general) by means of the categories, is equally so.*   (b)

––––––––––––

The idea of Self must be thought but cannot be known as an object in our experience. Why must we think it? We must think

* The "I think" is, as already stated, an empirical proposition, and contains within itself the proposition "I exist." But I cannot say "Everything which thinks, exists." For in that case the property of thought would render all beings which possess it necessary beings. My existence cannot, therefore, be regarded as an inference from the proposition "I think," as Descartes sought to contend—for it would then have to be preceded by the major premiss "Everything which thinks, exists"—but is identical with it. The "I think" expresses an indeterminate empirical intuition, i.e., perception (and thus shows that sensation, which as such belongs to sensibility, lies at the basis of this existential proposition). But the "I think" precedes the experience which is required to determine the object of perception through the category in respect of time; and the existence here [referred to] is not a category.

it because our awareness of succession presupposes the continuity of something that is aware. This argument is implicit in the considerations regarding the unity in our experience in Selection V. We cannot know the Self as an object because it never appears as an object in our experience. If knowledge to be knowledge has to be certain, then only what is necessary in experience i.e.—*a priori* truths, can be objects of knowledge. Notice the change if the possibility of uncertain knowledge is admitted. Knowledge becomes judgmental. Our knowledge of an object is the result of an inference the truth of which is only probable. But this kind of indirect—and hence incomplete—knowledge was not possible for Kant, and so he speaks of ideas which "must be thought" and cannot be known.

Rational Cosmology

For Kant, there are two ways of thinking about things. Both are essential for understanding and intelligibility, yet each precludes the other. On the one hand, we have the categories of science, and on the other, the categories of purposive activity. In order to explain both the activity and its results it appears necessary to think of objects as determined by their antecedent conditions, and at the same time to think of objects also as having an identity apart from those prior conditions. The antinomies of reason lay this dilemma bare. Kant believes the situation to be the result of employing Reason as a separate activity without any direct empirical reference. However, it needs to be pointed out that this dilemma is also a result of the manner in which reason is conceived—that is, the conception of the nature of knowledge, the particular type of logic involved, and the understanding of scientific demonstration. The antinomies are as much a demonstration of the inadequacy of the traditional conception of Reason as they are of what happens when Reason strays from its ground in experience. Kant himself shares this traditional view in many ways, yet struggles with it.

Selection IX:
THE IDEA OF THE UNIVERSE

...the cosmological idea extends the connection of the conditioned with its condition (whether this is mathematical or dynamical) so far that experience never can keep up with it. It is therefore with regard to this point always as Idea, whose object never can be adequately given in any experience.

In the first place, the use of a system of categories becomes here so obvious and unmistakable that, even if there were not several other proofs of it, this alone would sufficiently prove it indispensable in the system of pure reason. There are only four such transcendent Ideas, as many as there are classes of categories; in each of which, however, they refer only to the absolute completeness of the series of the conditions for a given conditioned. In accordance with these cosmological Ideas, there are only four kinds of dialectical assertions of pure reason, which, being dialectical, prove that to each of them, on equally specious principles of pure reason, a contradictory assertion stands opposed.   (a)

1

Thesis: The world has, as to time and space, a beginning (limit).
Antithesis: The world is, as to time and space, infinite.

2

Thesis: Everything in the world consists of [elements that are] simple.
Antithesis: There is nothing simple, but everything is composite.

3

Thesis: There are in the world causes through freedom.
Antithesis: There is no freedom, but all is nature.

4

Thesis: In the series of the world-causes there is some necessary being.
Antithesis: There is nothing necessary in the world, but in this series all is contingent.

Here is the most singular phenomenon of human reason, no other instance of which can be shown in any other use of reason. If we, as is commonly done, represent to ourselves the appearances of the sensible world as things in themselves, if we assume the principles of their combination as principles universally valid of things in themselves and not merely of experience, as is usually, nay, without our *Critique* unavoidably, done, there arises an unexpected conflict which never can be removed in the common dogmatic way; because the thesis, as well as the antithesis, can be shown by equally clear, evident, and irresistible proofs

—for I pledge myself as to the correctness of all these proofs—and reason therefore perceives that it is divided against itself, a state at which the skeptic rejoices, but which must make the critical philosopher pause and feel ill at ease. (b)

The first two antinomies, which I call mathematical because they are concerned with the addition or division of the homogeneous, are founded on such a contradictory concept; and hence I explain how it happens that both the thesis and antithesis of the two are false. (c)

Now if I inquire into the magnitude of the world, as to space and time, it is equally impossible, as regards all my concepts, to declare it infinite or to declare it finite. For neither assertion can be contained in experience, because experience either of an infinite space or of an infinite elapsed time, or again, of the boundary of the world by a void space or by an antecedent void time, is impossible; there are mere Ideas. The magnitude of the world, decided either way, would therefore have to exist in the world itself apart from all experience.... (d)

The same holds of the second antinomy, which relates to the division of appearances. For these are mere representations; and the parts exist merely in their representation, consequently in the division—that is, in a possible experience in which they are given—and the division reaches only as far as the possible experience reaches. To assume that an appearance, for example, that of body, contains in itself before all experience all the parts which any possible experience can ever reach is to impute to a mere appearance, which can exist only in experience, an existence previous to experience.... (e)

In the first (the mathematical) class of antinomies the falsehood of the presupposition consists in representing in one concept something self-contradictory as if it were compatible (that is, an appearance as a thing in itself). But, as to the second (the dynamical) class of antinomies, the falsehood of the presupposition consists in representing as contradictory what is compatible; so that while in the former case the opposed assertions were both false, in this case, on the other hand, where they are opposed to one another by mere misunderstanding, they may both be true. (f)

In appearance every effect is an event, or something that happens in time; it must, according to the universal law of nature, be preceded by a determination of the causal act of its cause—this determination being a state of the cause—which it follows according to a constant law. But this determination of the cause to a causal act must likewise be something that takes place or happens; the cause must have begun to act, otherwise no succession between it and the effect could be conceived. Otherwise the effect, as well as the causal act of the cause, would have always existed. Therefore the determination of the cause to act must also have originated among appearances and must consequently, like its effect, be an event, which must again have its cause, and so on; hence natural necessity must be the condition on which efficient causes are determined. Whereas if freedom is to be a property of certain causes of appearances, it must, as regards these, which are events, be a faculty of starting them spontaneously. That is, it would not require that the causal act of the cause should itself begin [in time], and hence it would not require any other ground to determine its start. But then the cause, as to its causal act, could not rank under time-determinations of its state; that is, it could not be an appearance, but would have to be considered a thing in itself, while only its effects would be appearances.* If without contradiction we can think of the beings of understanding as exercising such an influence on appearances, then natural necessity will attach to all connections of cause and effect in the sensuous world; though, on the other hand, freedom can be granted to the cause which is itself not an appearance (but the foundation of appearance). Nature and freedom therefore can without contradiction be attributed to the very same thing, but in different relations—on one side as an appearance, on the other side as a thing in itself.

We have in us a faculty which not only stands in connection with its subjective determining grounds [motives] which are the natural causes of its actions and is so far the faculty of a being that itself belongs to appearances, but is also related to objective grounds which are only Ideas so far as they can determine this faculty. This connection is expressed by the word *ought*. This faculty is called "reason," and, so far as we consider a being (man) entirely according to this objectively determinable reason, he cannot be considered as a being of sense; this property is a property of a thing in itself, a property whose possibility we cannot comprehend. I mean we cannot comprehend how the *ought*

---

* The idea of freedom occurs only in the relation of the intellectual, as cause, to the appearance, as effect. Hence we cannot attribute freedom to matter in regard to the incessant action by which it fills its space, though this action takes place from an internal principle.... It is only if *something is to start* by an action, and so the effect occurs in the sequence of time, or in the world of sense (for example, the beginning of the world), that we can put the question whether the causal act of the cause must in its turn have been started or whether the cause can originate an effect without its causal act itself beginning. In the former case, the concept of this activity is a concept of natural necessity; in the latter, that of freedom. From this the reader will see that as I explained freedom to be the faculty of starting an event spontaneously, I have exactly hit the concept which is the problem of metaphysics.

should determine (even if it never has actually determined) its activity and could become the cause of actions whose effect is an appearance in the sensible world. Yet the causality of reason would be freedom with regard to the effects in the sensuous world.   (g)

As to the fourth antinomy, it is solved in the same way as the conflict of reason with itself in the third. For, provided the cause *in* the appearance is distinguished from the cause *of* the appearances (so far as it can be thought as a thing in itself), both propositions are perfectly reconcilable: the one, that there is nowhere in the sensuous world a cause (according to similar laws of causality) whose existence is absolutely necessary; the other, that this world is nevertheless connected with a necessary being as its cause (but of another kind and according to another law). The incompatibility of these propositions rests entirely upon the mistake of extending what is valid merely of appearances to things in themselves and in confusing both in one concept.   (h)

The function of the antinomies is to show that reason, when it is used speculatively—without being tied down to percepts—involves itself in contradictions. There are four such contradictions. We shall consider the third, which deals with freedom and determinism.

On the one hand, the category of causation makes it impossible to think of a first element in the chain of causal sequences, since under that category every event is thought as being preceded and explained by another event. On the other hand, we must conceive of such a first cause, for without it, there is no sufficient reason for the causal series occurring at all.

If there is such a first cause, it must be unconditioned, free, and in fact, inexplicable, and an inexplicable cause is no explanation of a causal series. Thus, from the point of view of Reason, it is both logically necessary and impossible to assert either alternative. For example, from the phenomenal point of view we must regard the Self as determined, and for the reasons given previously, we must think of a Self outside of the phenomenal world, the noumenal Self. Kant solves the antinomy by saying that man must be conceived of as belonging to two worlds, the phenomenal world or the world of Nature, and the noumenal world or the world of Freedom.

Having separated the world of fact from the world of value, Kant has trouble explaining how the two worlds act together. That he intends to do so is evidenced by the fact that the third antinomy involves two conceptions of causation. One is the temporally conditioned relation between cause and effect, each of which is phenomenal; the other the nontemporal relation of ground and consequent, in which the consequent is phenomenal, but the ground is noumenal. Kant believes that while a given appearance may be understood through the categories as the effect of another appearance as cause, the same appearance may at the same time be the consequent of a self-determining, freely acting ground, or thing-in-itself. It is possible, then, that man as a self-determining ground, a noumenon, may be free. There is nothing that precludes this possibility because in Kant's theoretical formulation man as ground is not an object for understanding.

Rational Theology

Just as we cannot know the Self but must think of it as the sum total of the conditions of inner experience and must think of the idea of the Universe as the sum total of the conditions of outer experience, so the sum total of all the conditions of both Self and Universe, taken together, requires the idea of God. Without these regulative ideas, our attempt to know will have no guidance and no criteria of completeness. These three ideas function as ideals for the activity of knowing.

All of the attempts to prove the existence of God fall into three categories; the ontological, the cosmological, and the physico-theological. These arguments use either the transcendental approach, which argues from the nature of concepts, or the empirical approach, which argues from the determinate nature of the world. Kant's view of these arguments is that, no matter how they approach the problem, reason "stretches its wings in vain in thus attempting to soar above the world of sense by the mere power of speculation." [1]

The ontological proof purports to argue from the conception of "the most perfect being" to the necessity of its existence on the grounds that such a being would not be "most perfect" if it did not exist. This argument, which first appears in St. Anselm (1035–1109), is a perennial feature of the extreme rationalism of thinkers such as Descartes and Spinoza. Here we have Kant's famous refutation of it on the grounds that "existence is not a predicate" as well as the example of the "hundred real thalers."

[1] *Critique of Pure Reason,* Norman Kemp Smith (trans.) (London: Macmillan, 1929; New York: St. Martin's Press), p. 500.

The cosmological proof begins with the empirically founded idea that everything that exists is contingent on something else for its existence, and argues that a necessary cause, God, is required as the condition of all that exists. Kant's critique here is that, first, we have no experience of an idea of existence and, second, that the argument proceeds in the same manner as the ontological proof.

Both of these transcendental proofs involve an illusion. They take to be objective the subjective principles of reason—the principle of necessity and the principle of contingency. With regard to these two principles, which are "heuristic and regulative," Kant says:

> The one calls upon us to seek something necessary as a condition of all that is given as existent, that is, to stop nowhere until we have arrived at an explanation which is complete *a priori;* the other forbids us ever to hope for this completion, that is, forbids us to treat anything empirical as unconditioned and to exempt ourselves hereby from the toil of its further derivation.[2]

This passage shows that the idea of God is nothing but a regulative principle of reason, and reflects the general character of the antinomies as well.

The third proof, the physico-theological, begins with the particular facts of design in nature and proceeds to argue for an intelligent, supreme author of nature. While of all the arguments this one, Kant says, "deserves the most respect," it nevertheless falls back on the transcendental principles of contingency and necessity to make its inference beyond experience.

Selection X:
THE IDEA OF GOD

The Ontological Proof

There is one concept and indeed only one, in reference to which the not-being or rejection of its object is in itself contradictory, namely, the concept of the *ens realissimum*. It is declared that it possesses all reality, and that we are justified in assuming that such a being is possible (the fact that a concept does not contradict itself by no means proves the possibility of its object: but the contrary assertion I am for the moment willing to allow). Now [the argument proceeds] "all reality" includes existence; existence is therefore contained in the concept of a thing

[2] *Critique of Pure Reason*, p. 515.

that is possible. If, then, this thing is rejected, the internal possibility of the thing is rejected—which is self-contradictory.   (a)

"Being" is obviously not a real predicate; that is, it is not a concept of something which could be added to the concept of a thing. It is merely the position of a thing, or of certain determinations, as existing in themselves. Logically, it is merely the copula of a judgment. The proposition, "God is omnipotent," contains two concepts, each of which has its object —God and omnipotence. The small word "is" adds no new predicate, but only serves to posit the predicate *in its relation* to the subject. If now, we take the subject (God) with all its predicates (among which is omnipotence), and say "God is," or "There is a God," we attach no new predicate to the concept of God, but only posit the subject in itself with all its predicates, and indeed posit it as being an *object* that stands in relation to my *concept*. The content of both must be one and the same; nothing can have been added to the concept, which expresses merely what is possible, by my thinking its object (through the expression "it is") as given absolutely. Otherwise stated, the real contains no more than the merely possible. A hundred real thalers do not contain the least coin more than a hundred possible thalers. For as the latter signify the concept, and the former the object and the positing of the object, should the former contain more than the latter, my concept would not, in that case, express the whole object, and would not therefore be an adequate concept of it. My financial position is, however, affected very differently by a hundred real thalers than it is by the mere concept of them (that is, of their possibility). For the object, as it actually exists, is not analytically contained in my concept, but is added to my concept (which is a determination of my state) synthetically; and yet the conceived hundred thalers are not themselves in the least increased through thus acquiring existence outside my concept.   (b)

The Cosmological Proof

The *cosmological proof,* which we are not about to examine, retains the connection of absolute necessity with the highest reality, but instead of reasoning, like the former proof, from the highest reality to necessity of existence, it reasons from the previously given unconditioned necessity of some being to the unlimited reality of that being. It thus enters upon a course of reasoning which, whether rational or only pseudo-rational, is at any rate natural, and the most convincing not only for common sense but even for speculative understanding.   (c)

It runs thus: If anything exists, an absolutely necessary being must also exist. Now I, at least, exist. Therefore an absolutely necessary being exists. The minor premiss contains an experience, the major premiss the inference from there being any experience at all to the existence of the necessary.* The proof therefore really begins with experience, and is not wholly *a priori* or ontological. For this reason, and because the object of all possible experience is called the world, it is entitled the *cosmological* proof. Since, in dealing with the objects of experience, the proof abstracts from all special properties through which this world may differ from any other possible world, the title also serves to distinguish it from the physico-theological proof, which is based upon observations of the particular properties of the world disclosed to us by our senses. (d)

The Physico-Theological Proof

This world presents to us so immeasurable a stage of variety, order, purposiveness, and beauty, as displayed alike in its infinite extent and in the unlimited divisibility of its parts, that even with such knowledge as our weak understanding can acquire of it, we are brought face to face with so many marvels immeasurably great, that all speech loses its force, all numbers their power to measure, our thoughts themselves all definiteness, and that our judgment of the whole resolves itself into an amazement which is speechless, and only the more eloquent on that account. Everywhere we see a chain of effects and causes, of ends and means, a regularity in origination and dissolution. Nothing has of itself come into the condition in which we find it to exist, but always points to something else as its cause, while this in turn commits us to repetition of the same enquiry. The whole universe must thus sink into the abyss of nothingness, unless, over and above this infinite chain of contingencies, we assume something to support it—something which is original and independently self-subsistent, and which as the cause of the origin of the universe secures also at the same time its continuance. What magnitude are we to ascribe to this supreme cause—admitting that it is supreme in respect of all things in the world? We are not acquainted with the whole content of the world, still less do we know how to estimate its magnitude by comparison with all that is possible. But since we cannot, as regards causality, dispense with an ultimate and supreme being, what is there to prevent us ascribing to it a degree of perfection that sets its above *everything else that is possible?* This we can easily do—though only

* This inference is too well known to require detailed statement. It depends on the supposedly transcendental law of natural causality: that everything contingent has a cause, which, if itself contingent, must likewise have a cause, till the series of subordinate causes ends with an absolutely necesary cause, without which it would have no completeness.

through the slender outline of an abstract concept—by representing this
being to ourselves as combining in itself all possible perfection, as in a
single substance. This concept is in conformity with the demand of
our reason for parsimony of principles; it is free from self-contradiction,
and is never decisively contradicted by any experience; and it is likewise
of such a character that it contributes to the extension of the employment
of reason within experience, through the guidance which it yields in
the discovery of order and purposiveness.

This proof always deserves to be mentioned with respect. It is the
oldest, the clearest, and the best suited to ordinary human reason. It
enlivens the study of nature, just as it itself derives its existence and
gains ever new vigour from that source. It suggests ends and purposes,
where our observation would not have detected them by itself, and extends our knowledge of nature by means of the guiding-concept of a
special unity, the principle of which is outside nature. This knowledge
again reacts on its cause, namely, upon the idea which has led to it,
and so strengthens the belief in a supreme Author [of nature] that the
belief acquires the force of an irresistible conviction.   (e)

The physico-theological argument can indeed lead us to the point of
admiring the greatness, wisdom, power, etc., of the Author of the world,
but can take us no further. Accordingly, we then abandon the argument
from empirical grounds of proof, and fall back upon the contingency
which, in the first steps of the argument, we had inferred from the order
and purposiveness of the world. With this contingency as our sole
premiss, we then advance, by means of transcendental concepts alone,
to the existence of an absolutely necessary being, and [as a final step]
from the concept of the absolute necessity of the first cause to the completely determinate or determinable concept of that necessary being,
namely, to the concept of an all-embracing reality.   (f)

With this critique of the arguments for God's existence, his
examination of knowing comes to an end. The activity of knowing,
which is productive of the ever incomplete system of Nature, includes

1. The synthesis of the manifold of sense under the perceptual
forms of space and time.
2. The synthesis of the perceptual level by the constitutive act of
understanding, in which concepts are applied to percepts through the
use of the schemata of time and under the guidance of the unity
of apperception.

3. The continuing synthesis of reason as it regulates the attempt to complete the system of Nature on the basis of the three ideas of completion—Self, Universe, and God.

In so far as this activity is constitutive it is theoretical, and the result is the system of Nature—the phenomenal world as we experience it. But in so far as the activity is regulative, it is speculative, and the product is the system of ideas required to guide the activity. Since this speculative activity is directed towards a goal, it really is a part of practical reason: it involves the activity of willing. Therefore, the activity of knowing, if fully understood, involves the activity of willing.

Also, objectively, knowing involves interpretation according to two types of rules, the Categories and the Ideas, but subjectively, it involves imagination and the activity of judging.

PART II:
Of Reason in Willing (Practical Reason)

The Postulates of Practical Reason

Knowing, for Kant, is a purposive activity guided by certain ideals and producing a system of nature and science. In this enterprise Reason has the dual function of supplying the constitutive principles of the system and the regulative principles of the activity.

Willing is also a purposive activity involving goals and choice. For Kant this is the essential meaning of the idea that man is a rational being. Just as he is concerned with the rational structure of knowing, so he is concerned with the rational structure of willing. It is in this context of rational activity that we must understand Kant's ethics, with its imperatives and duties. We will consider first the regulative ideas necessary to carry on the activity of willing.

Kant's procedure is the same as before. He begins with the "moral law within," and declares it to be a fact by virtue of our sense of duty or obligation. We recognize that there are things we "ought" to do. Kant writes:

Duty! Thou sublime and mighty name that dost embrace nothing, charming or insinuating but requirest submission and yet seekest not to move the will by threatening aught that would arouse natural aversion or terror, but only holdest forth a law which of itself finds entrance into the mind and yet gains reluctant reverence (though not always obedience)—a law before which all inclinations are dumb even though they secretly work against it: what origin is there worthy of thee, and where is to be found the root of thy noble descent which proudly rejects all kinship with the inclinations and from which to be descended is the indispensable condition of the only worth which men can give themselves? [1]

The "moral law within" and its command of Duty presupposes three *a priori* principles of Practical Reason: Freedom, Immortality, and God.

Selection XI:
OF FREEDOM

The concept of causality as natural necessity, unlike the concept of causality as freedom, concerns only the existence of things as far as it is determinable in time, and consequently as appearances in contrast to their causality as things-in-themselves. If one takes the attributes of the existence of things in time for attributes of things-in-themselves, which is the usual way of thinking, the necessity in the causal relation can in no way be united with freedom. They are contradictory to each other, for the former implies that every event, and consequently every action which occurs at a certain point of time is necessary under the condition of what preceded it. Since the past is no longer in my power, every action which I perform is necessary because of determining grounds which are not in my power. That means that at the time I act I am never free. Indeed, if I assumed my entire existence were independent of any external cause (e.g., God), so that the determining grounds of my causality and even of my whole existence were not outside me, this would not in the least convert that natural necessity into freedom. For at every point of time I still stand under the necessity of being determined to act by what is not in my power, and the *a parte priori* infinite series of events which I can continue only by an already predetermined order would never commence of itself. It would be a continuous natural chain, and thus my causality would never be freedom.

Therefore, if one attributes freedom to a being whose existence is determined in time, it cannot be excepted from the law of natural necessity of all events in its existence, including also its actions. Making such an exception would be equivalent to delivering this being to blind chance.

[1] Immanuel Kant, *Critique of Practical Reason,* translated by Lewis White Beck, copyright © 1956 by The Liberal Arts Press, Inc., reprinted by permission of the Liberal Arts Press Division of the Bobbs-Merrill Company, Inc.; p. 89.

Since this law inevitably concerns all causality of things so far as their existence is determinable in time, freedom would have to be rejected as a void and impossible concept if this were the way in which we thought of the existence of these things as they are in themselves. Consequently, if we wish still to save it, no other course remains than to ascribe the existence of a thing so far as it is determinable in time, and accordingly its causality under the law of natural necessity, merely to appearance, and to attribute freedom to the same being as a thing-in-itself. This is absolutely unavoidable if one wishes to maintain both these mutually incompatible concepts; but in applying them, when one wishes to explain them as united in one and the same action and thus explain this union itself, great difficulties turn up, which seem to make such a unification unfeasable. (a)

Now in order to remove the apparent contradiction between the mechanism of nature and freedom in the case under discussion, we must remember what was said in the *Critique of Pure Reason* or what it implies, viz., that natural necessity, which cannot coexist with the freedom of the subject, attaches merely to the determinations of a thing which stands under the conditions of time, and consequently applies only to the acting subject as appearance. As a consequence, [it pertains to the subject] only so far as the determining grounds of any action of the subject lie in what belongs to the past and is no longer in his power; in this must be counted also his already performed acts and his character as a phenomenon as this is determined for him in his own eyes by those acts. But the same subject, which, on the other hand, is conscious also of his own existence as a thing-in-itself, also views his existence so far as it does not stand under temporal conditions, and to himself as determinable only by laws which he gives to himself through reason. In this existence nothing is antecedent to the determination of his will; every action and, in general, every changing determination of his existence according to the inner sense, even the entire history of his existence as a sensuous being, is seen in the consciousness of his intelligible existence as only a consequence, not as a determining ground of his causality as a noumenon. From this point of view, a rational being can rightly say of any unlawful action which he has done that he could have left it undone, even if as an appearance it was sufficiently determined in the past and thus far was inescapably necessary. For this action and everything in the past which determined it belong to a single phenomenon of his character, which he himself creates, and according to which he imputes to himself as a cause independent of all sensibility the causality of that appearance. (b)

Therefore, in the Dialectic of pure speculative reason it was found that the two apparently incompatible modes of finding the unconditioned for the conditioned (e.g., in the synthesis of causality, to find a causality which has no sensuous condition for the conditioned in the series of causes and effects in the world of sense) do not in fact contradict each other and that the same act, which as belonging to the world of sense is always sensuously conditioned, i.e., mechanically necessary, can at the same time, as belonging to the causality of the acting being in so far as it belongs to the intelligible world, have a sensuously unconditioned causality as its foundation. That is, it can be thought of as free.   (c)

Thus nothing remained but that perhaps an incontrovertible, objective principle of causality could be found which excluded every sensuous condition from its determination, i.e., a principle in which reason does not call upon anything else as the determining ground of the causality but rather by that principle itself contains it, thus being, as pure reason, practical of itself. This principle, however, needs no search and no invention, having long been in the reason of all men and embodied in their being. It is the principle of morality. Therefore, that unconditioned causality and its faculty, freedom, and therewith a being (myself) which belongs to the world of sense and at the same time to the intelligible world, are no longer thought merely indeterminately and problematically (which even speculative reason could detect as possible), but with respect to the law of its causality are determinately and assertorically known; thus is the reality of the intelligible world definitely established from a practical point of view, and this determinateness, which would be transcendent (extravagant) for theoretical purposes, is for practical purposes immanent.   (d)

In the last selection we saw Kant firmly grasping the second horn of the dilemma we pointed out in connection with the antinomies. In order to talk about human activity intelligibly, we must think of man as having an identity of his own, as a cause (Kant's term is "autonomy"), as being something more than the sum of the antecedent conditions. From the point of view of ethics, this "something more" is necessary for freedom as well as responsibility, and its source lies in the element of "spontaneity." In the mechanical world of phenomena each state is the direct product of a previous state. By the idea of spontaneity Kant wants to indicate that man has the power to initiate action at any given moment, that with respect to the present there is an element in man's nature that is unconditioned. Man as moral being is the cause of himself and not merely the product of his past states.

Kant is completely serious about the idea of freedom of the Will. It is as if he were saying that science and nature have no concern with purpose, but man does. Man can know scientifically in a nonpurposive way. He cannot understand his own thinking activity, however, outside of a purposeful context. To be human and not an animal is to put this activity in a purposeful context: no purposive context, no understanding; no understanding, no morality; no morality, no distinctively human activity. Even though the necessity is inner, these postulates and laws are pragmatically necessary if man is going to be autonomous in his activity. Kant sees the moral problem as the maintenance of rational nature as noumenon in the face of man's sensuous concern for happiness in the phenomenal world of nature.

Kant accepts not only "the starry skies above" but also "the moral law within." And this moral law that commands that man "ought" to maintain himself as a person presupposes not only man's freedom to chose to remain autonomous but also the possibility of attaining the commanded goal, the Good Will.[1] Since man as man is a part of the world of nature he can attain this goal only beyond this life. Hence, Kant arrives at the postulate of immortality.

Selection XII:
OF IMMORTALITY

The achievement of the highest good in the world is the necessary object of a will determinable by the moral law. In such a will, however, the complete fitness of intentions to the moral law is the supreme condition of the highest good. This fitness, therefore, must be just as possible as its object, because it is contained in the command that requires us to promote the latter. But complete fitness of the will to the moral law is holiness, which is a perfection of which no rational being in the world of sense is at any time capable. But since it is required as practically necessary, it can be found only in an endless progress to that complete fitness; on principles of pure practical reason, it is necessary to assume such a practical progress as the real object of our will.

This infinite progress is possible, however, only under the presupposition of an infinitely enduring existence and personality of the same rational being; this is called the immortality of the soul. Thus the

[1] See pp. 149ff.

highest good is practically possible only on the supposition of the immortality of the soul, and the latter, as inseparably bound to the moral law, is a postulate of pure practical reason. By a postulate of pure practical reason, I understand a theoretical proposition which is not as such demonstrable, but which is an inseparable corollary of an *a priori* unconditionally valid practical law.   (a)

In the third postulate of practical reason, God, Kant shifts his ground substantially. Unlike freedom and immortality, which are presuppositions of the moral law, the postulate of God is required to fulfill our conception of the Highest Good, of which the moral law is but a part. It is not clear what the credentials of this conception of the Highest Good are. Undoubtedly Kant was trying to combine noumenal "virtue" with phenomenal "happiness" as an ideal of completeness, and a God is needed to secure the ultimate connection of the two. But after urging and demonstrating at great length that man's good, which is the only condition of his value as rational creature, lies in the Good Will and not in happiness, it seems that Kant betrays his moral insight in introducing the notion of happiness on some ideal, to-be-hoped-for, and ultimate level without giving sufficient grounds for such a hope.

Selection XIII:
OF GOD

The moral law led, in the foregoing analysis, to a practical problem which is assigned solely by pure reason and without any concurrence of sensuous incentives. It is the problem of the completeness of the first and principal part of the highest good, viz., morality; since this problem can be solved only in eternity, it led to the postulate of immortality. The same law must also lead us to affirm the possibility of the second element of the highest good, i.e., happiness proportional to that morality; it must do so just as disinterestedly as heretofore, by a purely impartial reason. This it can do on the supposition of the existence of a cause adequate to this effect, i.e., it must postulate the existence of God as necessarily belonging to the possibility of the highest good (the object of our will which is necessarily connected with the moral legislation of pure reason). We proceed to exhibit this connection in a convincing manner.

Happiness is the condition of a rational being in the world, in whose existence everything goes according to wish and will. It thus rests on the harmony of nature with his entire end and with the essential determining ground of his will. But the moral law commands as a law of freedom through motives wholly independent of nature and of its harmony with our faculty of desire (as incentives). Still, the acting rational being in the world is not at the same time the cause of the world and of nature itself. Hence there is not the slightest ground in the moral law for a necessary connection between the morality and proportionate happiness of a being which belongs to the world as one of its parts and as thus dependent on it. Not being nature's cause, his will cannot by its own strength bring nature, as it touches on his happiness, into complete harmony with his practical principles. . . .   (a)

Therefore, the highest good is possible in the world only on the supposition of a supreme cause of nature which has a causality corresponding to the moral intention. Now a being which is capable of actions by the idea of laws is an intelligence (a rational being), and the causality of such a being according to this idea of laws is his will. Therefore, the supreme cause of nature, in so far as it must be presupposed for the highest good, is a being which is the cause (and consequently the author) of nature through understanding and will, i.e., God. As a consequence, the postulate of the possibility of a highest derived good (the best world) is at the same time the postulate of the reality of a highest original good, namely, the existence of God. Now it was our duty to promote the highest good; and it is not merely our privilege but a necessity connected with duty as a requisite to presuppose the possibility of this highest good. This presupposition is made only under the condition of the existence of God, and this condition inseparably connects this supposition with duty. Therefore, it is morally necessary to assume the existence of God.   (b)

In this manner, through the concept of the highest good as the object and final end of pure practical reason, the moral law leads to religion. Religion is the recognition of all duties as divine commands, not as sanctions, i.e., arbitrary and contingent ordinances of a foreign will, but as essential laws of any free will as such. Even as such, they must be regarded as commands of the Supreme Being because we can hope for the highest good (to strive for which is our duty under the moral law) only from a morally perfect (holy and beneficent) and omnipotent will; and, therefore, we can hope to attain it only through harmony with this will.   (c)

Therefore, morals is not really the doctrine of how to make ourselves happy but of how we are to be *worthy* of happiness. Only if religion is added to it can the hope arise of someday participating in happiness in proportion as we endeavored not to be unworthy of it.   (d)

The postulates of pure practical reason all proceed from the principle of morality, which is not a postulate but a law by which reason directly determines the will. This will, by the fact that it is so determined, as a pure will requires these necessary conditions for obedience to its precept. These postulates are not theoretical dogmas but presuppositions of necessarily practical import; thus, while they do not extend speculative knowledge, they given objective reality to the ideas of speculative reason in general (by means of their relation to the practical sphere), and they justify it in holding to concepts even the possibility of which it could not otherwise venture to affirm.

These postulates are those of immortality, of freedom affirmatively regarded (as the causality of a being so far as he belongs to the intelligible world), and of the existence of God. The first derives from the practically necessary condition of a duration adequate to the perfect fulfilment of the moral law. The second comes from the necessary presupposition of independence from the world of sense and of the capacity of determining man's will by the law of an intelligible world, i.e., the law of freedom itself; the third arises from the necessary condition of such an intelligible world by which it may be the highest good, through the presupposition of the highest independent good, i.e., the existence of God.   (e)

———————

It has often been pointed out that of the three postulates only the first, freedom, is of real importance to Kant's ethic. There is a sense in which this is true, which will become clear in the remarks that follow. There is a sense, however, in which to disregard immortality and God is to miss much of the significance of his doctrine of practical reason.

Kant holds man to be a rational being, and the use of reason to be a practical, purposive activity directed toward ends. In asking for the postulates of practical reason, Kant is asking for the conditions that make purposive activity possible.

The first condition is the "ability to choose." If it is not possible to choose between what will and what will not fulfill a purpose, no purposive activity is possible.

The second condition of purposive activity is time seen not as successive but as continuous. Noumenal activity is "non-temporal" in the "successive" sense, but there is temporal continuity between ground and consequent. If there is no continuity between a choice and its possible fulfillments, purposive activity is impossible.

The third condition is order. If there is no order to enable a choice of means to lead to the fulfillment of a purpose, then purposive activity is impossible. The generalization of these three conditions—choice, continuity, and order—yield freedom, immortality, and God. Purposive activity requires a real power of choice structured through time.

The Ultimate Condition of Rational Being

But Kant realizes that the dynamics of willing require that our concern be not merely with the end we aimed at. There is an integrity that we must maintain at all cost as the ultimate condition of all purposive activity. (And here is the sense in which Kant's ethics is concerned only with freedom.) The will in choosing can destroy its power of choice through a choice, and thus its freedom and practical reason. Man's ultimate concern then must be for the integrity of the will. What shall it profit a man if he gain the world and lose his soul—if he gain his end and lose his nature as rational being? For this reason, the nub of the Kantian ethic centers around the conditions of the Good Will.

We shall consider first the nature of the Good Will and then three different expressions of it: the rational will, the autonomous will, and the responsible will.

Selection XIV:
THE GOOD WILL—DUTY AND RESPECT

It is impossible to conceive of anything anywhere in the world or even anywhere out of it that can without qualification be called good, except a Good Will. Reasoning, wit, judgment, or whatever the *talents* of the intellect may be called, or such qualities of *temperament* as courage, determination and constancy of purpose, are doubtless good and desirable in many respects. But they may also be extremely evil and harmful unless the will be good which is to make use of these natural gifts and whose particular quality we therefore designate as *character*. The same is true of the *gifts of fortune*. Power, riches, honor, even health, all comfort and contentment with one's condition which is called *happiness* frequently engender together with courage also an insolence, unless a good will is present which properly directs and thus fits to a general purpose their influence upon the mind and with it the entire principle of activity. Even an impartial sane witness can never take pleasure in the uninterrupted well-being of a person who shows no trace of a pure and good will. Consequently the good will seems to be the indispensable condition even of being worthy of happiness.   (a)

The good will is good not because of what it causes or accomplishes, not because of its usefulness in the attainment of some set purpose, but alone because of the willing, that is to say, of itself. Considered by itself, without any comparison, it is to be valued far more highly than all that might be accomplished through it in favor of some inclination or of the sum of all inclinations. Even though by some special disfavor of fortune or because of the meager provision of a stepmotherly nature this will were entirely lacking in ability to carry out its intentions; if with the greatest of efforts nothing were to be accomplished by it, and nothing were to remain except only the good will (not, to be sure, as a pious wish but as an exertion of every means in our power), it would still sparkle like a jewel by itself, like something that has its full value in itself. Its usefulness or fruitfulness can neither add nor detract from its worth.   (b)

However, reason is not sufficiently adapted to guide the will with certainty in respect to its objects and the satisfaction of all our needs which it in part even mutiplies and for which purpose the inborn natural instincts would have served far better. Nevertheless reason has been allotted to us as a practical faculty, that is to say, a faculty which is meant to influence the *will*. Therefore, if we are to assume that nature in the distribution of its capacities has everywhere proceeded with expediency, the real destination of reason cannot be to serve as a means to other ends but to produce *a will good in itself*, for which reason is absolutely indispensable. Thus this will, though not the sole and entire good, must nevertheless be the highest good and a condition of every other, even of all desire for happiness.   (c)

Now, in order to develop the idea of a good will to be esteemed for no other reason than for itself, just as sound common sense already contains it and it therefore needs less to be taught than clarified, and which is foremost in the evaluation of all our actions and the condition of everything else, we will take the concept of DUTY. Duty includes the notion of a good will with certain subjective restrictions and hindrances. However, far from hiding and obscuring it, these rather serve to bring it out by contrast and make it shine forth all the brighter. (d)

For the will stands at the crossroads, as it were, between its *a priori* principle, which is formal, and its *a posteriori* drive, which is material. Since it must be determined by something, it follows that it must be determined by the formal principle of general volition, whenever an action is done from duty and consequently every material principle has been withdrawn from it. (e)

Since then an action from duty must eliminate entirely the influence of the inclinations and thus every object of the will, there is nothing left to determine the will, except objectively the *law* and subjectively *pure respect* for this practical law, that is to say, the maxim [1] to obey such a law, even at the expense of all my inclinations. (f)

In the boundless esteem for the pure moral law, removed from all advantage, as practical reason presents it to us for obedience, whose voice makes even the boldest sinner tremble and forces him to hide himself from it, there is something so singular that we cannot wonder at finding this influence of a merely intellectual idea on feeling to be inexplicable to speculative reason, and at having to be satisfied with being able to see *a priori* that such a feeling is inseparably bound with the idea of the moral law in every finite rational being. If this feeling of respect were pathological and thus a feeling of respect were pathological and thus a feeling of pleasure grounded on the inner sense, it would be futile to try to discover a relation of the feeling to any idea *a priori*. But it is a feeling which is concerned only with the practical, and with the idea of a law simply as to its form and not on account of any object of the law; thus it cannot be reckoned either as enjoyment or as pain, yet it produces an interest in obedience to the law, and this we call the moral interest. And the capacity of taking such an interest in the law (or of having respect for the moral law itself) is really moral feeling. (g)

Our taking this interest in an action of duty is not suggested by an inclination, but the practical law absolutely commands it and also actually produces it. Consequently, it has a very special name, viz., respect.

The concept of duty thus requires of action that it objectively agree with the law, while of the maxim of the action it demands subjective respect for the law as the sole mode of determining the will through itself. And thereon rests the distinction between consciousness of having acted *according to duty* and *from duty*, i.e., from respect for the law. (h)

---

[1] Maxim is the subjective principle of volition; the objective principle (that is, that which would also serve subjectively for all rational beings as a practical principle if reason had full power over the faculty of desire) is the practical law.

Therefore I have need of no far-reaching perspicacity to know what
to do in order that my volition may be morally good. Inexperienced in
understanding the course of the world, incapable of being prepared for
all that happens in it, I merely ask myself: Can you will that your
maxim becomes a universal law? If not, then it is unsound; and indeed
not because of a disadvantage arising from it for you or for others, but
because it is not suited as a principle for a possible universal code of
law. But reason forces upon me an immediate respect for this code,
even though I do not yet *comprehend* upon what it is based (that is a
matter for investigation by philosophers). But I at least understand
this much: that it is an appreciation of that value which far outweighs
all the worth of that which is esteemed by inclination; that the necessity of my action out of *pure* respect for the practical law is what constitutes duty and that, to duty, every other motive must yield because
it is the condition of a will good *in itself*, than which there is no greater
value.   (i)

Moral feeling is the subjective condition of the good will. The
question often arises whether Kant, after having ruled out completely the possibility of basing ethics on feelings because they are
transient, or on inclinations because they lead to bondage to external conditions, has not let them in at the back door. Kant himself
does not think so, and in several places distinguishes between a
feeling or inclination that precedes its object and one that is engendered by its object. The moral feeling is respect, caused by our
awareness of the moral law. Kant does not consider the moral law
to exist apart from us: rather it is the objective law of our own
structure as rational beings. He speaks of the feeling of respect that
we realize when we become self-conscious of our own rational
nature. The moral law, subjectively, is this feeling of respect, expressed as Duty. Objectively, it is formally stated as a law, expressed as the condition of all lawfulness. Reason, in essence, is
universal, and this condition makes law possible. Man, as a rational
creature and member of the intelligible world, is the particular
whose nature it is to be universal and lawful. It may not be possible
to fulfill this law all the time, but moral feeling is the recognition
that it is a law for my being. The difference between the subjective
feeling and the objective law is the difference (or distance) between the spring of moral being and its goal, its perfected form.

We now turn from the subjective ground of morality to its objective structure, the rational imperative. In the next selection Kant distinguishes between the "hypothetical" and the "categorical" imperatives. For anyone in our time, Kant's insistence on the categorical nature of the moral law presents difficulties. Not only is the idea of "absoluteness," which is part of what it means to be "categorical," out of fashion, but contemporary logic has collapsed the meaning of the categorical into the hypothetical. "All men are mortal" means, today, "If there are any men, then they are mortal." More often than not, it is denied that an unconditioned imperative is possible.

It must be pointed out, first, that Kant is talking about the expression of the rule for the activity of an autonomous being, and the rule of and for an unconditioned being can only be unconditioned itself. Second, Kant distinguishes hypothetical from categorical not only to mark off conditioned from unconditioned but also to mark off the temporal from the nontemporal. In the solution of the third antinomy, Kant distinguishes between phenomenal cause and effect and noumenal ground and consequent. Cause and effect is expressible in hypothetical terms in which the cause is temporally antecedent to the consequent.[1] The hypothetical mode of expression is consequential and nonethical. However, to follow the moral imperative is not to *become* a good will as a consequence in time. Rather, it is to *be* a good will. And this is expressible categorically as "All those who follow the moral imperative are good wills." It is true that Kant's traditional logic hampers him sometimes in the *Critiques*, but in this instance it is our contemporary extensional logic, which is a logic of conditioned being, that hinders our understanding of the one thing that Kant's traditional logic could express—unconditioned being. We must take the idea of the "categorical" in this way if we are to understand Kant's point of view.

Selection XV:
THE RATIONAL WILL AND THE CATEGORICAL IMPERATIVE

Each thing in nature works according to laws. Only a rational being has the faculty to act *according to the conception* of laws, that is according to principles, in other words has a will. Since the deduction of actions from laws requires *reason* the will is nothing but practical reason. If reason invariably determines the will then the actions which

[1] See pp. 133-4.

such a being recognizes as objectively necessary are subjectively necessary as well, that is to say, the will is the faculty to choose *that only* which reason, independent of inclination, recognizes as practically necessary, that is, good. But if reason of itself alone does not sufficiently determine the will, if the latter is dependent also on subjective conditions (certain impulses) which do not always correspond with the objective conditions; in a word, if the will is not *in itself* in full accord with reason (as is actually the case with men) then the actions which objectively are recognized as necessary are subjectively contingent, and the determination of such a will according to objective laws is *obligation.* ....   (a)

The conception of an objective principle in so far as it is obligatory for the will, is called a command (of reason), and the formula of the command is called an IMPERATIVE.   (b)

There are three kinds of Imperative: the technical, the prudential and the moral. Every imperative expresses an Ought, and thus an objective necessity, and indeed a necessity of the free and good will, for it is a property of the imperative that it necessitates objectively. All imperatives involve an objective necessitation, even on the assumption of a good and free will. The technical imperatives are problematical, the prudential imperatives are pragmatic and the moral imperatives are ethical.

Problematic imperatives imply a necessitation of the will in accordance with a rule to an arbitrarily chosen end. The means are stated assertorically, but the end is problematical. If, for instance, we set ourselves the task of constructing a triangle, a square, or a hexagon, we must proceed in accordance with the rules implied: the problem is at our choice, but having chosen it our means to it are defined. Geometry, mechanics, and, in general, the practical sciences contain technical imperatives.   (c)

Practical philosophy contains no technical rules: it contains only rules of prudence and of morality, and it is, therefore, pragmatic and ethical. It is pragmatic in respect of the laws of prudence, and ethical in respect of those of morality.

Prudence is the ability to use the means towards the universal end of man, that is, happiness. We, therefore, have here (as is not the case with technical rules) a determined end. Rules of prudence require us both to define the end and the means to be used to attain it. We need, therefore, a rule for judging what constitutes happiness and the rule for using the means to this happiness. Prudence is thus the ability to determine both the end and the means to the end. ....   (d)

But we can conceive an imperative where the end is governed by a condition which commands not subjectively but objectively. Moral imperatives are such. Take, for example: "Thou shalt not lie." This is no problematic imperative, for in that case it would mean, "If it harm thee to lie, then do not lie." But the imperative commands simply and categorically: "Thou shalt not lie"; and it does so unconditionally, or under an objective and necessary condition. It is characteristic of the moral imperative that it does not determine an end, and the action is not governed by an end, but flows from the free will and has no regard to ends. The dictates of moral imperatives are absolute and regardless of the end. Our free doing and refraining has an inner goodness, irrespective of its end.   (e)

When I conceive a *hypothetical* imperative in general I do not know what it will contain until the condition is supplied. But when I conceive a *categorical* imperative I know at once what it contains. For, since besides the law the imperative contains only the maxim to accord with this law, the law however contains no condition which limits it; therefore nothing remains but the universality of the law in general with which the maxim of action shall conform, and this conformity alone the imperative really represents as necessary.

Consequently there is only one categorical imperative and it is this: *Act only on that maxim which will enable you at the same time to will that it be a universal law.*   (f)

[For example, in order to discover] whether or not a deceitful promise is in accordance with duty, I ask myself: Would I indeed be satisfied to have my maxim (to extricate myself from an embarrassing situation by a false promise) considered a universal law? Would I be able to say to myself: Everybody has the right to make a false promise if he finds himself in a difficulty from which he can escape in no other way? In that manner I soon realize that I may will the lie, but never a universal law to lie. For according to such a law there really would be no promise at all, because it would be vain to make a pretense of my will in respect to my future actions to those who have no faith in my pretensions or who, if they were rash enough to do so, would repay me in my own coin. Therefore my maxim would destroy itself as soon as it got to be a universal law.   (g)

A person who is wearied with life because of a series of misfortunes that has reduced him to despair still possesses sufficient reason to be able to ask himself, whether it may not be contrary to his duty to himself to take his life. Now he asks himself, whether the maxim of his action could possibly be a universal law of nature. But this maxim reads: Out of love of self I make it my principle to shorten my life if its continuation threatens more evil than it promises comfort. But he will still ask, whether his principle of self-love is capable of being a universal law of nature. Then he will soon see that a nature, whose law it would be to destroy life by the very feeling which is meant to stimulate the promotion of life, would contradict itself and therefore not persist as nature. Accordingly the maxim cannot possibly function as a universal law of nature, and it consequently completely refutes the supreme principle of all duty.   (h)

Because the universality of the law according to which effects are produced constitutes what we really mean by *nature* in the most general sense (according to form), that is, the existence of things in so far as it is determined by universal laws, the universal imperative of duty may read thus: *Act as if the maxim of your action by your will were to become a* UNIVERSAL LAW OF NATURE.   (i)

One of the criticisms most often aimed at the categorical imperative is that it has no content and cannot be used to determine right and wrong action. If we consider action phenomenally, this criticism is justified. The categorical imperative, however, is not concerned with phenomenal action. That is the concern of prudence. The categorical imperative states the formal limits within which a will can act without losing its moral and rational character. It lays down the framework within which the will can maintain its integrity as autonomous and something in and of itself.

In our next selection, Kant talks about the nature of man as an end, and gives the justly famous second version of the categorical imperative: "Act so that in your own person as well as in the person of every other you are treating mankind also as an end, never merely as a means."

It should be noted that the same conditions that maintain my own person as an end maintain other persons as ends also. For Kant, the acceptance of the categorical imperative as applying to my acts precludes asking if it applies to the acts of others. I do not accept the categorical imperative for myself in any prudential sense. My recognition and acceptance of the categorical imperative involves all rational beings.

Kant also speaks of a Kingdom of Ends in which each person

will act according to laws given to himself by his own reason, and because all such laws will be rational, no actions will conflict. This is an ideal to be approached in political and social organizations. Elsewhere, in the light of this ideal, Kant gives one of the most interesting interpretations of the contract theory of the origin of such ideal structures. No law shall be passed which would not have been agreed to by the persons involved if it had been offered in the form of a contract to each person.

Selection XVI:
THE AUTONOMOUS WILL AND THE KINGDOM OF ENDS

Assuming, however, that there is something, the *existence of which of itself* has an absolute value which, *as end in itself,* could be the basis of definite laws; then the basis of a possible categorical imperative or practical law would lie in it and in it alone. (a)

If then there is to be a supreme practical principle and in respect to the human will a categorical imperative, then it must be one which, when we conceive what is necessarily an end for everybody because it is the *end in itself,* must constitute an *objective* principle of the will and therefore be able to serve as universal practical law. The basis of this principle is: *Rational nature exists as end in itself.* Man necessarily conceives his own being in this way, and therefore it is thus far a *subjective* principle of human actions. But every other rational being conceives his existence in the same way and on rational grounds identical with my own; therefore it is at the same time an *objective principle* from which as the supreme practical basis all laws of the will must be capable of being deduced. The practical imperative will then read as follows: *Act so that in your own person as well as in the person of every other you are treating mankind also as an end, never merely as a means.* (b)

For rational beings are all subject to the *law* that each one must treat himself and every other being *never merely as means,* but *always as end in itself also.* Consequently there results a systematic union of rational beings by means of common laws, that is to say, a realm which for the very reason that these laws are directed upon the interrelation of these beings as ends and means, may be called a realm of ends. (This is a mere ideal, to be sure.)

A rational being belongs as *member* to this realm of ends if he shares in the making of the universal laws but also is himself subject to these laws. He belongs as *sovereign* to this realm if he makes the laws and is not subject to the will of any other.

A rational being, whether as member or sovereign, must always consider himself as legislating in a realm of ends made possible because of the freedom of the will. He cannot maintain his position as sovereign merely by the maxim of his will, but only if he is a completely independent being without wants and of unlimited capabilities adequate to his will.

Morality then consists in the reference of all action to the making of laws by which alone a realm of ends is possible. This legislating, however, must exist potentially in every rational being and must be able to arise from his will. The principle of the will is then this: to undertake no act according to any other maxim than one can also count as universal law, and therefore to act so *that the will can consider itself at the same time as legislating universally by means of its maxims.*   (c)

In the realm of ends everything has either a PRICE or a DIGNITY. Whatever has a price can be replaced by something else as its equivalent. But what is raised above all price and therefore admits of no equivalent, has a dignity.   (d)

Morality is the condition under which alone a rational being can be end in himself because it alone enables him to be a legislating member in the realm of ends. Consequently morality, and humanity as capable of it, alone possesses dignity. Skill and industry have a commercial price; wit, vivid imagination and moods have an emotional price; however fidelity regards promises and good-will from principle (not instinct) have an intrinsic worth. Neither nature nor art contains anything by which the lack of these could be compensated; for then value does not consist of the effects which result from them, in the benefits or gains that they provide, but in the attitudes, that is to say the maxims of the will which are prepared to express themselves in such actions, even though success should not favor them.   (e)

The principle: In relation to every rational being, yourself and others, act so that in your maxim he can also be considered an end in itself, is basically the same as the principle: Act on a maxim which also contains within itself its own universal validity for every rational being. (f)

As a rational being and consequently belonging to the intelligible world man can never conceive the causality of his own will otherwise than under the idea of freedom; for freedom is independent from the determining causes of the world of the senses (and reason must always attribute such independence to itself). But with the idea of freedom the conception of *autonomy* is always inseparably connected and with this conception the universal principle of morality, which is ideally the basis of all the actions of *rational* beings just as the laws of nature are the basis of all appearances. (g)

The moral "ought" then is one's own necessary "I will" as member of an intelligible world, and is construed as an "ought" only because the person considers himself as also a member of the world of the senses.

(h)

In the previous selections on the Good Will we have read about (1) the "moral feeling" engendered by our recognition of the moral law within us, (2) the "categorical imperative" as the expression of man's nature as a rational being, and (3) the "kingdom of ends" as exemplified in the autonomous will legislating for itself. Kant gives the overall impression that the moral act, which is the rational or free act, follows from the categorical imperative. In his earlier works on ethics Kant seems to hold the view that to be moral, it is enough to be rational. This view, however, in no way explains how responsibility can be assigned for wrong acts. The moral law commands, and Kant holds that when we fail to follow it, we are to blame. But how can we be morally responsible for immoral acts if they are irrational?

In the next selection from the late work *Religion Within the Limits of Reason Alone*, Kant presents a theory of the fully responsible Will. In contrast to Nature, which is the realm of causal necessity, there is Freedom, which is the realm of causal spontaneity. If the idea of autonomy is taken seriously, then man as moral being must be self-determining. The nub of this freedom is the power of choice. Moral man is faced with choosing to act either in accordance with his inclinations and the sensible world, or in accordance with the law of his own being in the intelligible world. Both ways of acting are rational, both are moral in the large sense, and both are free; but the former is wrong and the latter is right, because the former destroys a responsible personality while the latter sustains it.

In the next selection Kant refers to the Will in two different ways.[1] One usage of the term "will" refers to its function of choosing what will determine its activity. In the selection whenever the

---

[1] For this distinction we are indebted to the work of Professor John R. Sibler in his introductory essay, "The Ethical Significance of Kant's Religion," found in *Religion Within the Limits of Reason Alone* (New York: Harper & Row) (Harper Torchbook).

term "will" refers to this function, the translators have placed a small "w" after it. The other usage of the term "will" refers to the essential nature of the willing activity itself, and there is no special mark in the translation. Thus the Good Will is the Will that chooses always to act in the light of its own nature as a willing Being. Kant frequently gives the formal version of the moral imperative: Act so that the maxim of your action can be universalized without self-contradiction. But this theory of Willing implies another version: Choose so that the maxim of your choosing does not destroy the possibility of further choosing. Such an ability to choose implies autonomous, self-determining and rational activity, and with it man is an end in himself. In discussing an organized product of nature as opposed to a mechanical product of nature Kant writes:

A thing exists as a natural purpose if it is (although in a double sense) both cause and effect of itself.[2]

and a little further on—

An organized product of nature is one in which every part is reciprocally purpose (end) and means.[3]

We have remarked previously that Kant understands man's moral and rational nature as purposive, and in man we have the purpose which is its own goal.

Selection XVII:
THE RESPONSIBLE WILL AND PERSONALITY

I. *Concerning the Original Predisposition to Good in Human Nature*

We may conveniently divide this predisposition, with respect to function, into three divisions, to be considered as elements in the fixed character and destiny of man:

(1) The predisposition to *animality* in man, taken as a *living* being;

(2) The predisposition to *humanity* in man, taken as a living and at the same time a *rational* being;

(3) The predisposition to *personality* in man, taken as a rational and at the same time an *accountable* being.*

---

[2] *Critique of Judgment*, p. 132.   [3] *Ibid.*, p. 133.

* We cannot regard this as included in the concept of the preceding, but necessarily must treat it as a special predisposition. For from the fact that a being has reason it by no means follows that this reason, by the mere representing of the fit-

1. The predisposition to *animality* in mankind may be brought under the general title of physical and purely *mechanical* self-love, wherein no reason is demanded. It is threefold: first, for self-preservation; second, for the propagation of the species, through the sexual impulse, and for the care of offspring so begotten; and third for community with other men, i.e., the social impulse....   (a)

2. The predisposition to humanity can be brought under the general title of a self-love which is physical and yet *compares* (for which reason is required); that is to say, we judge ourselves happy or unhappy only by making comparison with others. Out of this self-love springs the inclination *to acquire worth in the opinion of others*....   (b)

3. The predisposition to *personality* is the capacity for respect for the moral law as *in itself a sufficient incentive of the will*^{w}. This capacity for simple respect for the moral law within us would thus be moral feeling, which in and through itself does not constitute an end of the natural predisposition except so far as it is the motivating force of the will^w. Since this is possible only when the free will^w incorporates such moral feeling into its maxim, the property of such a will^w is good character. The latter, like every character of the free will^w, is something which can only be acquired; its possibility, however, demands the presence in our nature of a predisposition on which it is absolutely impossible to graft anything evil. We cannot rightly call the idea of the moral law, with the respect which is inseparable from it, a *predisposition to personality*; it is personality itself (the idea of humanity considered quite intellectually). But the subjective ground for the adoption into our maxims of this respect as a motivating force seems to be an adjunct to our personality, and thus to deserve the name of a predisposition to its furtherance.

If we consider the three predispositions named, in terms of the conditions of their possibility, we find that the first requires no reason, the

---

ness of its maxims to be laid down as universal laws, is thereby rendered capable of determining the will^w unconditionally, so as to be "practical" of itself; at least, not so far as we can see. The most rational mortal being in the world might still stand in need of certain incentives, originating in objects of desire, to determine his choice^w. He might, indeed, bestow the most rational reflection on all that concerns not only the greatest sum of these incentives in him but also the means of attaining the end thereby determined, without ever suspecting the possibility of such a thing as the absolutely imperative moral law which proclaims that it is itself an incentive, and, indeed, the highest. Were it not given us from within, we should never by any ratiocination subtilize it into existence or win over our will^w to it; yet this law is the only law which informs us of the independence of our will^w from determination by all other incentives (of our freedom) and at the same time of the accountability of all our actions.

second is based on practical reason, but a reason thereby subservient to other incentives, while the third alone is rooted in reason which is practical of itself, that is, reason which dictates laws unconditionally. All of these predipositions are not only *good* in negative fashion (in that they do not contradict the moral law) ; they are also predispositions *toward good* (they enjoin the observance of the law). They are *original,* for they are bound up with the possibility of human nature.... (c)

II. *Concerning the Propensity to Evil in Human Nature*

In this capacity for evil there can be distinguished three distinct degrees.... (d)

First: the frailty *(fragilitas)* of human nature is expressed even in the complaint of an Apostle, "What I would, that I do not!" In other words, I adopt the good (the law) into the maxim of my will^w, but this good, which objectively, in its ideal conception *(in thesi),* is an irresistible incentive, is subjectively *(in hypothesi),* when the maxim is to be followed, the weaker (in comparison with inclination).

Second: the impurity *(impuritas, improbitas)* of the human heart consists in this, that although the maxim is indeed good in respect of its object (the intended observance of the law) and perhaps even strong enough for practice, it is yet not purely moral; that is, it has not, as it should have, adopted the law *alone* as its *all-sufficient* incentive: instead it usually (perhaps, every time) stands in need of other incentives beyond this, in determining the will^w to do what duty demands; in other words, actions called for by duty are done not purely for duty's sake.

Third: the wickedness *(vitiositas, pravitas)* or, if you like, the *corruption (corruptio)* of the human heart is the propensity of the will^w to maxims which neglect the incentives springing from the moral law in favor of others which are not moral. It may also be called the *perversity (perversitas)* of the human heart, for it reverses the ethical order [of priority] among the incentives of a *free* will^w; and although conduct which is lawfully good (i.e., legal) may be found with it, yet the cast of mind is thereby corrupted at its root (so far as the moral disposition is concerned), and the man is hence designated as evil. (e)

Now the ground of this evil (1) cannot be placed, as is so commonly done, in man's *sensuous nature* and the natural inclinations arising therefrom. For not only are these not directly related to evil (rather do they afford the occasion for what the moral disposition in its power can manifest, namely, virtue) ; we must not even be considered responsible for their existence (we cannot be, for since they are implanted in us we are not their authors).... (f)

Neither can the ground of this evil (2) be placed in a corruption of the morally legislative reason—as if reason could destroy the authority of the very law which is its own, or deny the obligation arising therefrom; this is absolutely impossible.... (g)

In seeking, therefore, a ground of the morally-evil in man, [we find that] *sensuous nature* comprises too little, for when the incentives which can spring from freedom are taken away, man is reduced to a merely *animal* being. On the other hand, a reason exempt from the moral law, a *malignant reason* as it were (a thoroughly evil will), comprises too much, for thereby opposition to the law would itself be set up as an incentive (since in the absence of all incentives the will^w cannot be determined), and thus the subject would be made a *devilish* being. Neither of these designations is applicable to man. (h)

Man (even the most wicked) does not, under any maxim whatsoever, repudiate the moral law in the manner of a rebel (renouncing obedience to it). The law, rather, forces itself upon him irresistibly by virtue of his moral predisposition; and were no other incentive working in opposition, he would adopt the law into his supreme maxim as the sufficient determining ground of his will^w; that is, he would be morally good. But by virtue of an equally innocent natural predisposition he depends upon the incentives of his sensuous nature and adopts them also (in accordance with the subjective principle of self-love) into his maxim.... (i)

...Hence, the distinction between a good man and one who is evil cannot lie in the difference between the incentives which they adopt into their maxim (not in the content of the maxim), but rather must depend upon *subordination* (the form of the maxim), i.e., *which of the two incentives he makes the condition of the other.* Consequently man (even the best) is evil only in that he reverses the moral order of the incentives when he adopts them into his maxim. He adopts, indeed, the moral law along with the law of self-love; yet when he becomes aware that they cannot remain on a par with each other but that one must be subordinated to the other as its supreme condition, he makes the incentive of self-love and its inclinations the condition of obedience to the moral law.... (j)

Now if a propensity to this* does lie in human nature, there is in man a natural propensity to evil; and since this very propensity must in the end be sought in a will^w which is free, and can therefore be imputed, it is morally evil. This evil is *radical,* because it corrupts the ground of all maxims.... (k)

* [i.e., to the inversion of the ethical order of the incentives.]

We are not, then to call the depravity of human nature *wickedness* taking the word in its strict sense as a disposition (the subjective *principle* of the maxims) to adopt evil as *evil* into our maxim as our incentives (for that is diabolical); we should rather term it the *perversity* of the heart, which, then, because of what follows from it, is also called an *evil heart*. Such a heart may co-exist with a will which in general is good: it arises from the frailty of human nature, the lack of sufficient strength to follow out the principles it has chosen for itself, joined with its impurity, the failure to distinguish the incentives (even of well-intentioned actions) from each other by the gauge of morality; and so at last, if the extreme is reached, [it results] from looking only to the squaring of these actions with the law and not to the derivation of them from the law as the sole motivating spring.   (1)

Kant sees two incentives present to the Will—the moral and the sensuous. It is the presence of inclination that makes the moral incentive an obligation for our Will, and it is the presence of the moral incentive that makes the inclinations a temptation for our Will. Such a view is the result of regarding the idea of an organized product of nature as "reciprocally purpose (end) and means," and suggests that it is this reciprocal activity that constitutes the double-sidedness of the spontaneity of the Will. In so far as prudential activity is concerned with the phenomenal world and moral activity with the noumenal world, they should not be referred to as separate worlds or realms. Rather, they are mutually constituting and regulating activities of the Will. Instead of being separate, theoretical and practical reason become inseparable. But while Kant's thought can be taken to suggest these conceptions, it does not seem possible to state flatly that Kant ever understood his own work fully in this fashion. However, they do suggest the direction in which Kant's thought was developing.

Also, in so far as there is any justification for interpreting Kant in this way, the act of judging becomes central to the whole Critical philosophy in a different way than it seems to be in the earlier Kant.

It is important to point out that although Kant in his moral theory has achieved a theory of the Will that makes responsibility possible, this theory of the Will makes man solely and completely responsible to himself alone. His only Duty is to himself and every choice is his own; hence, forgiveness is impossible by man or God. One of the things the Kantian ethic has come to mean in history is the overpowering sense of isolation that individual man is burdened with. A comparison with Plato is instructive here.

Kant uses Reason in the broadest sense to include all human activities that contain within themselves their own principle of action. Plato too uses Reason in this way. For Kant man's sensuous nature has no principle of its own and attaches itself to outside sources, thus destroying the integrity of the self. Plato's man is much better off because he has an orderly and consistent world outside in which he can act. No such context is present for Kant's individual. The order and consistency of the world depend on the *a priori* principles within man, in short, upon man's rationality. But is man rational—is he inwardly consistent and autonomous? In one sense "yes," and in another, "no." As intelligible creature, man is rational, acts out of inner principles, and is good. But as sensuous creature, he is chaotic and prone to evil. Here are the ultimates in Kant's world. They are not outside but inside of man. Each is equally real, and each helps to constitute the other. What we have here is modern Protestant man, cut off from any world outside that is real in itself, and mortally wounded inside. His only recourse is to hold the world together by himself, and even this is ultimately of no use.

For virtually the same reasons Kant's ethic can be said to epitomize both the strengths and the weaknesses of the modern understanding of individual man.

PART III:
Of Reason in Feeling (Judgment)

We have spoken of the function of Judgment as mediating between the realms of Nature and Freedom.[1] We begin the third *Critique* with a selection that states in a general way how Kant conceives of this mediation.

Selection XVIII:
OF JUDGMENT AS MEDIATOR

The understanding legislates *a priori* for nature as an object of sense —for a theoretical knowledge of it in a possible experience. Reason legislates *a priori* for freedom and its peculiar causality; as the super-

[1]See p. 102.

sensible in the subject, for an unconditioned practical knowledge. The realm of the natural concept under the one legislation and that of the concept of freedom under the other are entirely removed from all mutual influence which they might have on one another (each according to its fundamental laws) by the great gulf that separates the supersensible from phenomena. The concept of freedom determines nothing in respect of the theoretical cognition of nature, and the natural concept determines nothing in respect of the practical laws of freedom. So far, then, it is not possible to throw a bridge from the one realm to the other. But although the determining grounds of causality, according to the concept of freedom (and the practical rules it contains), are not resident in nature, and the sensible cannot determine the supersensible in the subject, yet this is possible conversely (not to be sure, in respect of the cognition of nature, but as regards the effects of the supersensible upon the sensible). This in fact is involved in the concept of a causality through freedom, the *effect* of which is to take place in the world according to its formal laws. The word *cause*, of course, when used of the supersensible, only signified the *ground* which determines the causality of natural things to an effect in accordance with their proper natural laws, although harmoniously with the formal principle of the laws of reason. Although the possibility of this cannot be comprehended, yet the objection of a contradiction alleged to be found in it can be sufficiently answered. The effect in accordance with the concept of freedom is the final purpose which (or its phenomenon in the world of sense) ought to exist, and the condition of the possibility of this is presupposed in nature (in the nature of the subject as a sensible being, that is, as man). The judgment presupposes this *a priori* and without reference to the practical, and thus furnishes the mediating concept between the concepts of nature and that of freedom. It makes possible the transition from the conformity to law in accordance with the former to the final purpose in accordance with the latter, and this by the concept of a *purposiveness* of nature. For thus is cognized the possibility of the final purpose which alone can be actualized in nature in harmony with its laws.

The understanding, by the possibility of its *a priori* laws for nature, gives a proof that nature is only cognized by us as phenomenon and implies, at the same time, that it has a supersensible substrate, though it leaves this quite *undetermined*. The judgment, by its *a priori* principle for the judging of nature according to its possible particular laws, makes the supersensible substrate (both in us and without us) *determinable by means of the intellectual faculty.* But the reason, by its practical *a priori* law, *determines* it; and thus the judgment makes possible the transition from the realm of the natural concept to that of the concept of freedom.

As regards the faculties of the soul in general, in their higher aspect, as containing an autonomy, the understanding is that which contains the *constitutive* principles *a priori* for the *cognitive faculty* (the theoretical cognition of nature). For the *feeling of pleasure and pain* there is the judgment, independently of concepts and sensations which relate to the determination of the faculty of desire and can thus be immediately practical. For the *faculty of desire* there is the reason, which is practical without the mediation of any pleasure whatever. It determines for the faculty of desire, as a superior faculty, the final purpose which carries with it the pure intellectual satisfaction in the object. The concept formed by judgment of a purposiveness of nature belongs to natural concepts, but only as a regulative principle of the cognitive faculty, although the aesthetical judgment upon certain objects (of nature or art) which occasions it, is in respect of the feeling of pleasure or pain a constitutive principle. The spontaneity in the play of the cognitive faculties, the harmony of which contains the ground of this pleasure, makes the above concept [of the purposiveness of nature] fit to be the

All the Faculties of the Mind

Cognitive faculties		Faculties of desire
	Feeling of pleasure and pain	

Cognitive Faculties

Understanding	Judgment	Reason

A Priori Principles

Conformity to law	Purposiveness	Final purpose

Application to

Nature	Art	Freedom

mediating link between the realm of the natural concept and that of the concept of freedom in its effects, while at the same time it promotes the sensibility of the mind to moral feeling. The above table may facili-

tate the review of all the higher faculties according to their systematic
unity.*   (a)

It might be well to recall the problem in the fourth antinomy[1] in
order to clarify the mediation of judgment. On the one hand, the
category of causation makes it impossible to think of a first element
in the chain of causal sequences, since under that category every
event is thought to be preceded and explained by another event. On
the other hand, we must conceive of such a first cause, for without
one there is no sufficient reason for the causal series occurring as it
does. Also, if there is such a first cause, then it is unconditioned,
free, and in fact, inexplicable, and an inexplicable cause is an inadequate explanation of the causal series. Thus, from the point of
view of Reason, it is both logically necessary and logically impossible to assert either alternative. Kant's solution is to distinguish
the phenomenally conditioned realm from the noumenally unconditioned realm as two different types of causality.

It is through judgment that the effects, which are part of the
phenomenal, are ordered and made intelligible. We have seen that
practical activity required us to think of the Will as a supersensible
ground able to produce effects in nature. Such a Will is spontaneous
in action, free in choice, and obligated to the rule of its own being.
Subjectively, this Judgment, which Kant calls "aesthetical," relates
sensible objects to their supersensible ground. Immediately we must
ask: What reasons, are there for supposing that there is a supersensible ground for Nature? Just as practical reason requires the
noumenal Will, so here that part of theoretical reason that is speculative requires us to think of Nature as having a supersensible
ground so that we can complete a purposive system of Nature.
Ultimately just as purposive activity needs a purposeful actor, so a
purposive system of Nature needs a purposeful Author. There is an
analogy here between what Kant did for the system of moral activ-

---

* It has been thought a doubtful point that my divisions in pure philosophy
should always be threefold. But that lies in the nature of the thing. If there is to
be an *a priori* division, it must be either *analytical*, according to the law of contradiction, which is always twofold (*quodlibet ens est aut A aut non A*), or it is
synthetical. And if in this latter case it is to be derived from *a priori concepts* (not
as in mathematics from the intuition corresponding to the concept), the division
must necessarily be trichotomy. For according to what is requisite for synthetical
unity in general, there must be (1) a condition, (2) a conditioned, and (3) the
concept which arises from the union of the conditioned with its condition.
[1] See pp. 132-5.

ity and what he tried to do for the system of teleologically intelligible Nature. And even though teleological judgment is an activity of speculative Reason, the argument for an Author is based on practical and moral grounds.

In a very real way, this argument for an Author resembles the "cogito" argument of Descartes which Kant examined in the section on the idea of the Self (page 130). The principle applied here is the same: No activity without something that acts.[1] Whereas Descartes concluded that the Self exists as an item of knowledge, Kant concludes only that we must think about the Self in order to make human behavior intelligible. It is doubtful, however, that removing the Self from the body of knowledge we possess and placing it in the realm of what we must think removes the objection to the principle. Maintaining the separation between what we think and what we know becomes difficult as the order and intelligibility of what we know becomes more and more dependent on what we think.

Judgment in General

The requirement of order, like that of completeness in the Ideas of Reason, is a theoretical principle. Our phenomenal world of nature must be ordered if it is to be intelligible. The constitutive principles of the Understanding cannot accomplish this ordering by themselves, and the principles of Freedom have nothing to do with the theoretical problem of intelligibility. It is the faculty of Judgment that must complete the task.

In the *Critique of Judgment*, Kant treats the third activity of the soul, feeling, and the third cognitive faculty of man, judgment. Earlier, in connection with the Understanding and the synthetic activities appropriate to it, we said that all synthesis comes about through an act of judgment. Kant calls this constitutive act a "determinant" judgment in which a particular is subsumed under a general law. But judgment is grounded in the subjective aspect of perception as well. Kant speaks of the "imaginative" here just as he did in the section on the unity of Understanding; he is concerned with discovering principles for making intelligible given particulars. He calls this attempt to discover such principles "reflective" judgment, and its results are not a part of Nature, but are necessary to think in connection with Nature. Reflective judgments express the concern of Reason for completeness and intelligibility

[1] For clarification of this principle see p. 116, especially footnote 2.

in our world, and are grounded in the third activity of the soul, feeling.

Feeling, as such, is a subjective element in perception; that is, it has no cognitive connection with its object. But feeling is indicative of purposiveness which implies appropriateness. This feeling of appropriateness is reflected in aesthetic judgment and teleological judgment. Together they constitute the major division of the third *Critique.*

Aesthetic judgments are made on the basis of the harmony between the objective cognitive side of our experience and the subjective imaginative side. Such harmony records the pleasure produced when our perceptions are so ordered and constituted that the object experienced conforms to the ends of speculative reason. And since the aims of reason are the same for all men, aesthetic judgments, although subjective, hold for all men.

Susceptibility to pleasure from reflection upon the forms of things (of nature as well as of art) indicates not only a purposiveness of the objects in relation to the reflective judgment, conformably to the concept of nature in the subject, but also conversely a purposiveness of the subject in respect of the objects according to their form or even their formlessness, in virtue of the concept of freedom.[2]

Aesthetic judgment is not only of taste in relation to the beautiful, but also of "spiritual feeling" in relation to the sublime.

Teleological judgments, on the other hand, attribute the quality of appropriateness to the object of experience as such—for example, the structure of the eye is judged to be appropriate for seeing. Such a conception of the "things" of Nature is completely unwarranted on phenomenal grounds, and yet those "things" require more of an explanation than mechanical science can ever give. While Kant gives the impression in the first *Critique* that the Understanding is adequate to the task of knowing the system of Nature, in the third *Critique* he flatly states that the categories of the Understanding will always be inadequate. Teleological judgment is necessary for the system of Nature as well.

But the representation of purposiveness of the second kind (teleological), since it refers the form of the object, not to the cognitive faculties of the subject in the apprehension of it, but to a definite cognition of

2 *Critique of Judgment,* p. 28.

the object under a given concept, has nothing to do with a feeling of pleasure in things, but only with the understanding in its judgment upon them.[3]

In the following selections we shall consider aesthetic and teleological judgments particularly as they throw light on the nature of judgment as activity and its function as mediator between Nature and Freedom.

Aesthetic Judgments

The ground for this type of reflective judgment is the subjective feeling of pleasure given in perception. An object is judged beautiful when it is in harmony with the structure of the Understanding. In a different way, the experience of the sublime occurs in relation to the structure of Reason.

The beautiful in nature is connected with the form of the object, which consists in having [definite] boundaries. The sublime, on the other hand, is to be found in a formless object, so far as in it or by occasion of it *boundlessness* is represented, and yet its totality is also present to thought. Thus the beautiful seems to be regarded as the presentation of an indefinite concept of understanding, the sublime as that of a like concept of reason. Therefore the satisfaction in the one case is bound up with the representation of *quality*, in the other with that of *quantity*. And the latter satisfaction is quite different in kind from the former, for this [the beautiful] directly brings with it a feeling of the furtherance of life, and thus is compatible with charms and with the play of the imagination. But the other [the feeling of the sublime] is a pleasure that arises only indirectly; viz., it is produced by the feeling of a momentary checking of the vital powers and a consequent stronger outflow of them, so that it seems to be regarded as emotion—not play, but earnest in the exercise of the imagination.[1]

The next three selections deal with the Beautiful, the Sublime, and Art and Genius. Our comments will follow each selection.

Selection XIX:
THE BEAUTIFUL

Taste is the faculty of judging of an object or a method of representing it by an *entirely disinterested* satisfaction or dissatisfaction. The object of such satisfaction is called *beautiful*.   (a)

[3] *Ibid.*, p. 29.
[1] *Critique of Judgment*, p. 82 ff.

The pleasant, the beautiful, and the good designate three different relations of representations to the feeling of pleasure and pain, in reference to which we distinguish from one another objects or methods of representing them. And the expressions corresponding to each, by which we mark our complacency in them, are not the same. That which *gratifies* a man is called *pleasant;* that which merely *pleases* him is *beautiful;* that which is *esteemed* [or *approved*] by him, i.e., that to which he accords an objective worth, is *good.* Pleasantness concerns irrational animals also, but beauty only concerns men, i.e., animal, but still rational, beings—not merely *quâ* rational (e.g., spirits), but *quâ* animal also—and the good concerns every rational being in general. This is a proposition which can only be completely established and explained in the sequel. We may say that, of all these three kinds of satisfaction, that of taste in the beautiful is alone a disinterested and *free* satisfaction; for no interest, either of sense or of reason, here forces our assent. Hence we may say of satisfaction that it is related in the three aforesaid cases to *inclinaton,* to *favor,* or to *respect.*[1] Now *favor* is the only free satisfaction. (b)

The judgment of taste itself does not *postulate* the agreement of everyone (for that can only be done by a logically universal judgment because it can adduce reasons); it only *imputes* this agreement to everyone, as a case of the rule in respect of which it expects, not confirmation by concepts, but assent from others. The universal voice is, therefore, only an idea (we do not yet inquire upon what it rests). It may be uncertain whether or not the man who believes that he is laying down a judgment of taste is, as a matter of fact, judging in conformity with that idea: but that he refers his judgment thereto and consequently that it is intended to be a judgment of taste, he announces by the expression "beauty." (c)

Therefore it can be nothing else than the subjective purposiveness in the representation of an object without any purpose (either objective or subjective), and thus it is the mere form of purposiveness in the representation by which an object is *given* to us, so far as we are conscious of it, which constitutes the satisfaction that we without a concept judge to be universally communicable; and, consequently, this is the determining ground of the judgment of taste. (d)

There can be no objective rule of taste which shall determine by

[1] Understanding is bound by the categories, Reason bound by the moral law, but Judging is a free spontaneous act based on a free satisfaction.

means of concepts what is beautiful. For every judgment from this source is aesthetical; i.e., the feeling of the subject, and not a concept of the object, is its determining ground. (e)

Kant explains a judgment of taste in the light of the Unity of the Understanding (pages 165–168). The unity we create from the multiplicity of our phenomenal world has its ground in imaginative activity. This activity not only schematizes the diversity of the categories throughout our phenomenal experience, but also makes the "manifold of successive intuitions" into a unified "object for me" through an act of synthesis. The whole level of perception and intuition is part of the imagination that through its freedom and spontaneity serves as the ground for judgments of taste. The feeling of pleasure arises when the perceptual and imaginative level of intuition is in harmony with the unified conceptions of the categories of the Understanding. Kant writes:

> The subjective condition of all judgments is the faculty of judgment itself. This, when used with reference to a representation by which an object is given, requires the accordance of two representative powers, viz., imagination (for the intuition and comprehension of the manifold) and understanding (for the concept as a representation of the unity of this comprehension). Now because no concept of the object lies here at the basis of the judgment, it can only consist in the subsumption of the imagination itself (in the case of a representation by which an object is given), under the conditions that the understanding requires to pass from intuition to concepts. That is, because the freedom of the imagination consists in the fact that it schematizes without any concept, the judgment of taste must rest on a mere sensation of the reciprocal activity of the imagination in its *freedom* and the understanding with its *conformity to law*. It must therefore rest on a feeling, which makes us judge the object by the purposiveness of the representation (by which an object is given) in respect of the furtherance of the cognitive faculty in its free play. Taste, then, as subjective judgment, contains a principle of subsumption, not of intuitions under concepts, but of the *faculty* of intuitions or presentations (i.e., the imagination) under the *faculty* of the concepts (i.e., the understanding) so far as the former *in its freedom* harmonizes with the latter *in its conformity to* law.[1]

[1] *Critique of Judgment*, p. 129.

Selection XX:
THE SUBLIME

But the analysis of the sublime involves a division not needed in the case of the beautiful, viz., a division into the *mathematically* and the *dynamically sublime.*

For the feeling of the sublime brings with it as its characteristic feature a *movement* of the mind bound up with the judging of the object, while in the case of the beautiful taste presupposes and maintains the mind in *restful* contemplation. Now this movement ought to be judged as subjectively purposive (because the sublime pleases us), and thus it is referred through the imagination either to the *faculty of cognition* or *of desire.* In either reference the purposiveness of the given representation ought to be judged only in respect of this *faculty* (without purpose or interest), but in the first case it is ascribed to the object as a *mathematical* determination of the imagination, in the second as *dynamical.* And hence we have this twofold way of representing the sublime.   (a)

Nature is therefore sublime in those of its phenomena whose intuition brings with it the idea of its infinity. This last can only come by the inadequacy of the greatest effort of our imagination to estimate the magnitude of an object. But now, in mathematical estimation of magnitude, the imagination is equal to providing a sufficient measure for every object, because the numerical concepts of the understanding, by means of progression, can make any measure adequate to any given magnitude. Therefore it must be the *aesthetical* estimation of magnitude in which the effort toward comprehension surpasses the power of the imagination. (b)

We hence see also that true sublimity must be sought only in the mind of the [subject] judging, not in the natural object the judgment upon which occasions this state. Who would call sublime, e.g., shapeless mountain masses piled in wild disorder upon one another with their pyramids of ice, or the gloomy, raging sea? But the mind feels itself raised in its own judgment if, while contemplating them without any reference to their form, and abandoning itself to the imagination and to the reason —which, although placed in combination with the imagination without any definite purpose, merely extends it—it yet finds the whole power of the imagination inadequate to its ideas.   (c)

Now, in the immensity of nature and in the insufficiency of our faculties to take in a standard proportionate to the aesthetical estimation of the magnitude of its *realm,* we find our own limitation, although at the same time in our rational faculty we find a different, nonsensuous standard, which has that infinity itself under it as a unity, in comparison with which everything in nature is small, and thus in our mind we find a superiority to nature even in its immensity. And so also the irresistibility of its might, while making us recognize our own [physical] impotence, considered as beings of nature, discloses to us a faculty of judging independently of and a superiority over nature, on which is based a kind of self-preservation entirely different from that which can be attacked and brought into danger by external nature. This humanity in our person remains unhumiliated, though the individual might have to submit to this dominion. (d)

But although the judgment upon the sublime in nature needs culture (more than the judgment upon the beautiful), it is not therefore primarily produced by culture and introduced in a merely conventional way into society. Rather it has its root in human nature, even in that which, alike with common understanding, we can impute to and expect of everyone, viz., in the tendency to the feeling for (practical) ideas, i.e., to what is moral.

Hereon is based the necessity of that agreement of the judgment of others about the sublime with our own which we include in the latter. For just as we charge with want of *taste* the man who is indifferent when passing judgment upon an object of nature that we regard as beautiful, so we say of him who remains unmoved in the presence of that which we judge to be sublime: He has no *feeling*. But we claim both from every man. (e)

The feeling of the sublime is more complex than that of beauty. The first condition of it is nature in its more massive, powerful, and even destructive states. Such states surpass the mind's power to comprehend and order. They literally overwhelm the senses. This kind of aesthetic presentation produces the second aspect of the sublime—the contrast of our moral nature and worth as noumena with our sensuous phenomenal nature that is overwhelmed. In the experience of the sublime, we take pleasure in our superiority as persons over the blind, purposeless forces of nature. In the teeth of the gale man is reduced, and yet in being so, exalted. This is the root of the feeling of the sublime.

Of both the beautiful and the sublime Kant makes the following summaries.

If we take the result of the foregoing exposition of the two kinds of aesthetical judgments, there arise therefrom the following short explanations:

The *beautiful* is what pleases in the mere judgment (and therefore not by the medium of sensation in accordance with a concept of the understanding). It follows at once from this that it must please apart from all interest.

The *sublime* is what pleases immediately through its opposition to the interest of sense.

Both, as explanations of aesthetical universally valid judging, are referred to subjective grounds—in the one case to grounds of sensibility, in favor of the contemplative understanding; in the other case in *opposition to* sensibility, but on behalf of the purposes of practical reason. Both, however, united in the same subject, are purposive in reference to the moral feeling. The beautiful prepares us to love disinterestedly something, even nature itself; the sublime prepares us to esteem something highly even in opposition to our own (sensible) interest.[1]

Kant, in stressing the disinterestedness of the aesthetic feeling, is squarely in opposition to the bulk of contemporary interpretations of the beautiful, which most often understand it as the satisfaction of some personal need or desire. In contrast to this modern, subjective way of conceiving aesthetic experience, Kant harks back, in one sense, to an older, more realistic view that sees aesthetic experience as a response to objective external conditions. Yet in another sense, Kant is maintaining our fundamental relatedness to the external world, as he reinterprets the creativity of human reason in the context of aesthetic experience.

In the next selection Kant discusses both the creative process and the imagination as a function of the human "spirit." By "spirit" he means the person as a dynamic participant.

Selection XXI:
ART AND GENIUS

By right we ought only to describe as art, production through freedom, i.e., through a will that places reason at the basis of its action. For although we like to call the product of bees (regularly built cells of wax) a work of art, this is only by way of analogy: as soon as we feel that this work of theirs is based on no proper rational deliberation, we say that

---

[1] *Critique of Judgment*, p. 107.

it is a product of nature (of instinct), and as art only ascribe it to their Creator. (a)

But it is not inexpedient to recall that, in all free arts, there is yet requisite something compulsory or, as it is called, mechanism, without which the spirit, which must be free in art and which alone inspires the work, would have no body and would evaporate altogether; e.g., in poetry there must be an accuracy and wealth of language, and also prosody and measure. [It is not inexpedient, I say, to recall this], for many modern educators believe that the best way to produce a free art is to remove it from all constraint, and thus to change it from work into mere play. (b)

In a product of beautiful art, we must become conscious that it is art and not nature; but yet the purposiveness in its form must seem to be as free from all constraint of arbitrary rules as if it were a product of mere nature. On this feeling of freedom in the play of our cognitive faculties, which must at the same time be purposive, rests that pleasure which alone is universally communicable, without being based on concepts. Nature is beautiful because it looks like art, and art can only be called beautiful if we are conscious of it as art while yet it looks like nature. (c)

Genius is the talent (or natural gift) which gives the rule to art. Since talent, as the innate productive faculty of the artist, belongs itself to nature, we may express the matter thus: Genius is the innate mental disposition (*ingenium*) *through which* nature gives the rule to art. (d)

We thus see (1) that genius is a *talent* for producing that for which no definite rule can be given; it is not a mere aptitude for what can be learned by a rule. Hence *originality* must be its first property. (2) But since it also can produce original nonsense, its products must be models, i.e., *exemplary*, and they consequently ought not to spring from imitation, but must serve as a standard or rule of judgment for others. (3) It cannot describe or indicate scientifically how it brings about its products, but it gives the rule just as nature does. Hence the author of a product for which he is indebted to his genius does not know himself how he has come by his ideas; and he has not the power to devise the like at pleasure or in accordance with a plan, and to communicate it to others in precepts that will enable them to produce similar products. (e)

Spirit, in an aesthetical sense, is the name given to the animating principle of the mind. But that by means of which this principle animates the soul, the material which it applies to the [purpose], is what puts the mental powers purposively into swing, i.e., into such a play as maintains itself and strengthens the mental powers in their exercise.

Now I maintain that this principle is no other than the faculty of presenting *aesthetical ideas.* And by an aesthetical idea I understand that representation of the imagination which occasions much thought, without however any definite thought, i.e., any *concept,* being capable of being adequate to it; it consequently cannot be completely compassed and made intelligible by language. We easily see that it is the counterpart (pendant) of a *rational idea,* which conversely is a concept to which no *intuition* (or representation of the imagination) can be adequate.

The imagination (as a productive faculty of cognition) is very powerful in creating another nature, as it were, out of the material that actual nature gives it. We entertain ourselves with it when experience becomes too commonplace, and by it we remold experience, always indeed in accordance with analogical laws, but yet also in accordance with principles which occupy a higher place in reason (laws, too, which are just as natural to us as those by which understanding comprehends empirical nature). Thus we feel our freedom from the law of association (which attaches to the empirical employment of imagination), so that the material supplied to us by nature in accordance with this law can be worked up into something different which surpasses nature.

Such representations of the imagination we may call *ideas,* partly because they at least strive after something which lies beyond the bounds of experience and so seek to approximate to a presentation of concepts of reason (intellectual ideas), thus giving to the latter the appearance of objective reality, but especially because no concept can be fully adequate to them as internal intuitions.   (f)

Intuitions are always required to establish the reality of our concepts. If the concepts are empirical, the intuitions are called *examples.* If they are pure concepts of understanding, the intuitions are called *schemata.*   (g)

All intuitions which we supply to concepts *a priori* are therefore either *schemata* or *symbols,* of which the former contain direct, the latter indirect, presentations of the concept. The former do this demonstratively; the latter by means of an analogy (for which we avail ourselves even of empirical intuitions) in which the judgment exercises a double function, first applying the concept to the object of a sensible intuition, and then applying the mere rule of the reflection made upon that intuition to a quite different object of which the first is only the symbol.   (h)

Now I say the beautiful is the symbol of the morally good, and that it is only in this respect (a reference which is natural to every man and which every man postulates in others as a duty) that it gives pleasure with a claim for the agreement of everyone else. By this the mind is made conscious of a certain ennoblement and elevation above the mere sensibility to pleasure received through sense, and the worth of others is estimated in accordance with a like maxim of their judgment.... (i)

Kant's ideas on what constitutes art are especially applicable to those arts which are dynamic activities. One of the chief requirements of such an art is that it be "natural." It must not look labored. Yet, at the same time, we know that it is a purposive activity. Actually, these are criteria for excellence in performance, although Kant does not so restrict them. Just as there were serious objections to the adequacy of the categorical imperative for judging the consequences of an act to see if they are moral, so there are objections to the adequacy of these criteria for judging "objects of art" to see if they are art. Just as Kant's ethic is concerned with activities and not objects, so his aesthetic is concerned with activities and not objects. (Akin to the regulative function of Reason and not the constitutive function of Understanding.)

In art as well as in morality, the object is an activity, purposive in character and springing from a Will. We have in Kant's aesthetic theory, no matter what else you may apply it to, more information upon what it means to be a rational human Will. We have seen the moral qualities of a Good Will. Here we see the aesthetic qualities of perfected purpose in Willing. The Will has as a part of its dynamic not only an ethic because it requires choice, but an aesthetic because it requires judgment. Human purpose must not become mechanical or it will lose all "feeling." And it must retain form, or it will cease to produce the pleasure we find in harmony and balance. In this context "disinterestedness" is one of the criteria of balance.

These aesthetic intuitions of "appropriateness" have their application to the theoretical and speculative aspects of human activity as well. The demands of reason for completeness, have their criteria in the intuitions Kant finds in aesthetic judgment. These intuitions may be subjective, in that they refer to nothing in experience. However, they are always objective, indeed *a priori*, in that they indicate whether the requirements of reason are fulfilled. The schemata serve this purpose directly for the constitutive categories of the Understanding, and the aesthetic ideas indirectly for the regulative ideas of Reason. In this way the beautiful is the symbol of perfected

form and the sublime is the symbol of moral power. In an "organized" being, which Kant discusses in the next selection, the moral
and aesthetic dimensions are very closely interrelated.

c) Teleological Judgment

For the sake of theoretical knowlege, we have seen how man
must think in certain categories, and for the sake of practice, he
must act according to certain imperatives. Now, for the sake of
completeness under reason, man must combine the two by judging
Nature in the light of the concepts of purposiveness and appropriateness. What are we to make of this endeavor?

Kant is above all concerned with certainty in knowledge. and having realized that the connections and continuities that knowledge
clarifies cannot be grounded in our direct experience of an external
world, he proceeds to discover the grounds for that certainty within
man rather than in the external world. Perhaps the quest for certainty is doomed in either area, but in his internal search, Kant
finds his principles in the basic expressions of individual activity.
In the three *Critiques,* he treats these expressions as separate, but it
seems that he desires the world he constructs to be an organic whole
in the same way the individual is.

We have emphasized that individual activity is organic when it
uses the imagination to unify the categories of the Understanding,
the regulative ideas to unify the activity of Understanding, the
moral and purposive elements of Practical Reason to build an ethic,
and the aesthetic ideas as the basis for judgment. The focal point
of all this unification is man's rational nature as purposive being.

In this last section on teleological judgment, the question arises
whether there is any justification for attributing purpose to the
things of nature themselves. The first *Critique* gives the impression
that the categories of the Understanding are sufficient for the explanation of the system of nature in experience. But a scientific
understanding does not seem sufficient for intelligibility. Rational
intelligibility requires purpose, and we have already seen that human activity, the results of which are in the phenomenal world, cannot be understood scientifically. There would also appear to be other
objects and events in experience that cannot be understood apart
from some reference to a "noumenal ground" rather than to an
"antecedent cause."

Mechanical principles do not preclude the possibility of a purposive understanding, but whether there are any grounds for supposing that such purposive principles are needed is a question we shall deal with after the second of the three selections to follow.

In the first selection Kant discusses the nature of an organized being in contrast to a mechanical being. Although in recent years we have come to see how closely related are the organic and the mechanical, the difference still represents a crucial problem for our way of thinking about "the scientific" and "the world."

Selection XXII:
NATURAL PURPOSES AND ORGANIZED BEINGS

The teleological act of judgment is rightly brought to bear, at least problematically, upon the investigation of nature, but only in order to bring it under principles of observation and inquiry according to the *analogy* with the causality of purpose, without any pretense to *explain* it thereby. It belongs therefore to the reflective and not to the determinant judgment. The concept of combinations and forms of nature in accordance with purposes is then at least *one principle more* for bringing its phenomena under rules where the laws of simply mechanical causality do not suffice. (a)

In order to see that a thing is only possible as a purpose, that is to be forced to seek the causality of its origin, not in the mechanism of nature, but in a cause whose faculty of action is determined through concepts, it is requisite that its form be not possible according to mere natural laws, i.e., laws which can be cognized by us through the understanding alone when applied to objects of sense, but that even the empirical knowledge of it as regards its cause and effect presupposes concepts of reason. (b)

But in order to regard a thing cognized as a natural product as a purpose also—consequently as a *natural purpose,* if this is not a contradiction—something more is required. I would say provisionally: a thing exists as a natural purpose if it is [although in a double sense] both *cause and effect of itself.* For herein lies a causality the like of which cannot be combined with the mere concept of a nature without attributing to it a purpose; it can certainly be thought without contradiction, but cannot be comprehended. We shall elucidate the determination of this idea of a natural purpose by an example before we analyze it completely.

In the first place, a tree generates another tree according to a known natural law. But the tree produced is of the same genus, and so it produces itself *generically*. On the other hand, as effect it is continually self-produced; on the other hand, as cause it continually produces itself, and so perpetuates itself generically.

Secondly, a tree produces itself as an *individual*. This kind of effect no doubt we call growth, but it is quite different from any increase according to mechanical laws and is to be reckoned as generation, though under another name. The matter that the tree incorporates it previously works up into a specifically peculiar quality, which natural mechanism external to it cannot supply, and thus it develops itself by aid of a material which, as compounded, is of its own product.   (c)

Thirdly, each part of a tree generates itself in such a way that the maintenance of any one part depends reciprocally on the maintenance of the rest.   (d)

In a watch, one part is the instrument for moving the other parts, but the wheel is not the effective cause of the production of the others; no doubt one part is for the sake of the others, but it does not exist by their means. In this case the producing cause of the parts and of their form is not contained in the nature (of the material), but is external to it in a being which can produce effects according to ideas of a whole possible by means of its causality. Hence a watch wheel does not produce other wheels; still less does one watch produce other watches, utilizing (organizing) foreign material for that purpose; hence it does not replace of itself parts of which it has been deprived, nor does it make good what is lacking in a first formation by the addition of the missing parts, nor if it has gone out of order does it repair itself—all of which, on the contrary, we may expect from organized nature. An organized being is then not a mere machine, for that has merely *moving* power, but it possesses in itself *formative* power of a self-propagating kind which it communicates to its materials though they have it not of themselves; it organizes them, in fact, and this cannot be explained by the mere mechanical faculty of motion.   (e)

This principle, which is at the same time a definition, is as follows: *An organized product of nature is one in which every part is reciprocally purpose* [end] *and means.* In it nothing is vain, without purpose, or to be ascribed to a blind mechanism of nature.   (f)

————————

There are reasons why we cannot understand an organized being that is "both cause and effect of itself." First, an organized being requires the use of a "cause" that is not prior to its effect. Second,

it involves an inference from a directly observable effect to an un-
observable "ground" or "cause," a ground continuous with and con-
temporaneous with its effect and yet different from its effect. The
knowledge of such a ground, because indirect, would not be certain.
As Kant puts it, "It embraces in itself necessity and at the same
time a contingency of the form of the object." [1] What grounds
there are for supposing that we must think this way is the subject of
our last two selections.

Selection XXIII:
THE SYSTEM OF NATURE

Just as reason in the theoretical consideration of nature must assume
the idea of an unconditioned necessity of its original ground, so also it
presupposes in the practical [sphere] its own (in respect of nature)
unconditioned causality, or freedom, in that it is conscious of its own
moral command. Here the objective necessity of the act, as a duty, is
opposed to that necessity which it would have as an event if its ground
lay in nature and not in freedom (i.e., in the causality of reason). The
morally absolutely necessary act is regarded as physically quite contingent, since that which *ought* necessarily to happen often does not
happen. It is clear, then, that it is owing to the subjective constitution
of our practical faculty that the moral laws must be represented as commands and the actions conforming to them as duties, and that reason expresses this necessity, not by an "is" (happens), but by an "ought to
be." This would not be the case were reason considered as in its causality
independent of sensibility (as the subjective condition of its application
to objects of nature), and so as cause in an intelligible world entirely
in agreement with the moral law. For in such a world there would be no
distinction between "ought to do" and "does," between a practical law
of that which is possible through us and the theoretical law of that which
is actual through us.   (a)

But now it is at least possible to consider the material world as mere
phenomenon and to think as its substrate something like a thing in itself
(which is not phenomenon), and to attach to this a corresponding intellectual intuition (even though it is not ours). Thus there would be,
although incognizable by us, a supersensible real ground for nature, to
which we ourselves belong. In this we consider according to mechanical
laws what is necessary in nature regarded as an object of sense, but we
consider according to teleological laws the agreement and unity of its

[1] *Critique of Judgment*, p. 244.

particular laws and its forms—which in regard to mechanism we must judge contingent—regarded as objects of reason (in fact the whole of nature as a system). Thus we should judge nature according to two different kinds of principles without the mechanical way of explanation being shut out by the teleological, as if they contradicted each other.   (b)

In a thing that we must judge as a natural purpose (an organized being), we can no doubt try all the known and yet to be discovered laws of mechanical production, and even hope to make good progress therewith, but we can never get rid of the call for a quite different ground of production for the possibility of such a product, viz., causality by means of purposes. Absolutely no human reason (in fact no finite reason like ours in quality, however much it may surpass it in degree) can hope to understand the production of even a blade of grass by mere mechanical causes. As regards the possibility of such an object, the teleological connection of causes and effects is quite indispensable for the judgment, even for studying it by the clue of experience. For external objects as phenomena an adequate ground related to purposes cannot be met with; this, although it lies in nature, must only be sought in the supersensible substrate of nature, from all possible insight into which we are cut off. Hence it is absolutely impossible for us to produce from nature itself grounds of explanation for purposive combinations, and it is necessary by the constitution of the human cognitive faculties to seek the supreme ground of these purposive combinations in an original understanding as the cause of the world.   (c)

Hereon is based a privilege and, on account of the importance which the study of nature by the principle of mechanism has for the theoretical use of our reason, also an appeal. We should explain all products and occurrences in nature, even the most purposive, by mechanism as far as is in our power (the limits of which we cannot give an account of in this kind of investigation). But at the same time we are not to lose sight of the fact that those things which we cannot even state for investigation, except under the concept of a purpose of reason, must in conformity with the essential constitution of our reason and notwithstanding those mechanical causes be subordinated by us finally to causality in accordance with purposes.   (d)

———————

There is a difficulty here that is most often pointed out in connection with the first level of synthesis in the first *Critique*. It indicates real ambiguity in Kant's thinking. As long as you maintain that the "determinate judgments" of the Understanding are constitutive of the phenomenal world of experience, and that the "reflective judgments" of Reason concern only our relation to this phenomenal world, there are no grounds, by definition, for saying that mechanical principles will not explain a blade of grass simply because it is by virtue of these principles that you have the experience of "a blade of grass" as such. To say that the blade of grass cannot be explained by the principles that constitute it is circular and appears to be self-contradictory.

From one point of view, the categories constitute the blade of grass. From another point of view, the blade of grass can either be interpreted by use of the mechanical categories that are directly certifiable in experience scientifically, or it may be interpreted on the basis of purposive ideas that are never directly certifiable in experience. It is impossible from the first point of view to assert that the purposive alternative is real unless somehow the categories imply the ideas. The application of the categories presupposes the Ideas of Reason and in connection with this purposive way of thinking Kant mentions an "analogy," but such analogy must have a foundation in the blade of grass as well as in the activity of human reason (which is the only ground he mentions). This point of view appears to be similar to the way in which the sensuous (phenomenal) and the intelligible (noumenal) were understood in Selection XVII (p. 160 ff). But as strong as is Kant's emphasis upon creative reason, there is also very strong belief in an objectively real external world. Kant's problem then lies in reconciling the creative contribution of human reason with the reality of the external world. He never fully forges "creative realism" [1] because he tends to conceive of human reason and the external world in mutually exclusive ways. But his conception of the Will in *Religion Within the Limits of Reason Alone* and of organized being in this third *Critique* represent real progress towards a solution over his earlier conceptions of the problem.

For Kant there are no grounds for the analogy in the blade of grass from the point of view of theoretical reason and our knowledge of objects. Whatever grounds there are lie in the blade of grass, as an activity, from the point of view of practical reason. In a descriptive passage concerning our experience of the world (p. 139), Kant speaks of appropriateness and design, but never gives the basis

[1] Realism holds that the concepts, ideas, and distinctions in man's thought have a real foundation in the external world, and is opposed to the view that they are constructs of our minds reflecting our desires and interests only.

for such a description. It seems, however, that the basis for the analogy lies in practical reason and the faculty of desire. Granted the moral argument for a purposive creator, the blade of grass can be understood as a product of the purposive activity of this creator. Kant is affirming a relationship between this creator and Nature analogous to the relation between the noumenal self as ground for the purposive activity of practical reason and the consequences of this activity in Nature. With this relationship as a basis, teleological judgment as a mediation between Author and Nature is possible.

In order to clarify further this Author-Nature relation making teleological judgment possible as well as prepare for our next selection, let us consider the differing perspectives on God gained in our study of Kant. In Selection X (p. 137) on The Ideas of Reason, God is an idea of Speculative Reason embodying the total relatedness of all that is and, as regulative principle, making the task of knowing possible. In Selection XIII (p. 146) on the Postulates of Practical Reason, God is the guarantor of that continuity and connectedness of means to ends ensuring that a good will is a happy one. And in Selection XXIV, on Teleological Judgment, God is the creator and sustainer of that total relatedness of things through purposive activity which is Reason in Nature and in Freedom (the Will). Taken together these constitute the three aspects of God's activity and are exemplified in the Postulates of Practical Reason as the ultimate conditions of all willing (p. 148ff.). In our last selection Kant presents his famous moral argument for such a purposive creator.

Selection XXIV:
A PURPOSIVE CREATOR

Now we have in the world only one kind of beings whose causality is teleological, i.e., is directed to purposes, and is at the same time so constituted that the law according to which they have to determine purposes for themselves is represented as unconditioned and independent of natural conditions, and yet as in itself necessary. The being of this kind is man, but man considered as noumenon, the only natural being in which we can recognize, on the side of its peculiar constitution, a supersensible faculty (*freedom*) and also the law of causality, together with the object, which this faculty may propose to itself as highest purpose (the highest good in the world).

Now of man (and so of every rational creature in the world) as a

moral being it can no longer be asked why (*quem in finem*) he exists.
His existence involves the highest purpose to which, as far as is in his
power, he can subject the whole of nature, contrary to which at least he
cannot regard himself as subject to any influence of nature.   (a)

The moral law, as the formal rational condition of the use of our freedom, obliges us by itself alone, without depending on any purpose as
material condition, but it nevertheless determines for us, and indeed *a
priori*, a final purpose toward which it obliges us to strive, and this purpose is the *highest good in the world* possible through freedom.

The subjective condition under which man (and, according to all our
concepts, every rational finite being) can set a final purpose before himself under the above law is happiness. Consequently, the highest physical
good possible in the world, to be furthered as a final purpose as far as
in us lies, is *happiness*, under the objective condition of the harmony of
man with the law of *morality* as worthiness to be happy.

But it is impossible for us, in accordance with all our rational faculties,
to represent these two requirements of the final purpose to us by the
moral law as *connected* by merely natural causes, and yet as conformable
to the idea of that final purpose. Hence the concept of the *practical necessity* of such a purpose through the application of our powers does not
harmonize with the theoretical concept of the *physical possibility* of its
performance, if we connect with our freedom no other causality (as a
means) than that of nature.

Consequently, we must assume a moral world cause (an author of the
world), in order to set before ourselves a final purpose consistently with
the moral law, and in so far as the latter is necessary, so far (i.e., in the
same degree and on the same ground) the former also must be necessarily assumed, i.e., we must admit that there is a God.   (b)

We may then suppose the case of a righteous man [e.g., Spinoza], who
holds himself firmly persuaded that there is no God and also (because
in respect of the object of morality a similar consequence results) no
future life; how is he to judge of his own inner purposive destination,
by means of the moral law, which he reveres in practice? He desires no
advantage to himself from following it, either in this or another world;
he wishes, rather, disinterestedly to establish the good to which that
holy law directs all his powers. But his effort is bounded; and from
nature, although he may expect here and there a contingent accordance,
he can never expect a regular harmony agreeing according to constant
rules (such as his maxims are and must be, internally) with the purpose
that he yet feels himself obliged and impelled to accomplish. Deceit,
violence, and envy will always surround him although he himself be

honest, peaceable, and kindly; and the righteous men with whom he meets will, notwithstanding all their worthiness of happiness, be yet subjected by nature, which regards not this, to all the evils of want, disease, and untimely death, just like the beasts of the earth. So it will be until one wide grave engulfs them together (honest or not, it makes no difference) and throws them back—who were able to believe themselves the final purpose of creation—into the abyss of the purposeless chaos of matter from which they were drawn. The purpose, then, which this well-intentioned person had and ought to have before him in his pursuit of moral laws, he must certainly give up as impossible. Or else, if he wishes to remain dependent upon the call of his moral internal destination and not to weaken the respect with which the moral law immediately inspires him, by assuming the nothingness of the single, ideal, final purpose adequate to its high demand (which cannot be brought about without a violation of moral sentiment), he must, as he well can—since there is at least no contradiction from a practical point of view in forming a concept of the possibility of a morally prescribed final purpose—assume the being of a moral author of the world, that is, a God.   (c)

The subjective condition of the fulfillment of the moral law is happiness. However, since there is no connection between worthiness to be happy and happiness in experience, there is no ground for any expectation of happiness. The harmony of the conditions is not necessitated by the fact of the moral law.

There are some serious difficulties in Kant's argument for a purposive creator, and some doubts that he was able to bring about the reconciliation of Nature and Freedom he intended. To achieve this reconciliation, Kant presented in the third *Critique* the ideal of a purposive, organic system of Nature, expressive of a divine creator, that is necessary to the activity of man as rational creature. In the light of this ideal, man constructs a mechanistic understanding of things, which, though a marvel in itself, is ultimately inadequate. And how Kant conceives of this understanding in Nature is analogous to how he conceives of it in man. Ultimately, Freedom and Nature come together. But this cannot occur on the level of human activity until the creative art of freedom expressed in a constitution and a culture as a "kingdom of ends" shall become a "second nature" to man.

The whole field of human activity and understanding was broadened immeasurably through Kant's efforts. Kant was responsible for the death of the traditional conception of metaphysics as absolute knowledge about the most universal characteristics of Being and for our present understanding of it as the problem of determining the general categories of thought that will be most adequate to understand what actually is. There is hardly a school of thought or movement today that in some way does not stem directly from him. The idea that the human mind is an active agent in knowing and not merely a spectator has fathered the whole notion of commitment in man, which we hear so much about today. And last, Kant's moral insight, his conception of the capacity in man for responsible personality, and his liberal humanism represent a high point in the history of man's understanding of his world and, above all, himself.

RELATED PROBLEMS

1. Compare the function of the idea of God in speculative reason with its function in practical reason.
2. What distinguishes an analytic judgment from a synthetic judgment for Kant? for Hume?
3. Are the two expressions of the categorical imperative compatible with each other or not?
4. Does Kant consider freedom and reason in opposition to each other?
5. What would Kant reply to the criticism that the categorical imperative is no guide for making choices in practical life?
6. Having dismissed all concern for consequences in ethics, isn't the criterion of "universalization without self-contradiction" an appeal to consequences? Discuss.
7. Discuss how judgment mediates between thinking and willing?
8. Explain why it is a misunderstanding to describe Kant's theory of space and time as subjective.
9. Discuss Kant's conception of the Nature of Reason.
10. Why does Kant say that the aesthetic experience is "disinterested"? What are your views on this question?
11. What are Kant's objections to the sensuous desires and impulses of man?
12. What are the conditions for being "an end in itself"?
13. What are the characteristics of man's rational nature that emerge from Kant's interpretation of Genesis?
14. What was Kant's view of the relation between mechanism and teleology?
15. How do Kant's moral views differ from his metaphysical views?
16. Why does Kant think that we should take seriously the design argument for the existence of God?
17. Does Kant change his conception of freedom in his ethical writings? If so, how?

SPECULATIVE PROBLEMS

1. Compare Kant's view of mathematics as synthetic with Hume's view of it as analytic.
2. What is the function of imagination in Kant's Critical Philosophy?
3. Kant thought that his categories described the Newtonian world. What in fact would the experience produced by those categories be like?
4. Discuss Kant's distinction between constitutive and regulative principles. Can you conceive the operation of one without the operation of the other? Could a principle be both constitutive and regulative?
5. What led Kant to formulate the antinomies of reason?
6. What are the arguments for and against the temporal interpretation of the categorical imperative?
7. At the end of the Introduction to the *Critique of Judgment,* Kant explains the importance of "threefold" divisions in order to explain "synthetic unity." Is there any evidence in these selections that Kant understood this threefold dynamism in temporal terms, in the manner in which Hegel understood them? Recall here the relation between the subcategories, as well as the three *Critiques.*
8. Does the distinction between determinate judgments and reflective judgments parallel the distinction between constitutive and regulative principles?
9. Kant conceives of Reason as making a creative contribution to human endeavors. What does he mean by creativity in knowing, willing, and feeling?
10. Discuss the importance of Kant's analysis of space and time for human knowledge.
11. In what sense, if any, does Kant answer Hume's problem?
12. Kant held that the schemata are temporal expressions of the categories. If you look at each of the schema, do you find these categories implied in them?
13. In his writings Kant uses the terms "transcendental" and "transcendent." Distinguish between them.
14. Discuss Kant's criticisms of Descartes' "cogito."
15. Can you conceive of any other ways to solve the third and fourth antinomies than the way Kant does?
16. Discuss Kant's analysis of the ontological proof.

RECOMMENDED READING

Editions of Kant's Works

The Critique of Pure Reason. Norman Kemp Smith (trans.). London: Macmillan & Company, Ltd., 1929.

Critique of Practical Reason. Lewis White Beck (trans.). New York: Bobbs-Merrill, 1956 (The Library of Liberal Arts).

Critique of Judgment. J. H. Bernard (trans.). New York: Hafner, 1951.

Prolegomena to Any Future Metaphysics. Lewis White Beck (trans.). New York: Bobbs-Merrill, 1950 (The Library of Liberal Arts).

Religion Within the Limits of Reason Alone. Theodore M. Greene (trans.). New York: Harper and Row, 1960.

Immanual Kant: On History. Lewis White Beck (ed.). New York: Bobbs-Merrill, 1957 (The Library of Liberal Arts).

Lectures on Ethics. Louis Infield (trans.). New York: Harper and Row, 1963.

The Fundamental Principles of the Metaphysics of Ethics. Otto Manthey-Zorn (trans.). New York: Appleton-Century-Crofts, 1938.

Immanual Kant: Education. Annette Churton (trans.). Ann Arbor: University of Michigan Press, 1960.

The Doctrine of Virtue; Part II of The Metaphysics of Morals. Mary J. Gregor trans.). New York: Harper and Row, 1964.

First Introduction to The Critique of Judgment. James Haden (trans.). New York: Bobbs-Merrill, 1965.

Further Editions of Kant's Works

Immanuel Kant: Anthropology from a Pragmatic Point of View. Mary J. Gregor (trans.). The Hague: Martinus Nijhoff, 1974.

Kant: Philosophical Correspondence 1759-99. Arnuff Zweig (trans.). Chicago: The University of Chicago Press, 1967.

Immanuel Kant: Logic. Robert S. Hartman and Wolfgang Schwartz (trans.). New York: The Bobbs Merrill Company, Inc., 1974.

Immanuel Kant: Lectures on Philosophical Theology. Allen W. Wood and Gertrude M. Clark, (trans.). Ithaca: Cornell University Press, 1978.

Selected Works on Kant

Cassirer, Ernst. *Rousseau, Kant, Goethe.* Princeton: Princeton University Press.

Hendel, Charles W. *The Philosophy of Kant and Our Modern World.* New York: Bobbs-Merrill, 1957 (The Library of Liberal Arts).

Kroner, Richard. *Kant's Weltanschanung.* J. E. Smith (trans.). Chicago: University of Chicago Press, 1956.

Paton, H. J. *Kant's Metaphysic of Experience* (2 vols.). New York: Humanities Press, 1936.

Paton, H. J. *The Categorical Imperative.* Chicago: University of Chicago Press, 1948.

Sidgwick, Henry. *Lectures on the Philosophy of Kant.* New York: Macmillan, 1905.

Smith, Norman Kemp. *A Commentary on Kant's Critique of Pure Reason.* London: Macmillan, 1923.

Selected Works on Kant Since 1967

Acton, H.B. *Kant's Moral Philosophy.* London: Macmillan and Company Ltd., 1970.

Beck, Lewis White. *Early German Philosophy: Kant and His Predecessors.* Cambridge, Massachusetts: Harvard University Press, 1969.

Beck, Lewis White. *Essays on Kant and Hume.* New Haven: Yale University Press, 1978.

Beck, Lewis White (Ed.). *Kant Studies Today.* LaSalle, Illinois: The Open Court Publishing Company, 1969.

Benton, Robert J. *Kant's "Second Critique" and The Problem of Transcendental Agreements.* The Hague: Martinus Nijhoff, 1977.

Coleman, Francis K.J. *The Harmony of Reason: A Study in Kant's Aesthetics.* Pittsburgh: University of Pittsburgh Press, 1974.

Crawford, Donald W. *Kant's Aesthetic Theory.* Madison: The University of Wisconsin Press, 1974.

Gram, Moltke S. *Kant: Disputed Questions.* Chicago: Quadrangle Books, 1967.

Gram, Moltke S. *Kant, Ontology & The A Priori.* Evanston, Illinois: Northwestern University Press, 1968.

Hutchings P.A.E. *Kant on Absolute Value.* London: George Allen & Unwin, 1972.

McFarland, J.D. *Kant's Concept of Teleology.* Edinburgh: Edinburgh University Press, 1970.

Schaper, Eva. *Studies in Kant's Aesthetics.* Edinburgh: Edinburgh University Press, 1979.

Shell, Susan Meld. *The Rights of Reason: A Study of Kant's Philosophy and Politics.* Toronto: University of Toronto Press, 1980.

Sherover, Charles M. *Heideggar, Kant & Time.* Bloomington, Indiana: Indiana University Press, 1971.

Swing, Thomas Kaehao. *Kant's Transcendental Logic.* New Haven: Yale University Press, 1969.

Van De Pitte, Frederick P. *Kant as Philosophical Anthropologist.* The Hague: Martinus Nijhoff, 1971.

Ward, Keith. *The Development of Kant's View of Ethics.* Oxford: Basil Blackwell, 1972.

Werkmeister, William Henry. *Kant, The Archetectonic and Development of His Philosophy.* LaSalle, Illinois: Open Court Publishing Co., 1979.

Williams, T.C. *The Concept of the Categorical Imperative.* London: Oxford University Press, 1968.

Wolff, Robert Paul. *The Autonomy of Reason: Commentary on Kant's Groundwork of The Metaphysic of Morals.* New York: Harper & Row, Publishers, 1973.

INDEX

Abstract ideas: 20–21
Action: 55, 58–60, 64–65, 68, 82
Activity: 109, 110, 148, 149
Aesthetic, transcendental: 112, 115
Analytical: 105, 106, 107
Antimonies:
  analysis of, 131–133
  dilemma of, 186
  solution to, 135
A posteriori: 50, 105, 106, 107
Apperception, unity of: 120–123
A priori: 50–51, 104, 105, 106
Aristotle: 2, 40, 69
Art: 167, 176, 177, 179
Association of ideas: 21–23, 64
Autonomy: 145

Bacon: 9
Beauty:
  and the agreeable, 98
  grounded in taste, 172
  as a preparation, 176
  of social virtues, 77–78
  as a symbol, 178, 179
  taste for, 86–88, 98
  and the Understanding, 171
Belief:
  and cognition, 2
  and constant conjunction, 59, 61
  and custom, 59–61, 62–63
  and existence, 51, 52
  and feeling or sentiment, 62–63
Benevolence: 70–73, 74, 76–80, 82
Bentham: 3, 76, 77
Berkeley: 2, 13

Categories:
  deduction of, 119
  employment of, 126
  answer to Hume, 116
  nature of, 115, 116–117
  and perception, 120, 123
  phenomenal world, 115
  and the schemata, 127
  table of, 116, 117
  and time, 123
  as rule of unity, 125
Cause and effect (Causality):
  and association of ideas, 22
  and determinism, 133
  and First Cause, 135
  and Freedom, 144, 158
  not justified by demonstrative
    reasoning, 36
  dependence on experience, 33–37,
    58–61

and proofs of God's existence, 47–53
and matter of fact inferences, 25–27
its meaning, 27, 28–30
and necessity, 142
and necessary connection, 27–28, 30
as noumena, 136
and the passions, 31
as phenomena, 136
not justified by probability, 28, 36
Pyrrhonist critique of, 27–37
schema of, 123, 125
two conceptions of, 136
Choice, rational: 159
Cicero: 9, 87
Cogito: 116, 130
Conceptualism: 20
Conciousness:
  in general, 119
  unity of, 122–123
Cosmological Proof: 137, 138
Culture: 101
Custom: 2, 21, 58–61, 62, 64–65
Cynics: 6

Descartes: 1, 12, 116, 130, 136, 169
Desire: 96, 97, 98, 167
Duty: 142, 150, 151

Evil:
  cause of, 100
  conditions of, 116, 163
  three degrees of, 162
  judgments of, 116
  order of, 120
  unity of, 127
Existence:
  and belief, 51–52
  external, 24–25
  how inferred, 26–27
  and judgment, 51–52
  not an ordinary predicate, 23, 51–52
Experience:
  and action, 58, 68
  the central role of, 14
  as a collection of impressions, 65, 66
  components of, 116
  as experimental reason, 65–66, 82
  Hume's provisional account of, 15
  and intuition, 116
  judgments of, 116
  as temporal, 128
  unity and order of, 120, 127

Feeling: 14–15, 62–63, 82–83
Freedom:
  and the abyss, 97

PAPERBACKS AVAILABLE FROM PROMETHEUS BOOKS

PHILOSOPHY & ETHICS

____Animal Rights and Human Morality   *Bernard Rollin*   9.95

____Art of Deception   *Nicholas Capaldi*   6.95

____Beneficent Euthanasia   *M. Kohl, editor*   8.95

____Esthetics Contemporary   *Richard Kostelanetz, editor*   10.95

____Ethics and the Search for Values   *L. Navia and E. Kelly, editors*   13.95

____Exuberance: A Philosophy of Happiness   *Paul Kurtz*   3.00

____Freedom, Anarchy, and the Law   *Richard Taylor*   8.95

____Freedom of Choice Affirmed   *Corliss Lamont*   4.95

____Fullness of Life   *Paul Kurtz*   5.95

____Humanhood: Essays in Biomedical Ethics   *Joseph Fletcher*   8.95

____Infanticide and the Value of Life   *Marvin Kohl, editor*   9.95

____Introductory Readings in the Philosophy of Science   *Klemke, Hollinger, Kline, editors*   12.95

____Invitation to Philosophy   *Capaldi, Kelly, Navia, editors*   12.95

____Journeys Through Philosophy (Revised)   *N. Capaldi & L. Navia, editors*   14.95

____Philosophy: An Introduction   *Antony Flew*   6.95

____Problem of God   *Peter A. Angeles*   9.95

____Responsibilities to Future Generations   *Ernest Partridge, editor*   9.95

____Reverse Discrimination   *Barry Gross, editor*   9.95

____Thinking Straight   *Antony Flew*   5.95

____Worlds of the Early Greek Philosophers   *Wilbur & Allen, editors*   8.95

____Worlds of Hume and Kant   *Wilbur & Allen, editors*   7.95

____Worlds of Plato & Aristotle   *Wilbur & Allen, editors*   7.95

SCIENCE AND THE PARANORMAL

____ESP & Parapsychology: A Critical Re-evaluation   *C.E.M. Hansel* $9.95

____Extra-Terrestrial Intelligence   *James L. Christian, editor*   7.95

____Objections to Astrology   *L. Jerome & B. Bok*   4.95

____The Psychology of the Psychic   *D. Marks & R. Kammann*   9.95

____Philosophy & Parapsychology   *J. Ludwig, editor*   9.95

____Paranormal Borderlands of Science   *Kendrick Frazier, editor* $13.95

HUMANISM

____Ethics Without God   *K. Nielsen*   6.95

____Humanist Alternative   *Paul Kurtz, editor*   5.95

____Humanist Ethics   *Morris Storer, editor*   9.95

____Humanist Funeral Service   *Corliss Lamont*   3.95

____Humanist Manifestos I & II   1.95

____Humanist Wedding Service   *Corliss Lamont*   2.95

____Humanistic Psychology   *Welch, Tate, Richards, editors*   10.95

____Moral Problems in Contemporary Society   *Paul Kurtz, editor*   7.95

____Secular Humanist Declaration   1.95

____Voice in the Wilderness   *Corliss Lamont*   5.95

SEXOLOGY

____The Frontiers of Sex Research   *Vern Bullough, editor*   8.95

____New Bill of Sexual Rights & Responsibilities   *Lester Kirkendall*   3.95

____New Sexual Revolution   *Lester Kirkendall, editor*   6.95

____Philosophy & Sex   *Robert Baker & Fred Elliston, editors*   7.95

____Sex Without Love: A Philosophical Exploration   *Russell Vannoy*   8.95

LIBRARY OF LIBERAL RELIGION

____Facing Death and Grief   *George N. Marshall*   7.95

____Living Religions of the World   *Carl Hermann Voss*   4.95

THE SKEPTIC'S BOOKSHELF

____Atheism: The Case Against God   *George H. Smith*   7.95

____Atheist Debater's Handbook   *B.C. Johnson*   10.95

____What About Gods? (for children)   *Chris Brockman*   4.95

____Classics of Free Thought   *Paul Blanshard, editor*   6.95

____Critiques of God   *Peter Angeles, editor*   9.95

ADDITIONAL TITLES

____Age of Aging: A Reader in Social Gerontology   *Monk, editor*   9.95

____Avant-Garde Tradition in Literature   *Richard Kostelanetz, editor*   11.95

____Higher Education in American Society   *Altbach & Berdahl, editors*   9.95

____Israel's Defense Line   *I.L. Kenen*   9.95

____Pornography and Censorship   *Copp & Wendell, editors*   9.95

____Psychiatry, Mental Health Care, and Ethics   *Rem B. Edwards, editor*   9.95